PREACHING

ON THE BOOKS

OF THE

NEW TESTAMENT

PREACHING

ON THE BOOKS

OF THE

NEW TESTAMENT

BY

DWIGHT E. STEVENSON

HARPER & BROTHERS PUBLISHERS

NEW YORK

Library of Congress catalog card number: 56-6117

*To those who yesterday sat
in my classroom and today
stand in Christian pulpits in
two hemispheres*

✠

CONTENTS

vii

ACKNOWLEDGMENTS

The idea for this book really began in 1948 when editor Glenn McRae asked me to write a series of eight articles on "Discovering Books of the New Testament" for the *Bethany Church School Guide*. With the consent of Dr. McRae I have drawn upon these articles for some of the material in Chapters 6, 8, 10, 11, 13, 14, 19 and 24. The idea was further advanced by the writing of four study courses surveying the New Testament; a small amount of material from the fourth of these, *The Church Invades the Pagan World*, has been quoted in Chapters 20 and 21. Thanks are due the Bethany Press for permission to reprint these sections, especially as they bear upon James and Hebrews. The full flowering of the book idea, however, waited upon the demands of a course on the use of the Bible in preaching which I teach each year at The College of the Bible in Lexington, Kentucky. Both teacher and students, in an effort to capture the biblical message, have been driven to larger and larger units of scripture until book sermons have been one of the inevitable outcomes. The success of students in producing such sermons has redoubled my faith in the approach and has also given some urgency to the preparation of a guide for those attempting it.

Quite a number of the secretaries who serve the faculty of The College of the Bible have had a share in the typing of the manuscript. These include Dolores Van Nostrand, Jeanne Traugott, Jane Holliday, Barbara Wilson, Iona Kaetzel, and Ruth Conner. My wife, DeLoris, as always when I am working on a book, has been helpful by guarding me from interruptions, by constant spoken and unspoken encouragement, and by the critical reading of the entire manuscript.

I am grateful to several publishers for permission to quote copyrighted materials from various books. Sources quoted will be credited at the proper places throughout the volume. Except where otherwise indicated, the translation of the Bible used will be the Revised Standard Version, published by Thomas Nelson & Sons, and copyrighted 1946, 1952, by the National Council of the Churches of Christ in the United States of America.

Dwight E. Stevenson

Lexington, Kentucky

PREFACE

The minister who reads and uses this volume will be able to prepare twenty-seven sermons of his own upon the twenty-seven books of the New Testament, or a single sermon upon the message of any one New Testament book. It is not the author's purpose to provide a "homiletical pony" with finished sermons neatly wrought and ready for use. That way leads to plagiarism and to pulpit suicide. On the other hand, the author does aim at something more helpful than a general harangue on biblical preaching. The result is a book which is really a manual. The controlling word in its writing has been the word *how*. It tries to show a preacher how to study a New Testament book with a view to conveying its message in a single sermon.

It will be recognized that preaching on a whole biblical book is a type of expository preaching. Other types include sermons on persons of the Bible, on chapters and paragraphs, and on biblical ideas. There is no intention of disparaging these other types; on the contrary, they are to be encouraged. This book treats the more limited objective of book sermons, not upon the whole Bible, but upon the New Testament alone.

The first two chapters are devoted to a statement of general principles. These were set forth in outline form in 1952 in the author's chart, *A Guide to Expository Preaching*. Here they are developed and discussed more fully.

Each of the chapters following is focused upon a single New Testament book, except number eighteen which deals with all three Pastoral Epistles. For ready reference, the books are arranged in their accustomed order, beginning with Matthew and ending with Revelation. Quite obviously, there is no need to read these chapters in their biblical order. As a matter of fact, to give only one example, the chapter on The Letter of Jude should be read before the one on The Second Letter of Peter.

Each chapter falls into two main divisions: "I. Working Your Way into the Book" and "II. Preparing Your Book Sermon." Under the first division it will be noticed at once that the book constantly calls for the reading of specific verses from the New Testament. This feature of the present volume makes it different from most books; for this reason it cannot be read with reference to itself alone. Indeed, it is not designed primarily as a reading book, at all. It is designed as a guide to the study of the books of the New Testament. The proper object of study in each case is the New Testament book itself, with this volume as an aid toward grasping it. *Do not fail to read the italicized scriptural references as they are called for.* To neglect this integrated reading of scripture is to miss the main value of the present approach.

Perhaps it is also obvious that the book is hardly designed for one continuous reading at one sitting. This will become obvious when it is seen that the chapters call for the reading and rereading of every book in the New Testament itself, and that there is much consultation of scripture besides. Take it more slowly, a chapter at a time, and after the first two chapters, not more than one chapter per day. Such a program will make the book one of your study companions for at least a month, perhaps for a longer time. The whole message of all the books of the New Testament is not to be picked up easily or quickly. To deepen and clarify insights requires time. We ministers have an obligation to understand before we proclaim, to be clear before we try to be articulate.

PREACHING

ON THE BOOKS

OF THE

NEW TESTAMENT

I

REDIGGING THE WELLS
OF BIBLICAL PREACHING

PREACHING in every age is the music of a harp string, held taut by the tension between the novelty of the age and the antiquity of the gospel.[1] Its notes differ with the changes in the tension. This is to say that there is a new pulpit in every age.

I

The preaching of the apostles was the proclamation of a news story. In the second century, the apostolic fathers faced a new demand, that of squaring the gospel story with the Greek mind, and of making a rational case for it. With the rise of church order and the elaboration of ritual, preaching became ecclesiastical. Texts were taken from the *pericopes*,[2] and sermons were rooted in liturgy. When by the fourteenth century the church had sunk into corruption and needed reform, the pulpit became a prophetic voice, the instrument of an awakened conscience. The pulpit of the Protestant Reformation had two things to do: recover the Bible and refute Roman Catholics; in consequence, it became largely expository and controversial. With Wesley and Whitefield, in the eighteenth cen-

[1] Joseph Fort Newton, *The New Preaching* (Cokesbury Press, 1930).
[2] Official selections of scripture appointed to be read in the regular services of the church.

tury preaching became missionary and evangelistic. On into the nineteenth century up to the dawn of the twentieth, the watchword was the expansion of Christianity. "The world for Christ in this generation!" chanted the Student Volunteers, mirroring the age. "I look upon all the world as my parish," Wesley had said. These were the years of the Great Awakenings and of the missionary crusade. Today some of the momentum of revivalism still lingers, but its main force is spent. We have in our time another task, one that undergirds evangelism.

As we swing into the period through which we have recently passed, we can see that it has been a time of "applied Christianity" and of "philosophy of religion." Much missionary and evangelistic preaching had been for another world. This world was left to the Morgans and the Rockefellers and Tammany Hall. For more than forty years the pulpit has been grappling with the problem of bringing the world and the gospel together. That is to say, the message of the Christian pulpit in this twentieth century has been predominantly ethical. The kind of religion we have been interested in is applied Christianity. Most of us could not get very excited over evangelism—whatever outward honor we may have paid it—for it seemed to us little better than adding more half-converted pagans to the lot we already had in our congregations. Turning away from dogma and even from scripture, we have been saying "Christianity is life."

This might have worked, if the society to which we had been preaching had really known the Christian gospel and if it had honestly believed in it. Actually this half century only pretended to believe in Christianity. The creed it truly believed was the creed of materialism; its thoughts were "meat and money thoughts"; its world was a world of "coins and wires and motor horns." Consequently, along with Christian ethics, we preached apologetics. We tried to bring these modern fellow pagans within the churches to a genuine belief in the religion which they formally professed. Sermons on topics such as "Why I Believe in God," "Does Man Need Religion?" "What Religion Is and Does" were legion; they were trying to make a case for Christianity. A modern term for this type of thinking is "Philosophy of Religion." Its bearing on the deepest needs of people is seen in an analogy of Henry Nelson Wieman's.[3] Philosophy of religion, he said, is the dietitian who prepares the menu; theology is the cook who translates that menu into food for the table. Well, if hungering congregations in recent years looked up to us and were not fed, it may be that we were waiters carrying in the menu from an empty kitchen.

Ethics and philosophy of religion! There is only one thing wrong with this kind of preaching as a steady diet. It has no main course. Philosophy of religion led men to believe in the reasonableness of religion, and ethics spurred them to apply it, but how could they become religious in the first place? How could they acquire and grow in faith? That must have been a complete mystery to them, for we did not tell them.

II

Many signs indicate that we are turning the corner into a new era of the Christian pulpit. It has to do with the filling up of that hollow center which has developed during the first half of this century. Our people—perhaps we ourselves—are scripturally, theologically, and devotionally illiterate. We shall have to teach them, and we shall have to begin by teaching ourselves.

We shall have to return to the deep sources of our religion. And for the Christian pulpit, what are these deep sources? There are at least three. The first is *theology*. This will mean a change in our reading habits; we must stop looking for the easy book filled with usable illustrations, and begin reading the difficult ones that grapple

[3] In a class lecture at the University of Chicago.

with fundamental issues. We must stop stringing a few beautiful stories on a thread of generalizations and holding up the resulting necklace as an example of thinking. Instead, our sermons must be like chains, wrought out and linked together in white heat under the hammer blows of hard reasoning.

There will be dangers in this new preaching. There is the danger of dogmatism, for little minds can seldom follow great thinkers without pronouncing anathemas upon thinkers of other schools. There is the danger of obscurantism and technical jargon. There is the danger of resurrecting a dead theology of another day and of posing this animated corpse as the prophet of our living era. Real theology can be none of these, for it is nothing less than the translation of the Christian faith into the fresh, contemporary and meaningful thought forms of each living generation. Even in face of the dangers, modern preaching must become more theological, not that it should become any less ethical, but because ethics without theology soon declines into nagging.

The second deep source is *devotional life*. For the past fifty years ministers have grown steadily busier, with less time and less inclination to pray. We must learn, and we must teach our people. This will mean an increase in devotional literature and a return to the classics of the saints. It will mean a liturgical revival in public worship. We will no longer preach that apologetic sermon, "It Pays to Pray." Rather we will preach a teaching sermon, "Pathways of Prayer." Meantime, visions of monks atop high pillars and on long begging pilgrimages will warn us of the dangers which we must avoid in deepening our own spirit of devotion and of leading our people into the mysteries of divine communion.

The third source of the new preaching brings us to the subject of this book; it is the *Bible*. You may want to object that preaching has never departed from the Bible. By this, perhaps, you mean the preachers still "take a text." The late P. T. Forsyth hit the nail right on our thumb when he said, "The Bible is still the preacher's starting point, even if it is not his living source. It is still the usual custom for him to take a text. If he but preach some happy thoughts, fancies, or philosophies of his own, he takes a text for a motto." He sounded an unheeded warning when he went on to say, "The public soon grow weary of topical preaching alone, or newspaper preaching, in which the week's events supply the text and the Bible only an opening quotation."[4]

[4] P. T. Forsyth, *Positive Preaching and the Modern Mind* (Jennings and Graham, 1907).

III

What all of this may mean for preaching it is not possible for anyone to foresee clearly. There are some things that it does not mean. It does not mean Bible-centered preaching, or bibliolatry. It does not mean a return to proof texts. It does not mean a reincarnation of biblical preaching from any bygone age. The reason one can be so confident in these negatives lies in seventy-five years of recent history in which historical and literary scholarship have revolutionized our view of the Bible.

We must learn how to convey the positive fruits of biblical scholarship to our people. Up until now we have not done this to any marked extent. Some of us have kept silent, pretending that this was all very nice to know in seminary but of no possible use to us in our ministry. Others have rushed into the pulpit with a spirit of debunking. Where such negative preaching has prevailed it has not made the Bible a living book; it has taken the Bible from the people and given them nothing in return. The temper of such preaching is ridiculously illustrated by a seminary classmate of mine who went home to his wife after the first day in an Old Testament course, poked his head around the kitchen door and greeted his spouse with the blythe announcement, "There ain't no Abraham!"

The proper way of conveying a modern knowledge of the Bible to church congregations is still to be discovered. It calls for intellectual pioneering of the highest creativity, and for the courageous explorations and experiments by which that creativity can grow. In these efforts we have an urgent motivation, for scriptural illiteracy has made the Bible a closed book to the masses of modern Christians. In some cases, the Bible is closed because of a narrow literalism which turns it into a foreign book—a volume foreign to our real spiritual questions and our genuine moral struggles. Our motivation is urgent, for until the Bible again becomes a living book, Christianity cannot become a living faith.

The times are ripe for such a venture. The atmosphere of our times is far more biblical than any in which civilization has found itself for many centuries. Our long continued sense of crisis finds an echo in no other literature as it does in the Bible. Elton Trueblood reports the change of mood in his classic *Signs of Hope*:

In this recovery of urgency the Bible again makes sense to thoughtful readers. Once its language seemed overdrawn, but that is true no longer. It seems again to be a contemporary book because it is about refugees and dictatorships and colossal deceptions and wanton cruelty and urgent words. Once it was hard to understand Christ's words as he sent out the seventy disciples, for he told them to hurry, to avoid excess baggage and not to linger when people did not listen. His words were meaningless except in the context of crisis, but now we, for a generation, have lived in the mood of crisis. It is not so much that the Bible is a commentary on current history as that current history is a commentary on the Bible, making much of its ancient meaning suddenly clear.[5]

IV

The wells of biblical preaching have filled up with rubble during years of neglect. We must redig them, that the living water of the scriptures may flow again into our contemporary spiritual desert.

[5] Elton Trueblood, *Signs of Hope* (Harper & Brothers, 1950), p. 72.

But how shall we do this? The answer involves a temptation to be avoided and a challenge to be accepted.

First, look at the temptation. This is the easy road of a revived textual preaching. It is to be avoided because scraps of scripture can give people who hear them no sense of a whole message, no wide perspectives of meaning, no knowledge of unity and design. A contemporary theologian quipped, "When Paul wrote to Timothy, 'Study to show thyself approved unto God, a workman that needeth not to be ashamed, rightly *dividing* the word of truth,' he did not mean for us to chop the scripture up into mincemeat." And yet that is exactly what a constant diet of textual preaching does to the Bread of Life.

But there is an even deeper reason for resisting the allurements of textual preaching. This lies in the increasing paganization or secularization of our culture. There is an unwitting tendency for moral teachers to pick up their values from the culture in which they are immersed. When Christian values have permeated social mores and ethical codes, this tendency is not too disastrous; but when, as now, Christian values are being drained from culture, the tendency is exceedingly dangerous. For then we find our values in sub-Christian culture and seek our sanctions for them in the words of the Bible. Shakespeare long ago unmasked this danger when he made Bassanio say,

> What damned error but some sober brow
> Will bless it, and approve it with a text,
> Hiding the grossness with fair ornament?

The inference of hypocrisy in Shakespeare's lines is by no means necessary, for a man may be perfectly sincere and still hide a grossly sub-Christian idea even from himself beneath the fair ornament of a scriptural text. Take, for example, our culture's recent sanction of "the unlimited worth of the individual" which many have preached as a Christian idea. Of man the *individual*, entirely separate from other human beings and from responsibility toward them, the Bible knows nothing. It only knows of *persons* who are intended to live as children of God in the mutual harmony of a family. Today, with collectivism in the air we will have to be equally on our guard against distorting the truth of scripture to support the primacy of society and the unlimited claims of the mass. We can walk safely between these secular extremes only as we truly recapture the biblical world view.

Now for the challenge that must be accepted. We must begin to preach the scripture in large units and with long perspectives. This means single sermons on whole books of the Bible; it means sermons on ideas which run like highways clear across the Bible from JED and P to Second Peter. How much more it may mean we cannot foresee at present, except that we shall have to study the Bible in the future as we have never yet studied it. The Bible must become a world in which we are at home and where we know our way about. This will involve more than a knowledge of books and chapters and verses. It will require a kind of naturalization; we must become citizens of the Bible's spiritual order. "The minister must so live in it [the Bible] that he wears it easily," says Forsyth. "One reason why people are repelled by it is that the preachers cannot carry it with easy mastery. They are in Goliath's armour."[6]

In this present volume we are following only one of the many possible lines of exploration which lead out into biblical preaching with wider perspectives; this is the attempt to learn how to preach single sermons on whole books of scripture. This is one road back to an integrated understanding of our faith. The books are natural units. They were written and published separately and they were intended to be read as wholes. Sometimes we have been blinded to their unity by our analytic studies into the sources—JED P and "Q" and Porto-

[6] Forsyth, *op. cit.*

Luke and the "we" passages—and also by our study of literary types. The fact remains that the books which were compounded out of these sources are creative works having an organic unity of their own, and that the many literary strands are skillfully woven into fabrics having their own design. The analytic labor of the past generation of scholars was necessary and it has been immensely profitable, but our present task is that of seeing scriptural objects as wholes.

While we accept the challenge to help bring this synoptic view to pass, we must be under no illusion that there is only one way of doing it. No single approach will ever do justice to a book containing so varied a treasure, as no one mind will find there what others may discover, or fathom its depths at the first visit, for as Augustine reminds us, "Scripture contains pools at which lambs can drink, and depths in which elephants must swim."

2

SOME GUIDING PRINCIPLES

WITH the fashioning of individual sermons on whole books of scripture we shall probably find ourselves trying to navigate unfamiliar seas. Preachers of former generations may have known the sea lanes in these strange waters, but most of us have never before set sail upon them. We need, therefore, a preliminary glance at the map and a little exercise with the compass and sextant.

I

Let us begin by insisting that sermons on the books of the Bible are still subject to the canons of good preaching. They must aim at the wedding of divine truth with human need. A book sermon is something more than a Bible lecture, however well-informed it may be, just as a life-situation sermon is something more than a commentary on current events. When a minister stands up to preach he is there to make the truth plain and to make it moving. He is working to change attitudes, to secure commitments of purpose, to emotionalize ideas so that they will operate in stirring men to Christian action. A sermon exists in relation to hearers. It is addressed to a congregation, and it is always concerned with persons, first and last. No less than any other message from the pulpit, the book sermon is divine truth coming through personality to move men. If it is divine truth viewed impersonally as mere information it is not a sermon.

This creative tension between the divine and the human which ought to characterize all preaching was happily captured in a figure by Tholuck nearly a century ago when he said, "A sermon ought to have heaven for its father and the earth for its mother."

What this means for preaching the Bible was never more clearly expressed than by Dr. Harry Emerson Fosdick in that epochal *Harper's* article of July, 1928, "What Is the Matter with Preaching?" There the eminent New York clergyman accurately described the exact role which the scriptures play in proclaiming the living gospel: "The Bible is a searchlight, not so much intended to be looked at as to be thrown upon a shadowed spot."

How can this be done? Through a penetration to the timeless message at the heart of a biblical book. As a writing that emerged out of intense human struggles with real problems, many of which are the fundamental issues with which every generation must do battle, the Bible is a living book. It is chronologically remote from us, but psychologically near; externally foreign to our culture but inwardly akin to our spirits. There are ways of presenting the Bible which make it remote and foreign, but there are other ways of making it come alive. If, for example, a sermon on Hosea dwells upon the political surface of Israel's social and military struggles in the eighth century B.C. it will sound like an echo in a museum. If, on the other hand, it penetrates to the inner meanings which Hosea saw in those struggles and to the heart-rending sorrow which he felt over Israel's apostasy, it may speak in living accents. Under some such title as "News of God from a Broken Home," Hosea will speak again of the suffering love of God for a wayward world.

II

Furthermore, preaching on the books of the Bible is expository. This means that the idea of the sermon and its divisions are drawn from the book itself and in such proportion as to present only what the book says rather than some happy thoughts which it may arouse in us.

Expository preaching must aim first of all at a clear and objective picture of the scripture upon which it is trained. Years ago this was done largely through exegesis, but today something more is required. A proper rendition of difficult words and phrases, while essential, is less important than a clear-eyed view of the social and personal perspectives involved. It is not verbal translation that is needed so much as empathy. A successful expository preacher must live his way into a passage of scripture until he feels identity with it.

This means that the preacher's urge to organize the book quickly into sermon divisions must be deliberately held in check until he has studied it thoroughly and read it sympathetically. There will be a protracted period of preparation, many days or even several weeks long, during which the minister as a preacher is wholly absorbed into the minister as student. It is then that he will read the introductions, the commentaries (not homiletic commentaries!), consult the various versions, and even peer into the original tongues. Meantime, he will let none of these become a substitute for his participation in the living unity of the book itself. His one aim in appealing to the scholars is to prepare himself to read the biblical book with greater penetration and with deeper appreciation than he has ever yet achieved. Having done the spadework, he will read the book through at one sitting, and again at another sitting, and yet again, until he has become a naturalized citizen of its spiritual world. Then, and only then, may he safely trust himself to begin organizing the book for the purpose of a sermon.

Expository preaching is carefully organized. Every expository sermon is an organic whole with a few simple, discernible members. Not a miscellany of commentaries upon a passage nor a series of exhortations suggested by it, an expository sermon is the message of that passage itself so arranged as to be grasped in its entirety. If this can be done better by regrouping scriptural incidents or rearranging the sequence of verses and chapters, such reordering is to be commended. Veracity and simplicity strengthen each other. In a book sermon the book must be known and conveyed as an organic whole.

Moreover, in a true exposition, the sermon must lie down at full length upon the passage. The proportion of parts in the sermon must be a faithful mirror of the proportions within the scripture under study. There must be no distortion through the overemphasis or omission of main ideas.

III

In the presentation of the actual contents of a biblical book the preacher must be selective. He needs to remind himself that his sermon is no substitute for the reading of the book by his hearers. Rather, it should sharpen appetites for it. He can do this by reporting what is on the menu and by allowing his congregation to taste every dish, but he must not take time to count all the beans and every slice of bread. This is to say that a sermon on a book of the New Testament must be an experience of the book itself and not merely an introduction to it, but that it must not be exhaustive.

Such selectivity can best be achieved by locating the cardinal ideas of the book, key verses which express them, and a few typical word pictures and incidents which illustrate them. For example, suppose you are preaching on Jeremiah and have come to the cardinal idea that men as individuals must serve God even at the price of social nonconformity. A key quotation might be Jeremiah 15:20, "And I will make thee unto this people a fortified brazen wall; and they shall fight against thee, but they shall not prevail against thee, for I am with thee to save thee and to deliver thee, saith Jehovah" (A.S.V.). And a good illustrative incident would be found in chapter 26, where Jeremiah was threatened with death for speaking against the temple (26:8) and faced the prospect without flinching (26:14, 15). Nothing more is needed to clench this point, although both the quotation and the incident are selected from a vast amount of material that could have been used.

IV

Freshness is also important. In its nature any biblical sermon is an old, old story; but it must be organized in fresh ways and phrased in new words. Still more urgently, it must become contemporary through modern illustration and application. This can be done in part through a consistent use of modern titles for biblical books. Few moderns would be interested in such a sermon title as "Ecclesiastes" or its translation "The Preacher," but they might respond to such a title as "Living by False Goals," "When Life Eludes Our Grasp," or "The Empty Life." Similarly, the announcement of a sermon on "Galatians" for next Sunday would arouse little interest, but one might get an eager hearing for the same sermon bearing the modern title of "The Plight of Freedom."

Modern illustration is indispensable to freshness. Every sermon ought to have it, but expository preaching requires it. The Bible comes alive when the total destruction of Jericho in Joshua 6 is compared with the Nazi obliteration of Lidice, Czechoslovakia, in World War II, or when Samuel's mandate to Saul commanding the extermination of the Amalekites is seen as "the crime of genocide" against which the United Nations is now waging an international crusade. It is thus also that scriptural events are revealed in a universal light.

People who have heard a good biblical sermon in which modern illustration has been skillfully applied will never go away feeling that "it is all so remote; it happened a long time ago."

V

The modern mind wants to see an immediate contemporary relevance in an ancient truth without waiting for a delayed "application."

Exposition and application must be intertwined at every point throughout a biblical sermon, from introduction to conclusion. Modern insights into ancient scripture must have an implicit quality; they must not seem to be "tacked on."

Here, for example, is a book of sermons by the late G. Campbell Morgan bearing the title, *Living Messages of the Books of the Bible*. One does not need the copyright date of 1912 to tell that this was expository preaching geared to a bygone age; the method itself marks the sermons for another time. Every sermon is divided into two major parts, "A. The Essential Message" and "B. The Application." A contemporary preacher would insist upon combining the two. He would, in fact, feel that he could not really disclose the essential message of a book without indicating its modern application.

This intertwining of exposition and application is best seen in an actual sample of modern expository preaching such as George Arthur Buttrick's "The Sound of Thin Silence."[1] Preached the Sunday after the end of the war against Japan in 1945, it was based on 1 Kings 19, the scene which finds Elijah standing in the mouth of the cave at Mt. Horeb. Notice the parallelism of ancient and modern throughout the sermon:

Elijah, a victorious man in despair; we, after V-J day.

Elijah, a contender against the priests of Baal; we, contenders against Nazi paganism.

Elijah, killing the priests; we, subduing Axis armies.

Elijah, discovering that Baalism was not destroyed; we, aware that Nazism is not dead.

Elijah's agonizing despair; our misgiving.

The empty earthquake, wind, and fire; the futility of force.

The still small voice; the silent powers of the universe.

Elijah's alliance with the silent power of God; our alliance with that power.

[1] A. W. Blackwood (ed.), *The Protestant Pulpit*, pp. 180 ff.

There is artistry in this sermon, artistry such as exists at the top of a craft calling for severe disciplines; and it is the artistry of relevance. At every point of it from beginning to end scripture and application are interwoven into one fabric. The modern illumines the ancient and the ancient enlivens the modern. The message of such a sermon is something more than words to be heard; it becomes a program to live by. Such is the goal of good expository preaching, and of preaching on the books of the Bible, a department of expository preaching.

VI

Anyone who attempts to preach on the books of either Testament will soon discover that they present varying degrees of difficulty. The recognition of this fact should deter one from approaching the books of the New Testament in their natural sequence.

Ideally that book is easiest to treat in a sermon which has the most vivid concreteness and the most dramatic movement together with the strongest unity and the clearest simplicity within the briefest compass. Using these criteria—concreteness, movement, unity, simplicity and brevity—we can arrive at an approximate table of ascending difficulty, and having done that, we can decide to begin with the easiest books and work our way into the more difficult ones as we gain competence.

The Gospels are the most concrete and dramatic, but they are relatively long and are so surcharged with material that they are difficult to strip down to outline. Mark is the easiest of the group to handle and John the most difficult. Matthew and Luke, falling in between, are about equal in difficulty.

Romans and Hebrews, on the other hand, are the most abstract and logically formidable. Revelation, as the least simple, joins ranks with them to fill out a triad of the hardest books in the New Testament.

The fifteen easier books arranged in crude order of increasing difficulty would appear something like this:

Philemon
1 John
Philippians
The Acts of the Apostles
James
1 Thessalonians
1 Corinthians
1 Peter
2 John
3 John
Galatians
Mark
Matthew
Luke
John

The twelve more difficult books, beginning with the hardest, might be listed somewhat as follows:

Hebrews
Revelation
Romans
Ephesians
Colossians
2 Thessalonians
2 Peter
Jude
2 Timothy
1 Timothy
Titus
2 Corinthians

VII

In seeking to find some signposts to point the way toward an effective presentation of whole books of scripture in single sermons, we have arrived at these principles:

A book sermon, no less than any sermon, must preserve a creative tension between divine truth and present human need.

In idea, outline and emphasis, such a sermon must be faithful to the book which it aims to set forth.

It must be selective in content so as to bear the stamp of simplicity.

It must be fresh.

It must weld ancient truth and modern application into a radical unity.

The minister who undertakes this type of preaching will be wise to begin with one of the easier book   and work his way up the scale of difficulty by degrees.

3

THE FOUR GOSPELS
A General Introduction

THERE are many respects in which the Gospels are alike. The New Testament scholar, C. H. Dodd, has done us all a service in pointing out that the fundamental pattern of the proclamation (*kerygma*) of Good News can be found in all apostolic preaching from Peter's Pentecostal sermon onward, and that the written Gospels follow the same outline, which may be phrased as follows:

God's promises made to his people in the Old Testament are now fulfilled.
The Long-expected Messiah, born of David's line, has come.

He is Jesus of Nazareth, who went about doing good and wrought mighty works by God's power; was crucified according to the purpose of God; was raised by God from the dead and exalted to his right hand;

He will come again for judgment.
Therefore let all who hear this message repent and be baptised for the forgiveness of their sins.[1]

Even beyond this fundamental, shared outline many similarities among the Gospels could be pointed out, not the least of which is the amazing verbatim agreement of a large part of the Synoptics. Perhaps this impressive agreement is to be expected; after all, the

---

[1] As phrased by A. M. Hunter in *The Gospel according to Saint Mark* (SCM Press, 1948).

narratives do center in the same historical event and cluster around the same Person.

Nevertheless, there are differences—differences between John and the Synoptics, and among the Synoptics themselves. These differences could be discussed at great length and in detail; it does not suit our purpose to do so here. Instead of detailed differences we shall focus upon the various general impressions made by each of the books as a whole. We may say that John gives us the *influence* of Jesus as the Spirit living through all history and above history; that Matthew gives us the *intellect* of Jesus through his teachings; that Luke gives us the *mood* of Jesus through a portrayal of his penetrating human sympathy; and that Mark gives us the *action* of the Master. While no single word is adequate to convey the message of any of these books, these words—influence, intellect, mood, action—do serve as useful keys to an understanding of the different emphases of the Four Gospels.

There is another vivid way of setting off the contrasts; that is to give a title to the portrait of Jesus which emerges from each Gospel. Thus Matthew shows us "The Great Teacher"; Luke in a picture of the supreme friend of humanity reveals "The Great Physician"; Mark in bold strokes that quickly tell the story of humanity's moral hero unveils "The Strong Son of God"; and John in a portrait of a person who fills the earth and overflows it with divine life shows us "Our Eternal Contemporary."

A minister who is attempting to convey the message of the Four Gospels in separate sermons will do well to set his course for each by the central mood of each Gospel. Else there is no value in having four Gospels or in four sermons upon them; one would do as well.

Most preachers will not want to preach their first book sermon on one of the Gospels; they will feel more nearly adequate for so demanding a task after they have worked their way up through some of the shorter books, as was suggested in Chapter 2.

4

THE TEACHER SENT FROM GOD
The Gospel According to Matthew

To READ this book it is not required that you should begin from the high pinnacle of faith. You can begin where the disciples themselves began, as "men of little faith" (6:30; 8:26; 14:31; 16:8; 17:20). If you do you will find yourself being instructed until you are led deeper and deeper into the heart and mind of the one Great Teacher. You will find that the aim of this teacher is not to inform but to change you, as the first disciples themselves were changed. Read this book from a point of view—not that of a modern spectator who is safely detached and aloof from it all; nor that of Jesus himself, for he is our Saviour, not our example. But choose a group in the book and join it: the Pharisees and rulers whose deepest passions were aroused by Jesus, or the crowds who flocked after him but followed his meanings so haltingly, or the twelve. From one of these standpoints read the whole Gospel and let it do its work. We suspect that the author really wants you to think of yourself as one of the Disciples; within that favored group your identity shifts. You are Matthew and Peter and Judas in turn; but most of the time you are Peter, a wave being made into a rock.

I. WORKING YOUR WAY INTO THE BOOK

Previous study of the Synoptic Gospels has probably made you aware of Matthew, Mark and Luke as a general unit and acquainted you with the "sources." You know that Matthew used Mark (all but 55 verses) and "Q," a body of sayings about 200 verses in extent shared by Luke; you know that Matthew had in addition a source of his own—"M"—from which he derived no less than 400 verses. You have struggled, too, with questions of date and authorship. If you have done nothing else you have little more than "the synoptic *problem*," a curious predicament when it is remembered that the Gospel was not written to create a perplexity but is good news for solving life problems. Such critical questions are important but they are secondary to the book itself and its direct message. What is needed before all the reading *about* Matthew is simply the reading *of* Matthew itself; what must be experienced before the analysis of the book into sources is its wholeness and uniqueness as living literature. It is at this point that we should begin; and, after any study of critical questions, it is to this point that we should return.

Nearly all readers of Matthew are aware of the large collection of Jesus' sayings in chapters 5, 6 and 7 known as the Sermon on the Mount. Few are equally aware of the fact that this is only one of five such collections or discourses to be found throughout the book. For the others:

See Matthew 9:36-10:42; 13:1-53; 17:22-18:35; 23:1-26:1.

Even a casual examination will show that these five discourses are each unified about a theme, these being: (1) The new law of Christ, designed for the community which is to inherit the kingdom of heaven; (2) the apostleship, or the work of disciples when Christ chooses them and sends them out; (3) parables of the kingdom addressed to the crowds; (4) problems of life in the believing community; (5) the end of the age; divine judgment.

It will be seen too that the words immediately following each of the five discourses are verbally identical. They are: "and when Jesus had finished . . ."

Read Matthew 7:28; 11:1; 13:53; 19:1; 26:1.

We begin to suspect that these words are transitions used by the author to mark the boundaries between the main divisions of his book. There are five of them. Are there, then, five divisions in the book? If we assume an introduction (chapters one and two) and an epilogue (26:1-28:20), our expectation is fulfilled exactly. We are now ready to notice that the discourses come at the end of the five sections and that the chapters preceding them, though liberally filled with Jesus' sayings, are narratives. Thus the pattern for each section is the same: (A) Narrative, (B) Discourse. If the discourses have themes, what about the narratives? It will be seen that these do have themes closely related to the discourses which follow them, though they are not as strictly unified as the discourses.

Scholars like Benjamin Bacon were led by the above considerations to a division of Matthew into five books. When we go on to notice the author's marked interest in the Old Testament, his contrasts of Moses and Christ, his emphasis upon the church as the new nation to take the place of Israel, we begin to think of the "fulfilling of the law" as a kind of key idea for the whole book:

Read Matthew 5:17-20.

Matthew is putting the five books of Christ over against the five books of Moses! But his contrast is not a repudiation of Moses; it is a righteousness that exceeds that of Moses, and so fulfills it. Thus we see the marvelous artistry of this First Gospel: the structure expresses the purpose, which is to show Jesus Christ as the teacher greater than Moses who brings God's purpose first announced in Moses to fulfillment. Judaism naturally passes into Christianity, for that is its manifest destiny.

OUTLINE OF MATTHEW

Preamble: The genealogy and birth of Jesus, chapters 1, 2
Book I: Concerning discipleship, 3:1-7:29

A. Narrative: The beginning of Jesus' ministry, 3:1-4:25
   (Summary: 4:23-25)
B. Discourse: The new law, 5:1-7:29
   (Summary: 7:28-29)

Book II: Concerning apostleship, chapters 8-10
  A. Narrative: Jesus' mighty works, chapters 8, 9
  B. Discourse: When disciples become apostles, chapter 10
Book III: Concerning revelation and rejection, 11:1-13:58
  A. Narrative: Jesus' rejection, 11:2-12:50
    (Summary: Jesus' true family, 12:46-50)
  B. Discourse: Parables of the kingdom, 13:1-58
    (Summary: Jesus' townsmen reject him, 13:53-58)
Book IV: Life in the church community, chapters 14-18
  A. Narrative: Founding of the church, chapters 14-17
    (Summary: Christian freedom, 17:22-23)
  B. Discourse: Problems of Christian community, 18:1-35
Book V: Concerning judgment, 19:1-25:46
  A. Narrative: Jesus goes to Jerusalem, 19:1-22:46
    1. Demands of discipleship on the way, 19:3-20:28
    2. Two blind men healed, 20:29-34
    3. Events in Jerusalem, 21:1-22:46
  B. Discourse: Divine judgment, 23:1-25:46
Epilogue: Jesus' death and resurrection, 26:1-28:20

In a most stimulating study called *Creation Continues*,[1] the psychologist Fritz Kunkel has divided the First Gospel into seven parts which he has arranged as "a huge arch whose two halves are linked together in Peter's discovery": "You are the Christ, the Son of the living God." (16:16) Thus chapters 14-18, which contain this central idea, form the keystone of the arch. The blocks in the arch beginning with the left base are: I. The Gate, chapters 1-4; II. The Chart, chapters 5-7; III. The Way, chapters 8-13; IV. The Crossroads [Keystone], chapters 14-18; V. The New Way, chapters 19-23; VI. The New Chart, chapters 24-25; VII. The New Gate, chapters 26-28.

While we are noticing Matthew's superb sense of structure we must turn for a moment to his propensity for grouping of incidents and parables in units of three, five or seven parts. Thus the three miracles of 8:2-17; the seven parables of chapter 13; the seven woes of chapter 23; the five sayings about "little ones" in 18:1-14. There are numerous examples of this tendency which serves as an aid to

---

[1] Scribner's, 1947, pp. 10 and 11.

memory. Matthew's collecting and systematizing tendency can be seen in the gathering of miracles in chapter 9 from three different chapters of Mark, i.e., 2:1-22; 5:21-43; 10:46-52.

POINTS OF INTEREST

1. *The use of the Old Testament.* Leaf through the Gospel and notice the almost constant quotation from the Old Testament. In addition to those which stand out on the page of the Revised Standard Version because of special indentation, notice the following:

Read Matthew 2:15, 23; 8:17; 9:13; 11:5; 12:3-4, 7; 13:35; 21:5, 26:31.

The fulfilling of the law and the prophets is the key idea in these many quotations from, and references to, the Old Testament scripture. The Old Testament was for a long time the only scripture of the early Christian church. From the beginning the early Christian preachers saw the Christ and his church foreshadowed in the Old Testament, but no early leader was at greater pains to document this foreshadowing than the author of the First Gospel. This fact has led Theodore Robinson to a unique interpretation about authorship based upon one tradition which comes down to us from the church father Papias in the second century by way of Eusebius in the fourth. The quotation runs: "Matthew, then, compiled the oracles (*logia*) in the Hebrew tongue, and each interpreted them as he was able."[2] It has often been supposed that the "oracles" or "logia" (sayings) referred to by Papias were the sayings of Jesus in "Q," the document from which the First and Third Gospels derive so much of their common material. Robinson does not follow this suggestion. Instead, he offers the view that "logia" means quotations from the Hebrew Old Testament.

He says,

But it may well have been a collection of "oracles" dealing with the Messiah, such as might be used by the Christian to prove to the Jew that Jesus was the Christ. We know that such collections were current

[2] Eusebius, *Hist. Eccles.,* III, 39.

in the third century . . . but in the Jewish church the need for them would be immediate and urgent.[3]

It is quite possible that the Apostle Matthew made such a collection of Old Testament passages. Be that as it may, the First Gospel places a singular emphasis upon the fulfillment of the Hebrew scriptures by the Christian gospel.

Read Matthew 5:17; 13:52.

2. *The Christian church.* It cannot be said that Matthew is an ecclesiastical Gospel in the sense that it exalts the church as an institution or organization, but there is an intense interest in the church as a functioning community. Only so can we explain such passages as:

Read Matthew 16:18; 18:15-17; 13:37-43 (in that order).

The central section of the Gospel, chapters 14-18, is primarily concerned with the life of the Christian community.

3. *The Christian church as the new Israel.*

Read Matthew 21:42-43.

God works in history through a chosen community. At first this was the nation of Israel, but since Christ the community has been universalized to include believers from every race, nation and tongue. It is this community with Christ at the center which is the true Israel.

4. *A positive Christian morality.* As we have already seen, Christ came to teach a new law whose righteousness exceeds that of the Pharisees. The ethical teachings in this Gospel are always rooted in God and his kingdom but they are clear and challenging. Christian morality, which is to be practiced by believers in the community or with reference to their community of faith, is never equivocal. It sets the Christian off at once both from Jew and Gentile.

5. *The prominence of the kingdom of heaven.* This is Jesus' theme and Matthew's preoccupation. The church is a corner of that kingdom already present in time but the kingdom in its fullness is yet to come. When it comes it will appear not only in redemption but also

---

[3] T. H. Robinson, *The Gospel of Matthew* (Doubleday, 1928), p. xv.

in judgment. The kingdom has individual implications but it never is a purely individual, subjective "state of soul"; a corporate condition in history seems definitely to be involved. See particularly the parables of the kingdom in chapter 13.

6. *The prominence of Peter.* Before chapter 14 we do not suspect the growing importance of Peter but from that time to the close he comes more and more to stand out among the disciples as their representative, spokesman and leader. It is with Peter that the modern Christian reader naturally identifies himself; he sees in this wavering fisherman so much that is akin to his own spirit, and in Peter's growing strength under the Master's tutelage he sees his own hope of strength.

7. *The Christian's witness in the world.* Apostleship bulks large in the Gospel. Disciples have come to their teacher; having been taught they are sent out. They are to be "salt of the earth" and "light of the world" (5:13, 14) in the quality of their moral life, but they are also expected to bear explicit verbal witness to their faith:

Read Matthew 10:40-42; 28:18-20.

KEY PASSAGE

There are really two passages which deserve the distinction, but they are not of equal merit. In their order of importance they are:

1. Matthew 16:13-19.
2. Matthew 5:17-20.

These verses are selected from many which convey the same passionate concern for the Christian mission and the committed leaders to carry it out.

II. PREPARING YOUR BOOK SERMON

CARDINAL IDEA

Jesus is the Christ, the Son of God; he came not to destroy the law of Moses but to fulfill it and to teach us a more excellent way of

*life as members of a new community, the Christian church, which is
the new holy nation, destined to embrace all mankind.*

Shaping a Preaching Outline

A topical outline setting forth the cardinal idea just expressed
would have four main points:

I. Jesus Christ: the new lawgiver
II. The new Law: the Christian Way
III. The new community: the Christian church
IV. The Great Commission: the Christian witness

If such an outline is used, care must be taken to show the church
as community not as institution, and to relate it to the kingdom of
heaven. Each of the four points should be developed from the
material of the Gospel itself and applied to the modern situation.
Keep the standpoint of Peter or one of the disciples, that is, of a
member of the church who is being called to a more effective discipleship.

A second approach to outline may be made through 5:20, "For I
tell you, unless your righteousness exceeds that of the scribes and
Pharisees, you will never enter the kingdom of heaven." Here the
idea is a righteousness which first does all that the Pharisees do and
then goes on to surpass them. The Pharisees, of course, are activated
to righteousness by Moses the lawgiver; the Christians, on the other
hand, are impelled toward a more inward, more forgiving, more
inclusive righteousness by Jesus Christ as Saviour. Contrasts quickly
suggest themselves. The Pharisees are members of an exclusive
national community; Christians adhere to a universal community.
Pharisees make proselytes; Christians are even more passionately
missionary. Pharisees are conscientious moralists; Christians carry
these morals to the inward thought and disposition. The exact
development will unfold as you read the Gospel of Matthew from
this point of view.

A third door to outline is gained by way of the text of the book, Matthew 16:13-19. This is an epitome of the whole Gospel. Notice the relation to Old Testament expectation. Jesus is thought to be a Hebrew prophet. He is all that, and more. As the Christ, he creates a community, the church, using fallible human beings like Peter, and to them he commits the key for unlocking the kingdom of heaven to countless people who will hear their witness and respond to the higher way:

I. Jesus a Hebrew prophet, spokesman for God
II. Jesus as Christ and Son of God, the ultimate teacher
III. Faith in Christ as the foundation of a new spiritual nation, the church
IV. Believers as custodians of the keys of the kingdom

As a safeguard against distortion it will be well to check the sermon as it progresses against the cardinal idea and to supply illustrative sayings from all sections of the Gospel.

The fourth and last approach to outline to be offered here rests upon Matthew's own scheme of organization. There seem to be two general ways of going about this: A condensation of the Gospel into one's own words as it passes through the seven stages, including the five books and the Prelude and Epilogue. Such a "precis" will be found to have great power. The process is simple condensation; for example, the long genealogy of 1:1-16 is presented by J. P. Phillips in the following half-sentence: "The genealogy of Jesus Christ may be traced from Abraham, through forty-two generations, to Joseph, the husband of Mary, Jesus' mother. . . ." This omits details but it gets at the essence. One needs simply to continue along that line at the rate of about one page of sermon manuscript for every ten pages of scripture. Proportion will be achieved by faithfully adhering to the outline of the Gospel as given in this present chapter.

The second way of utilizing the Gospel's own scheme of organization is to select incidents and sayings that represent each part, setting them in enough general interpretation to show their import. For example, the beginning of Jesus' ministry in Galilee is summarized in 4:23-25; this can stand for the whole of chapters 3 and 4. There are several of these summaries in the Gospel; while they are hardly adequate alone, they do make an excellent core of the book's teachings. The summaries have been supplied as a part of the book outline given in this present chapter. In sections having no summary, sometimes a central key passage can be located as 8:14-17 and 8:23-27 for the miracles of chapters 8 and 9.

In all four main approaches sketched above the emphasis should be upon conveying the message of the Gospel of Matthew rather than making a lecture about the book. Such a message will have little time to mention such questions as relation to Mark and Luke, authorship and date. The purpose of the sermon is not a literary analysis; it is not even the presentation of the biblical book. Rather, it is the presentation through the book of the Teacher sent from God, Jesus Christ the Son of God and the Saviour of mankind. One fruit of attempting such a sermon will be a greatly heightened appreciation of the skill of the biblical writer!

A Modern Title

We have already chosen "The Teacher Sent from God" as our own preferred title for this chapter. By implication it is also a suitable name for the book sermon. Someone has said that the prominence of Peter in the Gospel might warrant a title like "The Gospel according to Peter." If "You" is substituted for "Peter" we have that direct personal involvement of every Christian which the Gospel itself accomplishes. "Surpassing the Pharisees" would seem to be an appropriate title for the sermon based on 5:20. "The Five Books of Christ" will have a certain appeal to those accustomed to hear about "The Five Books of Moses."

5

STRONG SON OF GOD
The Gospel According to Mark

A FEW YEARS ago the New Testament scholar, Edgar J. Goodspeed, wrote a book entitled *How to Read the Bible*, in which he said,

> Let us begin the reading of the Bible with the Gospel of Mark, and let us read it not piecemeal, as if it were very difficult; the Gospels are as a matter of fact very easy reading, full of interest and action. . . . If we ask, "How is the Gospel of Mark to be read?" the answer is, "At one sitting," as any close-packed, swiftly moving story should be read. It can easily be read aloud in an hour and a half, and to oneself in half that time.[1]

All that is essential to feeling the creative power of this Gospel is an open mind. We need not even bring faith with us, for this is not a book that requires faith; it produces it. Mark is so simple that a child can understand it and so powerful that dictators cannot reckon with it; so brief that it can be read in the time required to glance through the evening newspaper, and so searching that a man will spend his whole life trying to live up to it.

I. WORKING YOUR WAY INTO THE BOOK
Why not follow Dr. Goodspeed's suggestion? Read the Gospel of Mark at one sitting. Discard your theories about the Bible. For

[1] Winston, 1946, pp. 3-4.

the moment, free your mind of what you remember about Jesus. Exert no special effort to grasp the Gospel; let it grip and hold you by its own power.

Read Mark 1-16.

What were your impressions? Are you not a little out of breath? You have moved so rapidly, in such majestic company. Surely nothing compelled your attention more than Jesus himself. In this Gospel he is the towering, acting, serving, heroic one. He moves resolutely and purposefully into Galilee, strides designedly over it, retires from it to gather new resources of inward power, and returns marching unflinchingly toward Jerusalem and its cross. He acts and speaks in daring new ways. The story of such a life is truly a *Gospel*, for it *is* good news. Plainly Jesus' coming is no merely human event; it is a cosmic event, a happening guided by the hand of God.

FRESHNESS, ORIGINALITY

One of the things you will have noticed is how different Jesus was from others. His every doing and saying occasioned amazement. His teachings were different:

Read Mark 1:22; 4:33.

His attitudes toward traditional religious matters such as fasting, ritual, the sabbath were different:

Read Mark 2:18, 22, 27; 7:15.

His measures of greatness were the reverse of the world's measures of power, wealth, size, success:

Read Mark 8:33; 10:45; 12:43-44.

His love of sinners appeared to many to be scandalously different from the attitude of other religious leaders:

Read Mark 2:10-12, 16-17.

Above all, his picture of the Messiah was radically different from the picture of the conquering Davidic king or the overpowering heavenly messenger which was then popular:

Read Mark 8:31-33, 35.

In fact, the whole role of suffering was reversed by the teaching and example of Jesus. This was the crowning difference, and it occasioned the crowning amazement of the story:

Read Mark 15:39.

This Gospel also underscores the compassionate service of Jesus to human need:

Read Mark 6:34.

This one verse is a keynote of the Master's service. From the needy he could not turn away, be they leper, neglected paralytic, foreign woman or troubled ruler.

To no less a degree, Jesus is sensitive to the presence of God and responsive to his will:

Read Mark 1:35; 14:36.

THE POWER AND THE GLORY

And, pre-eminently, he is the Person of Power. He has the power of intellectual superiority:

Read Mark 3:4; 11:27-33; 12:17, 34b.

The most highly educated doctors of the law were quickly trapped in the intellectual snares which they had set for him. His was the power of intellect. His also was the power of moral authority, or of personal weight; this was real *authority*.

The power of Jesus extended from the minds to the bodies of men, to sickness, to spirits:

Read Mark 1:27, 31, 34; 3:11-12.

The power embraced nature:

Read Mark 4:41.

And the power was even victor over death:

Read Mark 5:42; 16:6.

THE RISE OF OPPOSITION

The rise of opposition against Jesus was early, as it was bitter. Officialdom was against him. The scribes mistrusted him from the start:

Read Mark 2:6-7.

And their mistrust quickly turned to enmity, and enmity into murderous plotting:

Read Mark 3:6.

Herod had killed John the Baptist and began to inquire about Jesus:

Read Mark 6:14.

The crowning opposition was that of the priests in the temple itself. When Jesus sought to make the temple a place of worship rather than a place of commercial traffic, the priests joined the conspiracy against his life:

Read Mark 11:18.

THE SHADOW OF THE CROSS

Thus it was soon apparent that tragedy would come. The shadow of the cross is cast over the narrative before it is scarcely half through:

Read Mark 8:31.

But it is shortly clear that the cross is not really a shadow so much as it is a light. Jesus goes before his disciples on the road to Jerusalem:

Read Mark 10:32.

He goes before them, showing them the way of the cross. He walks alone, for they are not yet equal to his terrible, lonely moral grandeur. And yet they follow, for the authority of his life is compelling. They follow, but as they follow they tremble, for their whole manner of life is shaken to its foundations. It is as if they are being broken down to be remade.

Yes, Mark is a Gospel of power, but the central power is that of the cross. What a strange reversal of the world's standards! In Charles Rann Kennedy's play *The Terrible Meek*, the Captain conveys the secret of this power to the Woman!

I tell you, woman, this dead son of yours, disfigured, shamed, spat upon, has built a kingdom this day that can never die. The living glory of him rules it. The earth is *his* and he made it. He and his brothers have been moulding and making it through the long ages: they are the only ones who ever really did possess it: not the proud: not the idle, not the wealthy, not the vaunting empires of the world. Something has happened up here on this hill today to shake all our kingdoms of blood and fear to the dust. The earth is his, the earth is theirs, and they made it. The meek, the terrible meek, the fierce agonizing meek, are about to enter into their inheritance.[2]

The tale of the resurrection is brief, but it is framed in mystery and highlighted with the joy of victory. Then the spell of this matchless life truly grips you. It holds you. You cannot cast it off, for you know that Jesus rose and that he lives.

That such an impact should have been made by such a book is all the more remarkable when you consider its brevity. The story of forty days in the wilderness and the temptation occupies two verses. The whole ministry appears to happen in a few days, not much more than a month in Galilee and a week in Jerusalem being recorded. There is restraint, but it is not the restraint of poverty. It is the restraint of massive power under superb control. We feel instinctively that what is told is a fraction of what could have been written. The economy of words, the careful selection of events and sayings, by their very restraint, heighten the power of the portrait.

AUTHOR AND CIRCUMSTANCES OF WRITING

Look now quickly at a few other points of interest.

Read Mark 14:51-52.

These verses are certainly unusual. Many have thought that this nameless young man was the author, John Mark, cousin of Barnabas

---

[2] Charles Rann Kennedy, *The Terrible Meek.* Copyright, 1912, 1933, 1939, by Charles Rann Kennedy; used by permission of the owner and Samuel French, Inc.

and missionary companion of Paul. He was also the son of Mary of Jerusalem in whose house the Christian church met in its earliest days following Pentecost:

Read Acts 12:12.

It seems highly probable that the Last Supper was eaten in this home. Thus, it is not unlikely that Mark was an eyewitness of Jesus' ministry—at least at the end. Three strands of evidence from early church fathers convey the unanimously accepted tradition about authorship:

Papais, shortly after A.D. 100, wrote: "Mark, having become the interpreter of Peter, wrote down accurately everything that he remembered, without however recording in order what was said or done by Christ."

The anonymous author of the *Anti-Marcionite Prologues to the Gospels,* writing between A.D. 160 and 180, said: "Mark, who was called stump-fingered because his fingers were small by comparison with the rest of his body, was Peter's interpreter and after Peter's decease wrote down this same Gospel in the region of Italy."

Irenaeus, about A.D. 180, agrees: "After their death [i.e., Peter and Paul's] Mark, the disciple and interpreter of Peter, himself also gave us a written record of the things preached by Peter."

The most ancient authorities agree that the Gospel of Mark was written in Rome and that it was based upon the preaching of Peter. It is worth noting that Peter is never presented in congratulatory terms in this Gospel.

All but about thirty verses of Mark are reproduced in the Gospels of Matthew and Luke, more than half of it word for word. The conclusion to be reached is that Mark was the first of the Gospels.

OUTLINE OF MARK

    I. Introduction: John the Baptist, the Baptism, and the Temptation,
       1:1-13
   II. The ministry in Galilee, 1:14-9:50

III. The journey to Jerusalem, 10:1-52
IV. The last week, 11:1-16:8

One can see from such an outline that the crucifixion, an event that happened on one day as the focal point of one week, really dominates the book. It is as if Mark were saying what Paul had written earlier: "I decided to know nothing among you except Jesus Christ, and him crucified" (1 Cor. 2:2). And the theme of the book might also have been stated in Paul's other words in that same Corinthian letter: "For the word of the cross is folly to those who are perishing, but to us who are being saved it is the power of God" (1 Cor. 1-18).

II. PREPARING YOUR BOOK SERMON

THE CARDINAL IDEA

God's own Son, who came to earth and became the centerpiece of humanity, disclosed the secret of divine power through a life of compassionate service and a death of vicarious sacrifice.

SHAPING A PREACHING OUTLINE

A good textual approach to Mark's message is found in Mark 10:43-45: ". . . whoever would be great among you must be your servant, and whoever would be first among you must be a slave of all. For the Son of man also came not to be served but to serve, and to give his life as a ransom for many."

The heart of the Gospel lies in the revolutionary idea of power and greatness epitomized in this text. Over against it is set the view of unregenerate humanity: "You know that those who are supposed to rule over the Gentiles lord it over them, and their great ones exercise authority over them. But it shall not be so among you." Even the religious authorities in Palestine seemed to have this worldly view of power and authority, with the result that the people were neglected and needy. When Jesus began to meet the deepest needs of these neglected people, it was inevitable that there should be a clash between the two kinds of power, with the seeming victory going to the protectors of vested interest, but with the actual victory going to Christ. Thus the movement of thought, which is also that of Mark, might be mile-posted: I. The new greatness of service; II. The clash of the great ones, new and old; III. New greatness as true greatness.

There is another verse of scripture which may be a helpful guide to a sermon outline, not so much as a text but as a picture or symbol: It is Mark 10:32. Here we have the picture of Jesus the moral leader going to Jerusalem to face martyrdom; he is physically and morally alone. Not even one of his disciples is equal to the demands of his companionship in such an hour, for he is showing them a way which is the opposite to the way of power in which they had so long trusted. They had wanted him to go to Jerusalem—as king; he was going to Jerusalem to be crucified. This had to be seen as the natural extension of his life of lowly service, for it too was an expression of his boundless love. Though they did not keep pace with their Master, nevertheless they followed him. He held them in thrall, and they could not escape the spell of his superior moral power. They went after him in amazement and in much trembling, but still they followed. I. In the way of service, Jesus walks in lonely power; II. This way leads to the cross; III. We are drawn, even against our fears, to follow in this way because we recognize it as the way of life.

A topical organization of the book may follow the great themes of the drama: service, popularity, opposition, sacrifice, victory. The background is the imperial city of Rome, spread over the earth as the paramount example of power after the old pattern. The Captain in Kennedy's *Terrible Meek* is spokesman for this kind of power:

We stretch out our hands, greedy, grasping, tyrannical, to possess the earth. Domination, power, glory, money, merchandise, luxury, these are the things we aim at; but what we really gain is pest and famine, grudge labour, the enslaved hate of men and women, ghosts, dead and death-breathing ghosts that haunt our lives forever.[3]

Then came Jesus, Strong Son of God, with another kind of power.

A Modern Title

"True Greatness," "Humanity's Moral Hero" are possible titles, but these pale when compared with "Strong Son of God."

[3] *Ibid.*

6

THE GREAT PHYSICIAN
The Gospel According to Luke

ONE WAY to find the spiritual stature of a man is to take the measure of his indignations. What and how big are the things that make him angry? By such a gauge, the author of the Third Gospel is a great soul. Consider some of the things that he hated: *Pious pretensions* and *self-righteousness* like those of the Pharisee praying in public to advertise his own excellence; *callousness to human suffering* like that of the priest and Levite who "passed by on the other side"; *vindictiveness toward penitent sinners* like the vindictiveness of the Elder Brother; *racial pride* such as the Jewish disdain of Samaritans; *greed* like the Rich Fool's. He saw these attitudes as disease which slay men as surely as smallpox or cancer; he saw them raging over the world as epidemics. But that is not all he saw; he also saw their power broken by the skill of the Great Physician and the empire of moral health extending its domain from a Galilean lakeside to world cities and thence to the farthest bounds of human habitation.

I. WORKING YOUR WAY INTO THE BOOK

The Gospel according to Luke is the first half of a two-volume work:

Read Acts 1:1-2; Luke 1:1-4.

These opening verses of Acts tell us clearly that the book to follow is volume two of an extended work, that it is addressed to Theophilus (meaning "one who loves God"), and that the first volume dealt with the ministry of Jesus and closed with his ascension. The opening verses of Luke introduce a book which fulfills all the conditions of volume one as described in the first verses of Acts. If we were expert in style and vocabulary, we should discover that the two books belong together and that they came from the same creative pen. There has never been any serious dissent from this view; and the literary excellence of the writing has never been contested. All would agree with Jerome's comment that Luke "of all the evangelists was the most polished in his use of the Greek language."

AUTHOR

Who was this writer? Th earliest church fathers to approach this question say that it was Luke, the physician, who was also a companion of Paul. There is no dissent from his opinion in early Christian literature, and when we look into the circumstances of Luke's life as they are revealed in a few brief references in the New Testament, we see that he could easily have been the author. There are only three verses of scripture in which Luke is mentioned by name:

Read Philemon 24; Colossians 4:14; 2 Timothy 4:11.

From reading these passages we learn that Luke was a physician, a prison companion of Paul, and a Gentile Christian for whom Paul had a great deal of affection. There is also much that we can learn from the so-called "we" passages in the book of Acts. These passages may have been taken directly from the travel diary of Luke: Acts 16:10-18; 20:5-21:18; 27:1-28:16. These verses tell us that the author was with Paul when he set sail from Troas to Macedonia on the second missionary journey and that he witnessed the clash with the soothsayers in Philippi. When Paul started back to Jerusalem for the last time, Luke joined him at Philippi and went with him the whole way. When, two years later and after his imprisonment at Caesarea, Paul was taken to Rome to stand trial before Caesar, Luke again accompanied him all the way. This would seem to say that he was in Palestine for two years—all through Paul's Caesarean imprisonment —and that he could have used this time to engage in the historical research and writing out of which came our two books.

There is one other minute clue that the author of our book was a physician:

Compare Mark 5:26 with Luke 8:43.

Jerome, who produced the Latin version of the scriptures known as the Vulgate, translating them in Palestine itself, recorded the tradition that Luke was a native of Syrian Antioch and a member of the church there. In Luke's universalism and missionary sympathies we certainly discover the Antioch spirit at its best. Were it not for the tradition, however, we might more easily suppose that Luke was "the man from Macedonia," and that he lived at Philippi.

Purpose

Luke's preface tells us something of his method and his purpose in writing his book: A somewhat various Gospel tradition carried by word of mouth and through several books gave a confused picture of the life and work of Jesus to Christians and other interested people who had not been eyewitnesses of the events. Luke determined to conduct careful research, to sort out the evidence, and to write an accurate and orderly account of the Gospel events. He had access to eyewitnesses of the original events, to books which certainly included Mark and the "Q" source also used by Matthew; but he also discovered a vast amount of material which he alone published. A consultation of a good harmony of the Synoptic Gospels will show these relationships: (1) How Luke uses about 60 per cent of the Gospel of Mark, (2) how he and Matthew parallel each other in a great deal of teaching material, especially in the Sermon on the Mount and many parables, (3) how Luke stands alone in nearly half of his work, especially in the opening chapters and the great middle section, from 9:51 to 19:28. It is in the study of the material peculiar to Luke that we discover the things that specially interested him and the purposes that drove him in the production of this literary master-piece.

Palestinian events are placed against a background of Empire happenings:

Read Luke 2:1-3; 3:1.

Luke is portraying a world religion, which has risen above racial and provincial limits, a religion which is a fulfillment and not a sub-version of Roman civilization with its universal state. Everywhere his sympathies are universal. The genealogies are traced back to Adam, the universal man, rather than to Abraham, the father of the Hebrews. Whereas the Jews had no dealings with Samaritans, he praises Samaritans (10:33) and pictures them in a good light more than once. When the Gospel is read together with the Acts the impression of Christian appreciation for the Roman State and its officials is greatly strengthened. Thus we come to see that Luke may have written in order to make a strong case for Christianity before the Roman world, and to disarm emerging misunderstanding and suspicion.

Special Interests

We have already mentioned Luke's passion for universalism. There are other interests closely allied to this:

1. Compassion for the poor finds its strongest New Testament outlet in this book. There is an intense concern for social justice shown in both volumes. Notice this in the following passages: The Song of Mary, 1:51-53; the preaching of John, 3:11-13; Luke's version of the Beatitudes, 6:20-26; and in the parables of Dives and Lazarus and the Rich Fool, 12:13-21. There are also some of the special sayings of Jesus which appealed strongly to Luke:

Read Luke 12:33; 14:12-14; 16:9, 14, 15.

Such compassion for the poor involves the stewardship of wealth and a harnessing of it to humanitarian purposes.

2. No writer in the New Testament is as interested in women or has a higher estimate of their worth. To see this read:

Luke 7:11-17, 36-50; 8:1-3; 10:38-42; 13:10-17; 23:27-31.

It can be seen that this interest in women is a natural correlate of Luke's universalism and humanitarianism. Luke cannot bear to tolerate the idea that there are second-class human beings anywhere.

3. Luke places special emphasis upon the prayer life of Jesus:

Read Luke 3:21; 5:16; 6:12; 9:18, 28; 23:46.

Thus we find Jesus praying after his baptism, after the cleansing of a leper, before the calling of the twelve, at the Transfiguration, and on the cross. Indeed, his last breath is spent in prayer.

4. Such an interest in prayer is naturally yoked to Luke's preoccupation with the Holy Spirit. Throughout the Gospel it is the presence of the Holy Spirit which directs Jesus. There is always the sense of the divine moving within the human life of Jesus as there was later the sense of the Holy Spirit living within the church:

Read Luke 4:1, 14; 10:21; 12:12.

5. Compassion for the penitent sinner might well be linked with compassion toward the poor. It has much of the same quality. Whole stories set forth this quality: The story of the penitent sinner, 7:36-50, the story of Jesus and Zacchaeus, 19:1-10, and the parable of the lost boy, 15:11-32, will suffice as a few out of many illustrations of Jesus' love for repentant sinners.

OTHER IMPRESSIONS

It is somewhat surprising to discover that the cross does not loom as large in The Gospel according to Luke as it does in Mark. Instead, the focus seems to be upon the resurrection and ascension. For example, Jesus' journey to Jerusalem to face the cross is introduced not through specific reference to the crucifixion at all but by reference to the ascension:

Read Luke 9:51.

Luke is hazy about the details of Palestinian topography. Several of his references to "Judea" appear to mean "Galilee." This bears out the tradition that Luke was a non-Jew:

Read Luke 6:17; 7:17.

Though Jesus appears throughout the story from the very beginning as divine Saviour, Luke has little theological interest when one compares him with Matthew or John. Luke is more pragmatic. He sees Jesus as one who brings deep, healing changes into the lives of persons. Luke never gets very far away from the sensitive humanitarianism of a conscientious physician; he finds people sick and in need of help, and he points them to their supreme Friend and Saviour.

OUTLINE OF LUKE

Introduction, 1:1-4:13
  I. The Galilean ministry, 4:14-9:50
  II. The Journey to Jerusalem, 9:51-19:28
  III. The last week, 19:29-23:56
  IV. The resurrection appearances, 24:1-49
Conclusion, 24:50-52

KEY PASSAGE

The Temptation narratives tell us much about the mission of Jesus by indicating what he rejected, but for what he accepted we are dependent upon the incident at Nazareth. Luke gives this to us at the very outset. Though it is chronologically out of place, Luke places it at the beginning of the ministry because it is the key to all that follows:

Read Luke 4:16-21.

Consider the mission of Jesus as shown here: (1) To preach good news to the poor is to lay the foundation for every bill of human rights. When fully applied, the insight of Jesus will wipe out poverty, ignorance and injustice all over the world. (2) To proclaim release to captives, sight to the blind and liberty for the oppressed is to liberate men from outward foes and inward fears. It is to set them free. (3) To proclaim the acceptable year of the Lord means to announce a social order acceptable to God. The vision calls for a perpetual Jubilee in which all social wrongs will be righted.

It is difficult to know just how far to press the details of the passage, but there can be no question that the section as a whole does set the tone and sound the motif of the whole Gospel. The Jesus who appears in these pages is Physician and Saviour of those in deepest need.

READING THE BOOK

Before reading the Gospel it may be helpful to browse through it, noticing some of Luke's special materials. These will be seen not only in the first three chapters but more particularly in the great middle section, 9:52-19:28. Little of this section has parallels in the other Gospels; much about the unique spirit of the Third Gospel is to be learned from it. It is here that we find the parables of the Rich Fool, the Good Samaritan, the Prodigal Son, the Pharisee and the Publican, and the story of the conversion of Zacchaeus, the despised tax collector. Only Luke has these.

Your browsing done, you will want to read the Gospel through at a sitting. Perhaps you will find it useful to do so with the outline of the book in view. Simply let the story take hold of you and carry you along; listen to what it has to tell you. Aside from the marks you may want to make on the page as you read, do not stop to take notes. Wait until you have finished; then write your impressions. Such writing after such a reading will be a devotional experience in itself, and in it will lie the beginnings of your book sermon.

I. PREPARING YOUR BOOK SERMON
CARDINAL IDEA

To every despairing person in every age and place, God sends a Saviour, Jesus Christ, who upon the condition of a man's trusting faith will liberate the sick soul from the disfiguring power of sin and inhumanity and set him healthy and strong as a member of the community where God's love reigns.

SHAPING A PREACHING OUTLINE

One clue to outline may be taken from the key passage. In our treatment above we tried to show how this key passage divides into three main goals: (1) To give men a sense of divine worth, (2) to set them free, and (3) to set up the will of God in the midst of interpersonal life. Using these three main goals as main divisions of the sermon it should be fairly simple to supply the material for each from the Gospel itself and from modern life.

A second clue to outline may be taken from the introductory paragraph of this chapter. What are the diseases which do not yield to treatment from lesser physicians, but which the Great Physician can cure? A reading of the Gospel from this point of view will prove highly rewarding. Here, for example, is a clinical report of a diseased condition: "He also told this parable to some who trusted in themselves that they were righteous and despised others" (Luke 18:9). Phillips renders it neatly, ". . . certain people who were confident of their own goodness and looked down on others." Spiritual snobbery, greed, guilt, hunger and sickness of body and mind— such are the diseases which the Great Physician can cure.

Still a third method of outlining the sermon is a narrative approach based upon a condensation of the Gospel itself. One of my students did this recently with powerful effect. He included a shortened version of some of the most notable parables, carefully selecting the events and sayings which would show the Great Physician actually at work in typical situations of need which are universally experienced. It sounds difficult, and it is, but such a message has much of the impact of the original good news; it will be heard with amazement and with gladness.

A fourth way of outlining the sermon is to use the principal interests of Luke as reflected in our discussion under "Special Interests" above. This would be a topical development of the work of Jesus as Saviour.

In any outline, however, we must be careful to put Jesus himself in the center, though we must also endeavor to see him through the eyes of Luke. For the purpose of the sermon we—the preacher and the congregation—are looking through Luke's eyes, we are Luke, telling the story of the life that heals in a broken and suffering world.

Modern Title

"The Great Physician" surely has priority. Written by Luke the physician about his Lord and Master, the book has the quality of personal tribute; but more, it shows Jesus at work as divine Saviour. Direct use of this emphasis upon salvation may prompt the title, "A Saviour for You." This second title has the virtue of bringing the universal appeal of the book directly home to each person. "Saviour of the World," though less personal, is nonetheless accurate. Other suggestions may include "Good News to the Poor" and "Release to the Captives."

7

OUR ETERNAL CONTEMPORARY
The Gospel According to John

IN THE Fourth Gospel the reader meets Jesus in Palestine during three years of an active and very human ministry. In the same pages he also meets the Christ of all peoples, humanity's Eternal Contemporary. Here he finds historical facts which pass into timeless symbols and symbols of eternity which root in definite historical fact. It is a book that can be read at two levels: by the outsider meeting Jesus as a historical personage for the first time, or by the committed Christian who is being led into a deeper communion with his living Lord. "Jesus, as he is seen by the writer of this Gospel, fills the earth and overflows it with divine life. Like the ocean, he is as near and as well known as the bays and tides along the shore of an island—as friendly to our boats, as much the source of life as is the sea to fishermen and sailors. But, like the ocean also, he is vast— vaster than the far horizon—mighty and majestic and mysterious."[1] This is the mood if our Gospel writer, whose reverent awe of Jesus prompted him to say, after he had tried to tell the story: "But there are many other things that Jesus did; were every one of them written, I suppose that the world itself could not contain the books that would be written" (John 21:25).

[1] From Dwight E. Stevenson, *The Fourth Witness* (Bethany Press, 1954), **p. 5.**

I. WORKING YOUR WAY INTO THE BOOK

As a reader of the Fourth Gospel where are you to be found within the book? You seem to have two possible identities there. You may be Thomas who says, "Unless I see . . . I will not believe."

Read John 20:24-29.

Thus, as the *alter ego* of Thomas, "who was not with them when Jesus came," because you live after his days in the flesh, you nevertheless come to an experience of the risen Lord which enables you to be one of "those who have not seen and yet believe."

Your other possible identity is with the unnamed "beloved disciple," who is also called "the other disciple."

Read John 19:26; 20:2, 3, 4, 8; 21:7, 20.

One suspects that this nameless member of the inner circle of Jesus' friends is not only the reverent author of the book but that he is also the believing Christian reader in any age. It is as if the book says to each reader, "You are yourself the disciple whom Jesus loves."

It is really clear that you are meant to be both persons in turn, first the late arrival, the outsider, who has to be convinced; and then the committed member of the inner circle who fully knows the love of Christ. The very structure of the book conduces to such a succession of identities. Up to the end of the twelfth chapter we find Jesus in the midst of crowds containing many who are merely curious and not a few who are hostile. In the rest of the book, except for the trial and crucifixion, the crowds are shut out and we find Jesus in the intimate circle of his friends.

The Purpose

The reader's dual identity within the book, as just discussed, disclosed the purpose of the writing. The Fourth Gospel is an invitation to come out of the shallows of existence and survival into the deeps of vital life; out of dry, unnourishing speculations about God into an experience of him; out of the darkness of self-centeredness and loneliness into the light of love.

Read John 20:30-31.

Such is the first purpose of the Gospel: to introduce the unbeliever to belief and to the life that faith brings.

It is also the purpose of the writer to deepen the Christian life of believers—to lead them into the richer meanings of Christ which keep unfolding to those who are taught by the spirit of Reality which is the living Christ.

Read John 16:12-14.

Thus, the two main goals of John may be said to be Christian conversion and Christian growth.

There are other, secondary aims which are instrumental to that main purpose. These include the building of a bridge of understanding from the Hebrew mind to the Greek mind, the refuting of messianic claims made on behalf of John the Baptist, the confounding of "docetists" and "gnostics," who were trying to substitute an abstract speculation for historical Christianity. These secondary aims were of vital importance to the first readers of the book; for the modern reader they are not so crucial.

AUTHOR AND DATE

Questions about author and date do not affect the message of the book, so we shall give them scant attention here. Overwhelming evidence from tradition supports the belief that the publication of The Gospel according to John took place at Ephesus, an important center of Hellenism, sometime near the year A.D. 100. According to many church fathers, John the Apostle died in old age at Ephesus. But it is generally thought that, although the witness of John the Apostle may stand behind the written Gospel, it was written by another hand. Some surmise that the real author appears briefly in the trial scene:

Read John 18:15.

Certainly the author was familiar with Jerusalem and the temple rites. He appears to have been a refined and highly educated Jew. Perhaps his name was John also. The church historian Eusebius says that "there were two of the same name in [the Province of] Asia, that there were also two tombs in Ephesus, and that both are called John to this day."

The exact identity of the author of the Fourth Gospel is therefore an unsettled question. But whatever his identity, we can tell from his book that he was a genius who possessed an intuitive and mystical mind, with a love for drama and allegory. He was a native, educated Jew who understood the Hellenistic mind and set himself with rare skill and artistry to capture that mind for the living Christ.

THE MAIN FEATURES

The Fourth Gospel, says Sir Edwyn Hoskyns, gives us a record not primarily of what eyewitnesses saw and heard, but what the disciples saw of the *glory* of the Word after Jesus had risen from the dead. A reader of John who has also read the Synoptic Gospels sense at once that he is in a different atmosphere. "Signs" and "sayings" are the two main bodies of material in John. The signs are deeds or things having an allegorical significance. Historically real, they are at the same time transparencies through which are seen religious truths of a moral and mystical nature. To get the feeling of allegory and symbol, read the allegory of the Good Shepherd in contrast with Luke's Parable of the Lost Sheep:

Read Luke 15:4-7; John 10:1-11.

We have in John a symbolic Gospel which sees things and events as the moving image of Eternity.

The "sayings" in John are long discourses and dialogues, each of them revolving around a central topic.

Compare Matthew 16:24-25 with John 15:12-17.

These long discourses and discussions lend to the Fourth Gospel a certain philosophical stamp. But this, far from becoming abstract, is quickly turned into the language of devotion. Note the characteristic "I am's" of John, and see how easily they change into prayer with the substitution of Thou for I: "Thou art the Light of the World. . . ."

Signs and sayings come in groups or episodes, each of which tends to be an epitome of the whole Gospel message. All the signs point to the crucifixion and resurrection, the great sign with which the book closes.

OUTLINE OF THE FOURTH GOSPEL

We shall follow the outline of C. H. Dodd in his masterful work *The Fourth Gospel, an Interpretation.* According to this distinguished British scholar, between proem (chapter 1) and appendix (chapter 21), the Fourth Gospel falls into two parts: The Book of Signs (chapters 2-12) and The Book of the Passion (chapters 13-20). The Book of Signs, in turn, is developed through seven episodes, each with its theme. Each of the seven episodes is presented in two phases, (1) narrative and (2) discourse. The narrative is a sign or symbol of deep spiritual meanings which are interpreted in the discourse following it. Thus in each episode narrative and discourse make a unified whole of symbol and interpretation, setting forth a single theme. The same scheme of narrative and interpretation is preserved in The Book of the Passion, but here discourse (chapters 13-17) precedes narrative (chapters 18-20), and the entire Book of the Passion is a single narrative. Such is the finely wrought pattern of the book. Now to look at it in detail:

OUTLINE OF FOURTH GOSPEL

The proem, chapter 1
 A. Prologue, 1:1-18
 B. The testimony, 1:19-51
I. The Book of Signs, chapters 2-12

    A. First episode: the New Beginning, 2:1-4:45
    B. Second episode: the Life-giving Word, 4:46-5:47
    C. Third episode: Bread of Life, chapter 6
    D. Fourth episode: light and life–manifestation and rejection, chapters 7, 8
    E. Fifth episode: judgment by the light, 9:1-10:42
    F. Sixth episode: the victory of life over death, 11:1-57
    G. Seventh episode: life through death, 12:1-36
II. The Book of the Passion, chapters 13-20
    A. The farewell discourses, chapters 13-17
    B. The passion narrative, chapters 18-20
The appendix, chapter 21

THE GOSPEL SUMMARIZED

We are not left in doubt for long about the main drift of the Fourth Gospel. The author summarizes the message at the outset; the Prologue is the gospel concentrated. In such a concentration it is possible to see that the gospel is good news of a deed which God performed for humanity through Jesus Christ, enabling men to come into their true inheritance of life. Omitting the verses pertaining to the Baptist, we get the following analytical picture of the Prologue:

    I. The divine life of the "Word," 1:1-5
      A. His eternity and divinity, vv. 1-2
      B. As the source of creation, v. 3
      C. As the source of human enlightenment, v. 4
      D. The "Word" in conflict with evil, v. 5
   II. The division of humanity over the "Word," 1:9-13
      A. The spiritually blind who exist in living death, vv. 10-11
      B. The children of light, born of the will of God, vv. 12-13
III. The "Word" incarnate in a man, 1:14-18
      A. The human life of the "Word," v. 14a
      B. The radiant spell of that life, v. 14b
      C. The boundless life which he gave out of his own fullness, v. 16
      D. The revelation of God which he gave out of his own fellowship vv. 17-18

Let us recapitulate the message of each of the three divisions of the Prologue: I (1:1-5). The God of beauty and of power and order in this amazing universe of atoms and stars is not foreign to the human heart. Indeed, as Augustine said, "If you dig deep enough in every man you will find divinity." II (1:9-13). Yet, the natural state of once-born humanity is one of sight without insight. In such a state the life of man is little more than a possibility in a bundle of confused desires which might as well be called death. What is even more astounding is that human perversity drives most of us to resist the light that would rescue us from this darkness, impels us to turn upon those who bear it, and to boast that we are "living" when in reality we only exist. This means martyrdom for the light-bearer and writes the law of the cross deep into human history. III (1:14-18). Now the Jesus of history enters and Christianity finds its central anchor in him. In him the living presence of God took up his dwelling in a tabernacle of flesh. His life had reality (truth), splendor (glory) and overflowing goodness (grace upon grace). This is a fact of history, of human experience. He brought the little-known God out of the shadows into the sunshine of love. All of this was in Jesus of Nazareth for the eye of faith to see; and what men saw has been a continuing vision of inspiration which will never die.

The attempt to translate *Logos* which is the central word of the prologue is always frustrating. *Word, Thought, Deed* have all been used. Perhaps for our age, enamored of *power*, that is the word that should be used. Here is my attempt to restate the prologue in terms of power:

The Cosmic Force which lies back of the world and out of which all nature sprang—indeed, without which there would have been universal emptiness—is also the secret of victorious living. This Cosmic Force battles with evil, and evil does not overcome it. As true Power, it is constantly in the world; it lies deep within every man. Yet, even though it is imbedded in human nature and is the very essence of full humanity, human beings, rebellious against God, seldom recognize the Power! It comes to the people of power in a power culture, but they reject it as weakness. Nevertheless, some men open their lives to it, and those who do so find themselves growing beyond ordinary humanity toward their inherent divinity. They begin to transcend their mortal beginnings and limitations. They experience the will and the power of God.

This Power has come to men as a human being who lived on earth among us, a life full of charm and reality. We saw him; he was radiant, glorious—none other than the Son of God. And from his overflowing life we all received boundless and everlasting enrichment. Before this, we knew about the law of God; now we experience his Love and his Reality. Formerly God was a dim, unclear figure to our minds; now in the life of this man, his Son, who knows God's heart, he stands revealed![2]

KEY VERSE

"For God so loved the world that he gave his only Son, that whoever believes in him should not perish but have eternal life" (John 3:16).

II. PREPARING YOUR BOOK SERMON

CARDINAL IDEA

Real Life, as contrasted with mere existence leading to extinction, may be had by personal commitment to Jesus Christ who came into the world as the incarnation of what is deepest in nature and highest in spirit; to reject him is to bring disaster, not upon him but upon ourselves; to accept him is to be born anew into endless and boundless life.

SHAPING A PREACHING OUTLINE

From the above survey of the Fourth Gospel two approaches will be at once apparent. One will be to begin from the key verse, which is appropriately known as "the golden text of the Bible." A textual division of the sermon according to the leading ideas of the verse will be faithful to the message of the book. This text should be read in the light of its immediate context, which is John 3:16-21. Some of the topics developed within this textual framework might be:

[2] *Ibid.*, p. 14.

The loving God, The perishing world, The incarnate love of God in the perishing world, Judgment and redemption.

The second obvious approach is to use the Prologue as the epitome of the whole book, as has been suggested. An outline somewhat more simplified than the analysis of the prologue already given, might follow these lines:

I. The Cosmic Christ
    A. His transcendence: Pre-existent and creative
    B. His immanence: the light of men
II. The Incarnate Christ
    A. His revelation
    B. His splendor
    C. His judgment
    D. His power of redemption

More simply still, it is possible to get a four-point sermon by using actual words of the Prologue:

I. The light shines in the darkness
II. The darkness has not overcome it
III. We beheld his glory
IV. To all who received him he gave power to become children of God

Bishop Gerald Kennedy in his Lyman Beecher Lectures at Yale devoted one lecture to the message of the Fourth Gospel. He set it forth under the title, "Good News of Eternity," and developed it through some of its outstanding ideas, with a Johannine text for each idea: (1) Revelation ("And The Word became flesh and dwelt among us, full of grace and truth . . ." John 1:14); (2) Eternal life in the commonplace ("And this is eternal life, that they know thee the only true God, and Jesus Christ whom thou hast sent." John 17:3); (3) The divine dwells in the human ("Abide in me, and I in you." John 15:4). This outline by Bishop Kennedy may stimulate you to select your own group of three or four texts which convey the thought of the Gospel in its most important stages.

A thematic approach is suggested by the seven episodes of the

Book of Signs, each of which illustrates one of the main themes of the Gospel. See the outline of the book, above.

The seven great "I am" passages offer another, quite similar road to outline. While seven points are unconventional for a sermon, the extraordinary importance of the message justifies them; because of their grandeur and familiarity, most of them are etched on the memory anyway:

1. "I am the bread of life."
2. "I am the light of the world."
3. "I am the door."
4. "I am the good shepherd."
5. "I am the resurrection, and the life."
6. "I am the way, and the truth, and the life."
7. "I am the true vine."

Chester W. Quimby in his book, *John the Universal Gospel*,[3]

[3] Macmillan, 1947, pp. 221-24.

concludes with "A Dictionary of John" in which some of the special terms of the Gospel are defined. This suggests a sermon hinging on the most important words in John's special vocabulary. While there are several of these special words, many of them are related in families; for example, *light* is directly related to *truth, darkness, judgment* and *believe*. *Love* is related to *know, glory* and *sanctify*. Each of these Johannine words carries its own unique meaning, and these meanings taken together summarize the teaching of the whole book.

A Modern Title

The central figure of this universal Gospel may best be called "Our Eternal Contemporary." If we want to shift attention to the object of Jesus' ministry, we might phrase it: "That You May Really Live," or "Lest You Die before You Live."

8

THE MARCH OF THE GOSPEL
The Acts of the Apostles

Like a mighty army
Moves the church of God;
Brothers, we are treading
Where the saints have trod.

To THE author of The Gospel according to Luke and The Acts of the Apostles the march of the gospel down the centuries is as unceasing and as victorious as the march of time itself; he writes his two-volume account of early Christianity in such a way as to include the centuries and the whole of Christendom. He writes of a continuing gospel. This procession, which began with Jesus' Triumphal Entry into Jersualem is not to be stopped! Luke means to say to us that the Tirumphal Entry did not take place in an obscure corner of the Mediterranean basin merely; it took place in the world. And it did not happen nearly two thousand years ago; it is still happening. Read the New Testament log of its progress: Jerusalem, Samaria, Caesarea, Antioch, Cyprus, Galatia, Philippi, Thessalonica, Athens, Corinth, Ephesus, Rome! At last the emperor of mighty Rome acknowledged, "O pale Galilean, thou hast conquered!" Then watch the procession moving down through history: Alexandria, Ethiopia, Spain, France, Germany, Britain. Christ's invasion of Britain was more important than that of William the Conqueror. See him still entering other lands, new continents, islands, cities, civilizations: India, Japan, China, the South Seas, Africa, Greenland, Tibet. All over this world our allied armies have gone, to find that the church was there ahead of them, in distant, secluded places, in jungles and huddled villages . . . at the ends of the earth. That is what Luke was writing about.

I. WORKING YOUR WAY INTO THE BOOK

At the beginning of the book of Acts you are greeted by the second installment of a continued story: "In the first book, O Theophilus, I have dealt with all that Jesus began to do and teach. . . ." (Acts 1:1). That word *began* is significant. The earthly ministry of Jesus was only the beginning of the Gospel. Turning to the end of the Acts and noticing its deliberately unfinished character, we conclude that the work of the Apostles was only the "end of the beginning." The author of these two books was telling a story of a gospel whose beginnings could be described but whose eventual outcome could be only dimly imagined.

The first volume in this story was, of course, The Gospel according to Luke (see Luke 1:1-4). Both books display the same beauty of style, the same passion for accuracy, the same lofty universalism, the same social conscience, and the same note of triumphant joy.

Who was Theophilus, to whom these two books were addressed? Aside from the fact that the name means "one who loves God" we are given no clue. He is addressed at the beginning of Luke as Festus is addressed in Acts 26:25, which leads some to think that he may have been a Roman governmental official. This is an interesting speculation, but no such individual is known to us. The guess that suits many best is that Theophilus means "Anyone who loves God." In that case the book is a general work addressed to all men of reverent mind in every place and age.

Since the book of Acts is the second of two volumes, the purpose of the first volume will be the purpose of this one as well. The reader is advised to turn to the discussion of Luke above for a review of that purpose. It is appealing to surmise that Acts was written by Luke while he was with Paul in Rome during the two years of the latter's wait for trial before Nero, and that the completed work as it stands was used as a brief at the hearing. As the book closed, the trial was about to take place.

For a discussion of authorship, we refer the reader to the chapter on The Gospel according to Luke, above. Our external knowledge of this Christian physician is scanty, but we can learn much about his character from the manner in which he wrote: he was modest and unassuming; he was a keen observer and an accurate reporter; he was highly educated; he was much interested in persons; he was a world citizen; he was an ardent admirer of Paul; and he was a thoroughgoing Christian.

CONTENTS OF THE BOOK

Turning now to the contents of the book itself, we find it dealing primarily with the spread of the Christian church. In the thirty years of this record, the church grew geographically until it had expanded from its religious center at Jerusalem, on the fringe of the Empire, to its capital at Rome. Spiritually, the church grew in this same period from a Nazarene sect within Judaism to the full stature of the church universal.

The story of this amazing expansion is not told comprehensively. It centers, for instance, largely upon Peter and Paul, while leaving the other apostles in the background. It deals with the westward expansion along the northern shores of the Mediterranean, while telling us little or nothing of the early penetration into Africa and eastward from Palestine toward India. We are told that there was a church at Rome, but we do not learn how it started. Plainly, Luke has given us typical incidents out of the first thirty years of the church's history. These are snapshots of living situations taken here and there to show how the church lived in its early years and how it grew. We may not learn all the "facts" about the early church from such a book, but we do something more important. We feel its pulse and know its spirit.

Moreover, these living situations are all organized around their main actors. Events are associated with persons. Two main personalities dominate the book, Peter the leader of the original twelve, and Paul, the foremost messenger to the Gentiles. But there are numerous others. In fact, there are no less than 110 personal names in the book.

The book falls rather naturally into two fairly equal halves: Chapters 1-12 and chapters 13-28. This makes it possible to read it at two sittings, and still to keep the sense of wholeness which is so valuable in studying a biblical book.

An Outline of the Book of Acts

Author's Preface, 1:1-5
I. The Acts of Peter, 1:6-12:25
    A. The church established at Jerusalem, 1:6-3:42
        1. Preparation, 1:6-26
        2. Pentecost, 2:1-47
        3. Growth of the Jerusalem church, 3:1-5:42
    B. The expansion of the church to Antioch: Gentiles admitted, 6:1-12:25
        1. Stephen and the first persecution, 6:1-8:3
        2. Philip in Samaria, 8:4-40
        3. The conversion of Saul, 9:1-30
        4. Peter receiving the first Gentile, 9:31-11:18
        5. The founding and the early life of the "mixed" church at Antioch, 11:26-12:25
II. The Acts of Paul, 13:1-28:31
    A. The missionary work of Paul and Barnabas, 13:1-16:4
        1. The commission at Antioch, 13:1-3
        2. Paul and Barnabas in Cyprus and Galatia, 13:4-14:28

POINTS OF INTEREST

1. **The parallel of Luke and Acts.** R. R. Williams, Bishop of Leicester, has said,

> The Gospel tells us how God "visited and redeemed his people" by sending His Son, Jesus Christ. The Acts tells how this event became "a light to lighten the Gentiles" through the witness of the Spirit-filled Church. The stories run parallel to each other, and almost certainly Luke meant them to appear so.[1]

If we inquire into the details of the parallel, we discover: birth of Jesus—Pentecost, birth of the church; healing and teaching ministry of Jesus—the ministry of the church, healing and teaching; the passion of Jesus—persecutions and suffering of Apostles, especially Paul's arrest, imprisonments, shipwreck. The resurrection of Jesus—Paul preaching unhindered in Rome. It is further interesting to notice that both stories cover a period of almost exactly thirty-three years. Beneath the parallel of events there lies the identity of message; both books proclaim the primitive *kerygma* outlined above on page 19.

2. **The Acts of the Holy Spirit.** Although this book is called The Acts of the Apostles, it is more properly the ministry of the Holy Spirit. Notice how it is the Holy Spirit which not only initiates the work in Jerusalem but also opens the way to the Gentiles. The story

---

[1] Williams, *The Acts of the Apostles* (London: SCM Press, 1953), p. 26.

of the birth and growth of the church is more than a human affair.

3. Everything is turned to account for the expansion of the church. Christians are scattered by persecution, but they go preaching the word in new places (8:4). Imprisonments are used for the conversions of jailers (16:31). Every adversity is turned into an opportunity.

4. The Jerusalem conference of Acts, chapter 15, is a crucial turning point for world Christianity. It was then that Christianity graduated from its former status as a sect within Judaism to a universal religion destined for the world. We shall not here undertake to untangle the difficult questions about the relation of Galatians 2 to Acts 15; how the problem is settled does not vitally affect the essential message of the book, in any case.

5. No biblical book contains so many speeches, and these in turn show us the message of the Christian preachers. Notice how each speech is suited to the situation in which it is delivered. Notice also how each one moves quickly to a positive declaration of the main facts of the gospel. Each is a declaration of a divine event, a proclamation of "the mighty acts of God through Christ."

6. Key passages. The "outline" of Acts is disclosed in 1:8, "But you shall receive power when the Holy Spirit has come upon you; and you shall be my witnesses in Jerusalem and in all Judea and Samaria and to the end of the earth." Less exact as to detail, but just as faithful in spirit is 12:24: "But the word of God grew and multiplied."

7. Jerusalem and Antioch. Jerusalem, the mother church, is a kind of Moses who never enters the promised land. Born within Judaism, she never wholly escapes from it. Her sympathies, like her vision, are not quite large enough for the world task of the Gospel. Because she cannot grow up to her vision or rise to the challenge of the Holy Spirit, God finds it necessary—reluctantly and sorrowfully—to turn from her to Antioch, the daughter church.

Antioch, in turn, becomes the mother of the mission to the Gentiles.

The whole movement from Jews to Gentiles is repeated many times throughout the book; as at Pisidian Antioch, "It was necessary that the word of God should be spoken first to you. Since you thrust it from you, and judge yourselves unworthy of eternal life, behold, we turn to the Gentiles" (13:46).

8. Universalism. The world-wide implications of an interracial, international and intercultural fellowship are present in the church from the beginning, but they win their way against strong internal and external opposition. The overcoming of the external opposition is placarded by Gamaliel in 5:38, 39: ". . . keep away from these men and let them alone; for if this plan or this undertaking is of men, it will fail; but if it is of God, you will not be able to overthrow them. You might even be found opposing God!" The overcoming of internal prejudice, on the other hand, is signaled by Peter in his reply at the hearing over the admission of the Gentile Cornelius: ". . . who was I that I could withstand God?" (11:17).

9. The church as a fellowship. While the book of Acts tells the story of the expansion of the church, it is not the story of an institution or an organization; it is the warm narrative of a fellowship of Christian personalities. This distinction between *community* and *institution* should be a continuing one; it is one most frequently noticed on the mission fields, where community is strong and institution weak. Over against this, American and European churches have weak community and strong institutions. If there must be a choice, we know where the emphasis of Acts will fall.

With these clues, it is time now for you to read the book of Acts.

II. PREPARING YOUR BOOK SERMON

Cardinal Idea

The love of God for man, which found its first incarnation in Jesus Christ, is incarnate for the world in the church, the true com-

munity of his followers; under the power of God himself this church in spite of pettiness within and opposition without, is marching down the centuries and it is crossing all human boundaries.

Shaping a Preaching Outline

One outline, based upon the growth of the church, looks at two aspects of this growth, each constituting a main division of thought in the sermon: The church outgrew its geographic homeland, moving from Jerusalem to Rome, and, in the centuries since, from Rome to the ends of the earth. The church also outgrew its cultural infancy within Judaism, moving from a Jewish sect to a world faith. It refuses to be confined to any provincialism, even our modern Western provincialism. The church that grew thus was born of the Spirit, and it lives on in spite of hardships and seeming defeat, conquering by the power of God, provided it is truly the church, which it is when it devotes itself "to the apostles' teaching and fellowship, to the breaking of bread and the prayers" (Acts 2:42).

A second possible outline focuses upon the church as community, growing in four main areas: Brotherhood religion, a community of worship; brotherhood economics, a community of mutual service in life's necessities; brotherhood citizenship, a community of constructive citizens living from Christ-instructed consciences; brotherhood evangelism, a witnessing community which gradually becomes an interracial, intercultural and international fellowship. Preliminary to these four main points is a discussion of the true church as togetherness of those called out by Christ, inspired by the Holy Spirit; the church is constituted of those who come together because they have come to Christ and live in him.

Still a third outline comes from an attempt to present Christianity as a procession. The key is taken from the Triumphal Entry, as Jesus enters Jerusalem, where the church began. As the sermon progresses it shows Jesus entering world cities and villages, as this event of Palm Sunday becomes a cosmic happening at the core of human history. The sermon might bear the title, "Stop the Procession." Not only the Gospel but the Acts as well assert a movement that cannot be stopped. "Teacher, rebuke your disciples," the Pharisees pleaded. Jesus answered, "I tell you, if these were silent, the very stones would cry out." There is a strange, unconquerable but conquering persistence in Christianity; it cannot be stopped. A kingdom without frontiers, it keeps moving. Someone has said that you can't get away from Christ in morals and religion any more than you can get away from Copernicus in astronomy. Why? Because as Copernicus disclosed the truth about the stars, and the stars in their courses confirm his story, so Jesus disclosed the truth about man and the universe, and the whole world through every living cell cries out in support of him. If he stood alone against an alien sky, we could dispose of him and ignore his church as one more human institution. But it is not so. Where he goes, there goes all that is noblest and most powerful, all that man is and is meant to be —where he goes, there goes God.

A Modern Title

The third sermon can bear the title, "Stop the Procession!" The second is "The Church Conquering the World." Other titles for sermons on this book may be "The Continuing Gospel," "The Church on the March" or "The March of the Gospel."

9

THE GREAT REDEMPTION
The Letter of Paul to the Romans

O URS has been called the age that does not believe in sin; we have
explained it away into complexes and cultural lag. At the same
time, ours has been called the age of the guilty conscience. We are
not at peace with ourselves, and God is a stranger. We may be
skillful at self-justifying excuses and rationalizations but when the
truth is told we simply do not accept ourselves. This is shown not
only by our fear of being alone and silent but also in our ravenous
appetite for books about peace of mind. There is an Appalachian
folk song one line of which captures the present mood perfectly:
"Give my heart ease, O give my heart ease!" This uneasy heart is
also fearful; it lives in an age of broken community and of war—
hot war, cold war. In a word, our situation is a predicament and we
need to be delivered, to be saved, rescued, redeemed.

The Letter of Paul to the Romans is addressed to this predicament.
It contains good news of redemption—from the uneasy heart, from
the divided mind, from human strife, from cosmic loneliness. To
those who have been "slaves to death all their lives" Paul says,
"Wake up and live!"

I. WORKING YOUR WAY INTO THE BOOK

Luther called the book of Romans "the clearest Gospel" in the
New Testament. We do not want to contradict Luther but we may

have our doubts. To many readers it seems difficult, theological, almost obscure. Why should it seem so? Because they read it not in its own light as a story of deliverance from our human predicament, but in the light of the creeds as a doctrinal treatise. They do no expect to see themselves mirrored here; they expect to look into a dark cave of abstractions and theories which have nothing to do with them. This turn of opinions would have made Paul very angry. For theories and speculations he had nothing but contempt. His passion was facts, deeds, human lives. His book is not a treatise; it is a news story about the rescue of persons.

Occasion

The letter carries its own information about time and circumstances of writing:

Read Romans 1:9, 10; 15:23-29.

Paul had finished his work in the eastern Mediterranean and was about to return to Jerusalem with a gift from the churches for the poor Christians of the Holy City. Immediately after the completion of this pilgrimage, he hoped to sail to Rome for a brief visit with the church in the capital of the Empire. Then he would move on by plan to new mission fields in Spain.

Read 1 Corinthians 16:1-6; 2 Corinthians 9:1-5; Acts 20:1-6.

The above verses show us exactly where Paul's words to the Romans fit best—at Corinth, during his three months before starting for Jerusalem in company with the gift-bearing representatives of the Macedonian and Achaian churches. This event is dated by the British scholar C. H. Dodd in February of A.D. 59. Some would place it two years earlier, none later.

Why did Paul write to the Roman Christians? Two reasons are suggested by the letter itself. One was to prepare them for his coming. Paul had many detractors, not to say ardent foes, at work within the church of the Empire. He knew not what rumors about his preaching had come to Rome or what picture of him the Romans had. How could he better set the record straight than to send a letter giving them the main outlines of his message? Moreover, as we see from the letter itself, Paul was conscious of being at a milestone. He was completing his mission to the eastern Mediterranean world and was about to turn west. To summarize the message he had been preaching throughout the years of the eastern mission was the most natural thing in the world. And to send this summary to the church at the capital of the Empire was certainly fitting.

A second reason for the letter which may have existed in Paul's mind was related to his proposed mission to Spain. We know that it was the practice of the early church to aid its missionaries by giving them hospitality on their way through a given city, and provisions and money for their forward journey. It seems not unlikely that Paul was offering the Roman Christians the opportunity of sharing in his mission to Spain. What else can be the full meaning of Romans 15:24, "I hope to see you in passing as I go to Spain, and to be sped on my journey there by you, once I have enjoyed your company for a little."

We must remember that Paul was proud of his Roman citizenship, and that he thought of himself as the accredited apostle to the Gentiles. The chief Gentile city was Rome. Although he had not planted Christianity there, he felt an obligation to the Roman community, as he himself said:

Read Romans 1:13-15.

He was about to come to them to preach the gospel. His letter is an advance installment.

THEME

It is universally recognized among students of the letter that the theme is that verse which was so pivotal in the experience of Martin Luther, Romans 1:17. Couple it with the preceding verse and you have the epistle in a nutshell.

Read Romans 1:16, 17.

The paraphrase of these verses in Dummelow's one volume Bible commentary is enlightening:

[16] I am not ashamed to preach the message of Christ even in great Rome, for it is the divine power whereby God brings salvation to all who have faith in Christ. [17] For in it is revealed that God accepts men as righteous solely on the condition of faith, as is shown in the OT."[1]

There is more to the righteousness of God than this paraphrase shows, however. To get the full meaning, we can scarcely do better than to rely upon C. H. Dodd's interpretation.

The meaning of the words "the righteousness of God is revealed," says Dodd, is that "God is now seen to be vindicating the right, redressing wrong, and delivering men from the power of evil."[2] The rest of the verse, "through faith for faith," Dodd says, means very simply that this work of conquering righteousness in the Gospel is a "matter of faith from start to finish." On the human side, nothing is required to make it possible but faith and faith alone.

But what is faith? It is neither simple loyalty to God nor intellectual belief in propositions. Rather,

Faith is that attitude in which, acknowledging our complete insufficiency for any of the high ends of life, we rely utterly on the sufficiency of God. It is to cease from all assertion of the self, even by way of effort after righteousness, and to make room for the divine initiative. By such faith a man enters into life, in every sense in which that phrase can be used. . . .[3]

Thus we see that faith is a radical trust in the all-sufficient God, leaving no room for human merit of any kind.

It may be argued, as indeed it was by Paul's critics in his own

[1] J. R. Dummelow (ed.), *A Commentary on the Holy Bible* (Macmillan, 1941), p. 866.
[2] *The Epistle of Paul to the Romans* (Harper, 1932), p. 13.
[3] *Ibid.*, p. 15.

day, that such a reliance upon faith leads to passivism, even to moral indifference. The opposite is true. When I decide at last to let God act through me I no longer need to waste my energies in an internal tug of war; I can act freely and one-directionally for an unconditional right. There is no limit to what I may strive to achieve; the fret and the care are taken out of my striving. I no longer undertake it to compensate for a guilty conscience or to win favor with men and God. The favor has been bestowed. I have been accepted. Now I work in gratitude, and my labor expresses the sense of oneness with men and God which has come to me out of God's active, all-embracing love. The important thing is that I myself have been changed by giving in to God absolutely, and that this change is not my own doing but is the power of God working in me. Whereupon I can really go to work at last, and since I do not need to work for myself, I can work for God and his kingdom.

OUTLINE OF THE LETTER

Introduction, 1:1-17
    A. The address, 1:1-7
    B. Opening remarks, 1:8-15
    C. Theme of the letter, 1:16-17
  I. The evil predicament of all mankind, 1:18-3:20
    A. The pagan world, 1:18-32
    B. The Jewish world, 2:1-3:20
 II. Deliverance by God from the power of evil, 3:21-4:25
    A. Justification stated, 3:21-26
    B. Justification and its corollaries, 3:27-31
    C. The principle illustrated through an allegory, 4:1-25
III. Induction by God into a new life, 5:1-8:39
    A. The theme of salvation stated, 5:1-11
    B. The two natures contrasted, 5:12-21
    C. New life in Christ, 6:1-8:13
       1. Union with Christ in death and resurrection, 6:1-14
       2. An illustration from slavery, 6:15-23
       3. A second illustration, from marriage, 7:1-6
       4. Sin and salvation in experience, 7:7-25

From the above outline we can see how clearly and how systematically Paul sets forth his thought in this letter. He finds the whole human race in a predicament—living in sin and death, hunting peace but never finding it, thirsting for power and knowledge but doomed to weakness and ignorance, clutching at ideals but never attaining them. God appears through the historical Christ to give guilty man a new status; he removes the barrier of unforgiven sin and accepts man as his son, if man will come to him in complete acceptance of the love that Jesus showed. Thereupon man experiences salvation, which is simply a new order of life in which the old tensions are eliminated and a new freedom and power are experienced. This new life has within it such a victorious quality that it imparts the hope of everlasting life to those who have it. It works itself out in the Christan ethic. Men having his new status with God and this new life from God behave differently; from the motive outward their actions are transformed.

Paul has hardly sketched this grand design before he stops to mourn over Israel, his own nation. It is a matter of history in his time that the Jews have rejected this gospel of Christ, and that the new people of God are recruited principally from among the Gentiles. Paul can never be content with this. He would gladly give up his own salvation if his people could be saved. But he cannot believe that the Jews will forever reject him. Christ is destined to be victor, and to bring all things both in heaven and on earth into his dominion; therefore, the Jews will come in at last. This he believes, and he injects this deep personal concern into the letter. The letter can be read without these chapters (chapters 9-11), though, of course, Paul's sublime vision of the ultimate victory of God in history is not complete without them.

The heart of the letter is found in chapters 5 through 8. Together with the theme in chapter 1, this section may very well be read and reread. Again, the very center of these chapters is found in 5:1-11. Thus, a student may move in one of two different directions in reading and understanding the letter as a whole. He may begin with the theme, 1:16-17, and move on to the heart of the central section of the letter, 5:1-11, following it with the central section, chapters 5-8. He is then ready to read the whole letter from beginning to end. Or, beginning with the whole letter, he may move intensively in reverse order until he has summarized it all in the two short verses of the theme.

Vocabulary

From such an understanding of the letter, however, we are sometimes barred by one simple fact: Paul uses terms which may be opaque to us. After we have read through "salvation," "righteousness of God," "through faith for faith," and "the wrath of God" —all of which occur in the first chapter—we begin to realize that our understanding of Paul's meaning is becoming fuzzy already. To correct this ambiguity of thought—ours not Paul's—we shall have to see what he meant by them.

The wrath of God. We would be more inclined to say "disaster," and we would be correct if by it we meant the disaster that men bring upon themselves by human sin in a moral universe. The capricious element of human temper and anger must not be imputed to God. His wrath is the experienced disorder within and among persons who have tried to build their lives on shaky moral foundations.

Justification. This is an analogy from the law courts. In the language of personal counseling, we would say "acceptance." To be justified is not to be made righteous, but simply to be accepted by God, to be acquitted, not to be treated as a criminal but like a wandering and repentant son who has come home. Justification, therefore, can be read as acceptance or forgiveness.

Ransom. Here is an analogy based upon the institution of slavery. A too literal application of this analogy has led to extreme theories of the atonement. The term means simply the act of redeeming, the freeing of a slave. A good equivalent would be *emancipation*. The historical background is the emancipation of the Jews from bondage in Egypt. To be ransomed is to be set free; it is this act of freeing that Paul focuses upon, rather than the method. A theology of the method of atonement which is built upon the analogy of ransom has gone afield.

Propitiation. This analogy is taken from the practice of animal sacrifice at temples. All of Paul's readers both Jewish and Gentile would understand it. When it is seen as a sacrifice to appease God, it does violence to the character of God as seen in Christ; therefore, it must mean very simply "the means by which sin is forgiven."

Blood. For a Jew blood was the equivalent of life. The meaning, then, is "the consecrated life of Christ." That is what shows God's saving love to us.

Salvation. This is simply deliverance from death and from bondage to sin. Positively, it means the rule of love in human motives. It is more than an ideal; it is a way of living which has sufficient resources of power "to will and to do his good pleasure." It is the undivided life—inwardly united in a harmony of wishes and powers, outwardly joined to the solidarity of God's family. It is genuine life, now and forever.

Flesh. Paul uses the term in a double sense to mean either our physical bodies or our lower selves. Generally he uses it to denote our lower selves. He means life organized around a selfish center; the mind is included in such a life for there is such a thing as "the mind of the flesh."

Spirit. Do not be misled into Greek dualism of mind and body. By spirit Paul means human life, including physical existence, organized around the will of God. It is equivalent to our true nature, the image of God within us, our higher selves. This spirit is dynamic, not passive, and it comes from God to those who are willing to receive it.

Adam. This is our corporate humanity organized upon the basis of egoism. It is wrongdoing as a racial characteristic and a racial heritage. Adam is not one who merely lived and died thousands of years ago. Adam is the merely human in each of us, and "each man is the Adam of his own soul."

Death. Paul means a good deal more than physical extinction. He means a twisted existence, an existence corresponding to various analogies such as being "in bondage," "at war," "darkened in their minds." It is frustrated, self-destructive living. It is spiritual and not physical death that Paul is talking about.

One other key to the understanding of Romans is essential. This is a constant awareness of the earthly life of Jesus. When Paul thought about the manner of God's love toward men, he was always remembering the demonstration of that love in the life of Jesus. We must never be led away from that historical center of our faith. It is in Jesus that we understand love and forgiveness and find life abundant. Let the awareness of the life of Jesus in the flesh be a constant check upon the feverish imagination of theologians who like to begin with the analogies of Romans and build their systems of atonement. Nothing in these theories that does violence to the life and spirit of Jesus can be allowed to pass.

II. PREPARING YOUR BOOK SERMON

CARDINAL IDEA

Deliverance from our human predicament in frustrated, self-destructive ways of living can be found in the strength of God as we accept his love and are accepted by him, as we give up all imposition of our selfish will, all pride in our own good achievement, and let God work through us to lift us into a completely new kind of life now and forever.

SHAPING YOUR PREACHING OUTLINE

Effective preaching of the message of Romans will depend upon the pastoral heart much more than upon the theological mind. If you are acutely aware of the persons before your pulpit as men and women who have been "in bondage to death all their lives," if you see a world weak in its vaunted power, ignorant in the pride of its education, poor in spite of its natural resources, its inventions and its money, you will have the proper place to begin. If, in addition to this keen awareness of sin as a dominion of death in the lives of men, you have a personal knowledge of man's inability to extricate himself from it by his own power, if you have tried yourself unsuccessfully to win through to an easy conscience while clinging to your pride and your self-sufficiency, if in spite of all your good deeds you could never raise enough moral capital to pay off your conscience, if your goodness was always *your* goodness, a duty but seldom a joy, and your life was filled with ideals but void of power and inner peace—if you have experienced man's inability to save himself— you will have the second qualification for a sermon on Romans. What more? This: that you shall have died with Christ and experienced his resurrection, that you shall know yourself as a forgiven sinner, and taste the glorious liberty of the sons of God, that this shall be in your life no phrase or doctrine, but an experienced reality, so that the peace of God is yours and the power of God your daily portion. Then you will be morally and spiritually prepared to proclaim the great redemption. Failing that, there is no preparation with commentaries, lectionaries and books of theology that will avail; the man who understands Romans with his reason alone does not understand it at all.

Begin with man in need of God, with man lost in his own sin or self-righteousness. That is where Romans itself begins. There are two possible starting places in the letter itself. One is in the opening section, 1:18-3:20, where we see the failure both of the rebellious, sinful life and of the prideful, righteous pursuit of merit. This is our situation; we may hesitate to call it death but we are not entirely opposed to the label. We are experiencing enough of "the wrath of God" to make the label significant. Notice that Paul addressed these chapters to the capital of the Roman Empire, the very center of political and military power, the seat of culture and of education. It was these enlightened, privileged men who were "futile in their thinking," and whose "senseless minds were darkened." Proof enough that Paul would not be cowed today in New York or Washington. His message to our age would be much the same. Is this life that we live? Hardly.

The second possible starting place in the letter is found in 7:7-25 where Paul gives his searching psychological analysis of a mind that tries to merit forgiveness and peace. It corresponds somewhat loosely to Aristotle's account of the four stages of moral maturity: (1) Downright wickedness; (2) incontinence, knowing what is right but failing to do it; (3) continence or self control, doing the right but through struggle and intense effort, and therefore without joy; (4) temperance, personality harmonized, doing the right effortlessly and cheerfully. The word *temperance* is not a happy label for us, but the reality it signifies is what eluded Paul in his pre-Christian days. He lived then at Aristotle's third stage, in unsatisfying moral struggle.

The points of the sermon will naturally follow the unfolding stages of thought in the letter itself. These can be phrased variously:

1. Man's sin and the futility of moral struggle.
2. God's answer in judgment and redeeming love.
3. The new moral disposition of the redeemed man.

The above outline is suggested by a paragraph from *Sent Forth to Preach* by Jesse Burton Weatherspoon, though he does not state the points so briefly or in outline form. A second manner of stating the basic outline of the book comes from one of my own students:

1. Indications show man's need for God.
2. One's salvation comes through justification by faith.
3. Justification means a new order of life.
4. God needs all of his children (chapters 9-11).
5. The Christian life must prove itself ethically.

A third statement of points comes from the outline of the book given in the present chapter:

1. The evil predicament of all mankind.
2. Deliverance by God from the power of evil.
3. Induction by God into a new life.
4. God's plan for history.
5. The manner of the new life.

A very interesting sermon could be framed upon an extension of Paul's own method in 2:1-3:20, which is a dialogue between Paul and his readers. He reverts to this method in 6:1-2. It would be possible to set up the whole message of Romans in questions and answers. A gripping sermon should result.

Then, too, a sermon could be framed upon a skeleton of key verses chosen from each section of the letter. Each division would have its individual text; the text for the whole sermon would be the theme in 1:16-17. You will want to make your own list of key texts; meantime here is one suggestion:

Romans 2:12; 3:22b-25a; 6:3-4; 11:12; 12:1-2.

The special interest of Paul in the Jewish people is not so vital to us as it was to him. The omission of the chapters dealing with it would not alter the essential message of the book and it would greatly simplify the problem of presenting the book in a single sermon. If such an omission is elected, the various outline suggestions given above will need to be revised accordingly.

Notice that the ethical implications of faith are strongly stated and insisted upon by Paul. He himself was aware of the dangers of a gospel of free forgiveness without explicit moral claims. Not only does he devote chapters 12 through 15 to these moral claims, but he more than once refers to them in preceding chapters. We do well to insist upon Paul's own emphasis.

MODERN TITLE

"Man's Disorder and God's Design" may be borrowed from the theme of the constituting assembly of the World Council of Churches. It seems to fit very well. "The Great Redemption" sounds rather theological, but it is accurate. "God's Emancipation Proclamation" is certainly not theological; in some sections it may be more appealing than a more conventional title.

10

THE CHURCH AND THE PAGAN WORLD
The First Letter of Paul to the Corinthians

THE TENSIONS between the Christian church and the pagan world to be found in The First Letter of Paul to the Corinthians are captured amazingly well in Paul's own phrase of greeting: "To the church of God which is at Corinth. . . ." Corinth was the most licentious city of the Roman Empire. To plant and nurture a Christian church in such a sinkhole was to generate a moral collision.

One is reminded of a Presbyterian church in modern Jerusalem which stands near the valley of Gehenna. It is sometimes laughingly referred to as "the only church on the brink of Hell." In all seriousness some such designation of the church at Corinth would have been appropriate; it was a church not so much on the brink as in the midst of a Roman hell. That was the unpromising setting for a company of Christians "consecrated to Christ Jesus, called to be saints. . . ."

Hazards of the conflict were intensified by the fact that the opposing "world" not only surrounded the church, but had also invaded the church and was wreaking its hate from within.

I. WORKING YOUR WAY INTO THE BOOK

Some of the most beautiful passages of scripture you know are to be found in First Corinthians. Consider only three of the many that the letter contains: The church as the body of Christ (12:12-

31); the greatest thing in the world (13:1-13); the resurrection hymn (15:12-57). These verses throb with song. Nevertheless, the letter which contains them is written to a church which was filled with strife and immorality, to "saints" who were relapsing into paganism; and it was wrung out of the anguished heart of an apostle who watched all he had worked for tottering upon the rim of ruin. The Corinthian letters show us in vivid detail just what Paul meant when he wrote about "the care of all the churches" that rested upon him.

ESTABLISHING THE CHURCH

To read First Corinthians it is necessary to begin with the book of Acts.

Read Acts 18:1-18.

Paul came to Corinth directly from Athens on his second missionary journey, probably in the year A.D. 50. He found there two Jews, Priscilla and Aquila, who had been driven out of Rome by Claudius in A.D. 49 when a wave of antisemitism had engulfed the imperial city. With them and with Silas and Timothy, who soon joined them, Paul gathered a strong church, drawing his converts from the synagogues and from the pagan cults—largely from the latter. He remained in Corinth for a year and a half, a time made stormy by the bitter hostility of his own fellow Jews. This hostility finally broke into mob violence.

The ministry of Paul at Corinth was the longest of his career to date. Its length was exceeded later at Ephesus, but by no other local ministry in his apostolic labors.

When Paul left Corinth at the end of a year and a half, it was for a hurried pilgrimage to Jerusalem, whence he returned as far as Ephesus, to set up headquarters for three years. It was probably from Ephesus that First Corinthians was written, possibly in A.D. 55.

Corinth, the capital of the Roman province of Achaia, had a population of 600,000. It was the wealthiest city in Greece. Sitting astride the isthmus, with the port of Cenchreae eight miles to the east and that of Lechaeum two miles to the west, Corinth sat in walled eminence as the queen of Mediterranean commerce. Mariners considered the rounding of Cape Malea such a dangerous voyage that their smaller vessels were dragged on rollers across the narrow isthmus, passing just north of Corinth, and the cargoes of larger vessels were transported by land from one port to the other. Thus everything conspired to make Corinth a "Cosmopolitan Vortex," a Mediterranean crossroads of all nationalities, religions and cultures. It was the most unashamedly profligate of cities in the Empire. Upon Acrocorinthus, a rock towering 1,800 feet at the edge of the city, gleaming, gold-gilded temples housed one thousand prostitutes of the goddess Aphrodite. Corinth also sheltered temples to Poseidon, to Serapis, Isis, Demeter and Apollo. Every philosophy and faith and every dissipation made themselves at home here.

At Ephesus—News of Corinth

When, therefore, Paul approached the latter days of his long stay in Ephesus it cannot have surprised him that perils of paganism and strife were about to swallow up the Christianity that he had planted at Corinth. He has already written them a letter warning them not to admit immoral men into the church.

Read 1 Corinthians 5:9-11.

It may be that we have a fragment of this early letter in 2 Corinthians 6:14-7:1. Upon reading it you will notice that this fragment is not a connected part of Second Corinthians and that it does sound very much like the letter summarized in 1 Corinthians 5:9-11.

The problems of the Corinthian church which caused Paul to write our present letter were brought to his attention from three sources:

1. From Chloe's people:

Read 1 Corinthians 1:11.

These were probably slaves from the household of Chloe, recently removed from Corinth to Ephesus.

2. From former members of the congregation, Stephanas, Fortunatus and Achaicus:

Read 1 Corinthians 16:15-18.

3. From a letter written to Paul by the Corinthian church itself:

Read 1 Corinthians 7:1.

This letter may have been written partially in reply to Paul's earlier letter, but its main object seems to have been to raise a series of practical questions.

Thus from three sources, when taken together, Paul learned of a nest of vicious problems at Corinth. In much earnestness and anxiety he dictated a letter to deal with these threats to the life of the church there. What were the problems?

There were quarreling factions in the church:

Read 1 Corinthians 1:11.

The church was split three ways, around three honored personalities, Apollos, Paul and Peter.

Some were becoming arrogant about their superior Christian knowledge and virtue:

Read 1 Corinthians 4:8-13.

One man was living in an open sexual union with his own stepmother:

Read 1 Corinthians 5:1.

Christians were suing one another in the civil courts:

Read 1 Corinthians 6:1.

There was much uncertainty as to what Christianity taught about marriage and sexual relations:

Read 1 Corinthians 7:1, 9, 25.

Many did not know what to do about the meat that the public markets had on sale, for most of it had been offered to idols:

Read 1 Corinthians 8:1.

Some members had apparently challenged Paul's apostolic authority:

Read 1 Corinthians 9:1.

There was a great problem about the status and activity of women, so recently converted out of a paganism where forward women were immediately branded:

Read 1 Corinthians 14:33b-35.

Unconventionality in Corinth usually implied one thing and only one—immorality. But the new freedom of Christianity encouraged unconventionality!

There were drunkenness and gluttony at the Love Feast which preceded the celebration of the Lord's Supper:

Read 1 Corinthians 11:21

There was great public disorder in the worship service—a confusion of offices and gifts, clashes of leadership, and the hubbub of meaningless ecstatic speaking:

Read 1 Corinthians 12:29-31; 14:2.

Some Christians were telling their fellows that there was no resurrection of the dead:

Read 1 Corinthians 15:12.

This is a bewildering array of problems. Can we classify them in any way? We have seen that there were the three clear-cut parties centering around the great personalities. These were divisions. The other problems were also outgrowths of divisiveness. Clarence Tucker Craig in *The Interpreter's Bible* discovers five basic quarrels: (1) That of libertines against ascetics (6:12 *versus* 7:36-38); (2) that of emancipationists *versus* traditionalists in the question of the status of women; (3) meat-eating *versus* vegetarianism (10:23 *versus* 8:10); (4) ecstatic speaking *versus* articulate proclamation; and (5) a quarrel over the denial of the resurrection of the dead. Thus, following Craig's scheme, we see that all Corinthian problems may be summarized under a single text: ". . . there is quarreling among you, my brethren. . . . Is Christ divided?" (1:11, 13).

Paul managed to write in answer to these problems, but he did more than that. He wrote with prose that broke into poetry, with faith that hurdled obstacles. In one sense First Corinthians was a business letter; it even ended discussing the collection of money! But, if so, it was a business letter that became world literature.

OUTLINE OF THE BOOK

Introduction, 1:1-9
  I. The problem of factions, 1:10-4:21
  II. The problem of sex, 5:1-7:40
     (Lawsuits in 6:1-8 may have grown out of sexual misbehavior)
  III. The problems of freedom and license, 8:1-11:1
  IV. Various problems of public worship, 11:2-14:40
  V. The problem of the resurrection of the dead, 15:1-58
  VI. Personal matters, 16:1-12
Conclusion, 16:13-24

KEY PASSAGE

We may say that the dominant theme of the letter is "love of the brethren" expressing itself in the church as the body of Christ, but we have neglected an important aspect of the theme until we see that all of this is rooted in the divine foolishness of God—the Christ who went to the cross. The spiritual center of gravity in this letter, therefore, is found in 1 Corinthians 1:18-2:5. Paul was suggesting that, as Jesus was crucified, so every new convert to Christianity had to be crucified and rise to a personal resurrection. He had to die to pagan ways and rise to the mysterious, seemingly absurd ways of Christ. This crucifixion would change everything, and it would create not only a new kind of person but a new type of community.

It is now time for you to read the whole of First Corinthians at one sitting.

II. PREPARING YOUR BOOK SERMON

THE CARDINAL IDEA

The pagan world is corrupt and competitive; when Christians wander away from Christ this pagan world invades and despoils their fellowship and they behave like pagans—their minds are divided and they are divided among themselves. The cure is such a vital union with Christ as will enable them to die at the cross and rise in self-forgetfulness to a new kind of life—a life of brotherly love.

SHAPING A PREACHING OUTLINE

One preaching outline will emerge rather quickly from an effort to classify the stages of thought contained in the cardinal idea as just expressed. The result may look something like this:

I. The world in Christ's church
   A. Carnal-minded persons
   B. A competitive society
II. The Christ in his church
   A. A new kind of person
   B. A new kind of fellowship

A second approach to outline may be made through the problems of the Corinthian church, which constitute the organizing principle in the letter itself. Before this can be done, however, the problems must be universalized so that they can be seen to be modern as well as ancient. They are five in number:

1. *Sectarian spirit.* It is not difficult to see this as a modern problem. Whether in Corinth or in Cleveland, schism is the scandal of Christendom. Its cause is putting men in the place of Christ (1:13-17). Its cure is in a genuine return to Christ as center and soul of all being (1:30-31).

2. *Problems of Sex.* All of the Corinthian problems of sex and marriage are with us today, though their exact form may be a little different. The problem lies in the tension of two extremes: a libertin-

ism which holds that "all things are lawful" (6:12), and an asceticism which refuses all sexual intercourse in or out of marriage. The solution is neither indulgence but denial; it is a sacramental view of the human body (6:13, 15, 19), whether in or out of marriage.

3. *Freedom to follow conscience.* The problem arises from the fact that the conscience of one Christian may be in direct conflict with that of another. Even though the conscience of one may be mature and that of the other childish, the problem is not thereby eliminated (8:1, 4, 7). The pagan way of meeting the difficulty is a head-on collision through the selfish assertion of private rights, for what is clearer in its self-assertion than a clear conscience (8:9)? This is destructive of others; it violates the law of brotherhood. The cure is found in a renunciation of rights (10:24, 33; 8:1), and in a sacramental view of all appetites (10:31).

4. *A church in turmoil.* What title better expresses the public life of the Corinthian church? Problems of dress, of communion, of public witness tore this church asunder. There was strife (11:17-18). The cure of the trouble was manifold. For the Lord's Supper, what was needed was a spirit of self-examination together with the serious effort to use the bread and wine sacramentally to discern Christ. In the disordered life and worship of the church, what was needed was the recognition that there can be spiritual unity in organizational and functional diversity (12:4); and the realization that this spirit works in love, which must be put first among our aims. In fact we will have the correct picture of the church when we think of it as Christ's own body with ourselves as members of that body, controlled by that one mind. When we get this central thing worked out, other matters will work out; the rivalry and disorder will cease.

5. *An earthbound vision.* That was what the denial of the resurrection amounted to (15:12). The result of such a denial was to make Christ a phantom who lived in memory alone (15:16, 17), but who has no enduring cosmic significance. The practical outcome

of such a doubt is life gone secular and soft (15:32). But the out-come of positive faith in the resurrection is victorious life (15:22, 57).

At first it may seem that chapter 16 drags in extraneous matters, but on second view it should be apparent that the call for contribu-tions to the saints is integral to the letter. Wholehearted, generous giving of a missionary sort is not only an antidote to self-centered-ness and shallow Christian commitment, it is also a proof that the giver has been able to lift his eyes out of his own little rut to God's wide horizons. It is one way of getting out of Corinth and of getting the Corinthian spirit out of the church.

A third approach to outline can be made through a text. A good one is 12:4-6. What Paul describes here is the solution to be found by the church when Christ is in it; then there are varieties of gifts, services, functions with the *same* Spirit. But when the world is in Christ's church, these varieties shatter the unity of the Spirit; then there become varieties of spirits. The sermon will begin with a discussion of the varieties of the spirit caused by a pagan competitive-ness.

Still another textual door to the sermon may be opened through the use of the contrast between "the nonsense of God" and "the wisdom of men" in 1 Corinthians 1:18, 25[1] It is the wisdom of men to see knowledge as power, justice as the defense of one's own rights, the pursuit of a man's own pleasures as his own private affair. It is perhaps no accident that this "wisdom" comes to its flower in rivalry degenerating into open strife. Love shows us a far more excellent way, the way of the cross, which is "the nonsense of God." If we would be strong we must be willing to be broken; only when we shed our self-assertiveness, our pursuit of conscientious rights, in the interest of doing God's will can we come to understand this wis-

[1] E. J. Goodspeed, *The New Testament: An American Translation* (Univer-sity of Chicago Press, 1928).

dom and to experience its healing power. Then something more important than having our own way begins to happen to us, and it is no longer we who live but Christ (humanity resplendent and godlike) who lives in us.

A Modern Title

"The Church and the Pagan World" is the title chosen for the present chapter; it could be the name of the sermon. A rephrasing of the same tension might give us "The Secular Mind in the Household of Faith." "Paganism Goes to Church" conveys the same idea. For a biblical title, one might well settle on "Man's Strength and God's Weakness" or "The Wisdom of Men and the Nonsense of God."

THE MINISTRY OF RECONCILIATION
The Second Letter of Paul to the Corinthians

THE CORINTHIAN congregation was a problem-ridden church. It seems scarcely possible that anything could have been added to the disorder which is reflected in First Corinthians. Nevertheless, even while Paul was endeavoring to put things to rights, the situation worsened. Some Judaizers from Jerusalem, with malice toward Paul, arrived in Corinth; they carried glowing letters of recommendation and claimed authoritative leadership. Clearly they sought to undermine Paul's authority. They were encouraged and aided by a particularly arrogant Corinthian.

Read 2 Corinthians 3:1; 11:5; 2:5 (*in that order*).

The situation looked almost hopeless. But Paul did not give up. With tremendous energy and much agony of spirit Paul poured himself into the task of saving this church, and he succeeded.

I. WORKING YOUR WAY INTO THE BOOK

Paul wrote and dispatched the letter which we now call First Corinthians. He sent Timothy, perhaps as bearer of the letter, or perhaps as an apostolic messenger to follow quickly upon it. In any case, Timothy was to be there in order to add personal weight to the letter and to do what he could toward effecting a reform.

Read 1 Corinthians 4:17; 16:10.

Paul himself planned to visit them shortly, and he began getting his affairs in shape to that end:

Read 1 Corinthians 4:18-19; 16:2, 5-7.

Paul made this visit somewhat more hurriedly than he had anticipated when writing about it. The letter had been unsuccessful. Timothy had failed. Paul decided to go himself.

Read 2 Corinthians 2:1; 12:14; 13:1.

It turned out to be a painful and unsuccessful visit. The church had refused to discipline the member guilty of sexual immorality (see I Corinthians 5:1-2). The offender himself had been arrogant, and in the clash of wills that followed Paul had taken abuse such as he had never borne from within the church. Even his apostolic authority had been questioned. Insulted, humiliated and frustrated, Paul returned to Ephesus and wrote a scorching letter. This we know from his own words:

Read 2 Corinthians 2:3, 9; 7:8-12.

It seems certain that the bearer of this severe letter was Titus, and that he had agreed to meet Paul in Troas or in Macedonia to report the result. Paul was in great agitation about it:

Read 2 Corinthians 2:12-13; 7:5-6.

Do we have any trace of this severe letter? Most biblical scholars feel that we have a large portion of it in 2 Corinthians, chapters 10-13. We therefore suggest that you work your way into Second Corinthians by reading these chapters first. Before doing that, however, glance at the following outline.

OUTLINE OF 2 CORINTHIANS 10-13

I. Paul's defense of himself against his detractors, 10:1-12:13
    A. Paul counterattacks and affirms that his authority is from Christ, 10:1-18
    B. With mingled apologies and denunciations, Paul boasts of what he had done and suffered, 11:1-12:13

II. Paul announces his plan to visit them, a third time, 12:14-13:10
III. Parting advice, salutation and benediction, 13:11-14

Laying this book aside, take up Second Corinthians and read the chapters which we have just outlined. We shall then look at some special points of interest.

OBSERVATIONS ON THE "SEVERE LETTER"

This severe letter abounds in stinging sarcasm, but Paul is writing in this vein not so much to justify himself as to drive his readers to repentance and to make them ready for reconciliation. There is an impassioned, oratorical quality about the letter; the apostle is pleading a case with his utmost energy. And in these flaming lines he pours himself out, revealing more about himself than we can learn from any other single letter. He tells us about apostolic hardships and adventures of which the book of Acts gives us no hint (11:23-27), and he recounts a great deal of his own personal history, particularly in chapters 11 and 12.

From this "severe letter" we discover some of the insults which had been heaped upon Paul at the time of his "painful visit." Someone had implied that Paul was a coward when he was confronted by them face to face and that he was bold and courageous only in his letters (10:1, 9-10). Someone had accused Paul of boasting (10:13, 15). He had been called a poor speaker (11:6). He had even been ridiculed for the poverty which he brought upon himself by refusing pay from them. And this, ironically, was construed as a sign that he did not love them! Or, again, it was construed as a cleaver device for getting under their skin, so he could exploit them for his own purposes (11:7, 11; 12:16)! Much to his discredit, Paul had been compared to other "superlative apostles" (11:20, 21; 12:11-13).

Meantime, Paul did not retreat from the position he had taken in First Corinthians. He did not desist from his demand that no one could belong to the body of Christ without turning from immorality (12:21; 13:2, 11).

KEY OF THE "SEVERE LETTER"

The key to Paul's purpose in writing the whiplash sentences of the severe letter is contained in the Apostle's own words in 2 Corinthians 2:4: "For I wrote you out of much affliction and anguish of heart and with many tears, not to cause you pain but to let you know the abundant love that I have for you." We see at once that there is a difference between love and amiability. At no time in this stormy correspondence did Paul violate Christian love. This is not to say that he was always complimentary and polite. Sometimes love is compelled to be surgical. Paul was not engaged in a popularity contest at Corinth; he was trying to grow Christians and to create a community of Christlike minds. Politeness, amiability were not enough. Something as courageous as genuine love was required.

WAITING FOR THE OUTCOME

The letter that was written with so much passion was dispatched in great anxiety. Paul fell ill or was imprisoned, in Ephesus; at any rate, hovered near death for a season (2 Cor. 1:8-9). When he recovered or was freed it was to hurry to Troas where he expected to meet Titus. Not finding him, he pressed on across the Aegean to Macedonia. He almost regretted having written the letter. His earlier plan to visit Corinth in person was suspended until he should learn directly from Titus how things had gone:

Read 2 Corinthians 1:15-17, 23; 2:1, 4.

It was while Paul was in such an agitated state of mind that Titus finally joined him, perhaps at Philippi or Thessalonica. The news which Titus bore was good news:

Read 2 Corinthians 7:5-16.

There had been a complete capitulation and repentance. The offending member had been excommunicated, after which his arrogance had turned into humility and true penitence:

Read 2 Corinthians 2:5-8.

Paul's relief knew no bounds. He planned to speed on to Corinth for a meeting of reconciliation, but before he went he wrote another letter, overflowing with joy. This joyful letter is generally identified with 2 Corinthians 1-9. (We have previously seen that 2 Corinthians 6:14-7:1 is probably a fragment of a first warning letter which Paul wrote many months before, back at the beginning of the Corinthian disorders; these verses seem not to be an integral part of the joyful letter.)

OUTLINE OF THE JOYFUL LETTER

  I. Salutation and thanksgiving, 1:1-11
 II. Paul tells them of his feelings and conduct during the breach between Corinth and himself, 1:12-7:16
    A. His sincerity, 1:12-14
    B. The explanation for the delay of his visit, 1:15-2:11
    C. His anxiety and suspense while waiting for Titus, 2:12-17
    D. A defense of his actions, 3:1-6:10
    E. His love for the Corinthians, 6:11-8:4
    F. His joy when Titus came, 7:5-16
III. Paul urges them to provide a generous offering for the saints of Jerusalem, 8:1-9:15
    A. The fine example of the Macedonian churches, 8:1-6
    B. His plans and hopes for them, 8:7-24
    C. Direct appeal for their liberality, 9:1-15

The next logical step in working your way into the book is to read 2 Corinthians 1-9 as a unit.

PURPOSE OF THE JOYFUL LETTER

Clearly the purpose of this joyful letter was to express Paul's relief and joy at the repentance of the Corinthians, and to move quickly to the deeds of reconciliation. There was also a minor purpose. Paul urged the Corinthians to forgive and restore the penitent offender who had nearly wrecked the whole enterprise (2:5-11). Notice the many expressions of Paul's sense of solidarity with the Corinthian Christians. He evidently feels that his life is so closely intertwined with them that they are a part of him (1:6).

KEY VERSES

Two key passages appeal to us, one more localized in the Corinthian situation, the other a universalization of the principle demonstrated by the solution to the Corinthian troubles:

A local statement: "For even if I made you sorry with my letter, I do not regret it (though I did regret it), for I see that that letter grieved you, though only for a while. As it is, I rejoice, not because you were grieved, but because you were grieved unto repentance" (2 Cor. 7:8, 9). This key is from a wider passage, 7:2-16, which may be read as a whole; it shows in personal terms what Paul had hoped and feared and points unmistakably to his reasons for writing again.

A universal principle: "Therefore, if any one is in Christ, he is a new creation; the old has passed away, behold, the new has come. All this is from God, who through Christ reconciled us to himself and gave us a ministry of reconciliation. . . . So we are ambassadors for Christ, God making his appeal through us. We beseech you on behalf of Christ, be reconciled to God" (2 Cor. 5:17, 18, 20).

GIVING AS FELLOWSHIP

The eighth and ninth chapters of the "joyful letter" deal with Paul's plans for an offering for the poverty-stricken Christians at Jerusalem, a project which had been proposed at Corinth, where there had been more than ordinary enthusiasm for it. Corinthian enthusiasm had spread to Macedonia. Paul asked the various contributing churches to appoint messengers to accompany him to Jerusalem as bearers of the gift and as emissaries of good will from Christian Gentiles to Christian Jews. The offering, as Paul conceived it, was to fulfill a twofold purpose: (1) To alleviate the dire need of Jerusalem Christians, for there was much poverty there; and (2) to serve as an expression of the solidarity of the whole church, an indication that the breach between Jews and Gentiles had been healed within the Christian fellowship. Therefore, the collection from the Jerusalem saints may be seen as a part of the Apostle's larger ministry of reconciliation. Giving was not only charity; it was also fellowship. By sharing in it, the Corinthians not only carried out their original suggestion, but they also engaged in a healing affirmation of fellowship within their own congregation and with the whole Christian world. When Paul later wrote to the Roman church from Corinth, the collection was complete and he was about to depart in joy for Jerusalem:

Read Romans 15:25-28.

Paul was reconciled to the wayward church which he loved. In fact, he had loved it back to Christ. When the church again took up its creative role, it was drawn back into the joy of internal fellowship and made to share in the solidarity of the Church Universal.

II. PREPARING YOUR BOOK SERMON

The fact that Second Corinthians as we now have it is a union of parts of two letters from Paul—a severe letter and a joyful one—may seem to argue against a single sermon on the book. Certainly it is possible to preach separately on the two units, but a single message on the whole book is by no means impossible. In fact, the contrast between love in the mood of chastisement and love in the mood of joy sets a tension which should greatly add to the interest and the power of sermon.

THE CARDINAL IDEA

If love is to perform its full ministry it must probe deeply enough into the moral lives of others to produce repentance and it must lay such profound claims upon us that we will generously forgive, thus making possible the birth and growth of a Christlike fellowship.

SHAPING A PREACHING OUTLINE

Second Corinthians shows us the drama of love in three acts: Act I, Chastising Love; Act II. Forgiving Love; Act III. Sharing Love.

Act I is played out in chapters 10-13 in the "severe letter." Here in a love that goes beyond amiability and politeness, Paul has the courage of a surgeon. He is not painless, but he does aim to heal the Corinthians of their pagan, anti-Christian ways by driving them to repentance. He strives to show them their immorality, their arrogance, their defection from the spirit of Christ. And he succeeds. In just this way the reconciling love of God seeks to win us out of our sins of pride and sensuality to genuine repentance.

The script for Act II is found in chapters 1-7. There Paul not only forgives all personal affronts which he has suffered; humiliations, insults, libels have been numerous and without foundation, but Paul wipes the slate clean of them. They are like a lovers' quarrel, forgotten in the joy of reconciliation. Paul also urges foregiveness by the Corinthians of the arrogant, offending member; this member by his penitence has come to a new mind. The church must be as quick to restore him as it had been to discipline him. In fact, if there were no willingness to restore him when repentant, their discipline was exposed as lacking in love. The modern implications of love as forgiveness and restoration are fairly obvious.

Act III is performed on a world stage. Unrepentant, quarreling Corinth was a walled town, ingrown and self-centered; but Corinth repentant and reconciled was a world city with a mission of reconciliation toward all mankind. The script for Act III is chapters 8-9. The imperative of sharing our money with the whole church is here presented. Missionary giving is the result. But the missionary giving must be an outgrowth of a true missionary spirit, and that roots back in the key scripture: ". . . God through Christ reconciled us to himself and gave us the ministry of reconciliation. . . . So we are ambassadors. . . ."

Much the same movement of thought may be developed by dwelling upon 5:16-21. The term "ambassadors" is the final stage in the work of reconciliation which has passed through two previous steps: men formerly at odds with God have been made at one with him. The three possible relationships of men to God quickly disclose themselves as I. Enemies of God; II. Allies; III. Ambassadors.

A Modern Title

"The Healing Power of Love" gives the preacher an opportunity to contrast love's surgical action with the healing ministry of reconciliation; the analogy at the base of the sermon is medical. "Beyond Amiability" suggested the deeper reaches of love which are plumbed in this letter. "The Ministry of Reconciliation" is a direct quotation from the letter itself, but the phrase is current enough for use, and none is more comprehensive or more accurate as a covering title for the book we are studying.

12

THE FIRST FREEDOM

The Letter of Paul to the Galatians

THE LIBERTY BELL is cracked; it sounds a discordant note these days. Why? (1) Some people have mistaken liberty for license. In word and in pantomime they say, "I'll do as I please. What business is it of yours?" Moral anarchy results. Plato correctly assessed the moral confusion of such "free" men: ". . . insolence they term breeding, and anarchy liberty, and waste magnificence, and impudence courage." (2) Many of these same people have grown tired of their "freedom" and have bound themselves over to authoritarian masters —a totalitarian state, ideology or religion. The cause of this headlong desertion from freedom to authority was the abuse of freedom. Again, as Plato saw so clearly, "the excessive increase of anything often causes a reaction in the opposite direction. . . . The excess of liberty, whether in States or individuals, seems only to pass into excess of slavery."[1]

The twin perils to freedom just mentioned are the perils of *betrayal* and *denial.* Denial follows betrayal. The danger from both is real; millions have been engulfed by that danger. (3) But there is a more subtle danger which is no less real; that is the identification of Freedom (in this case capitalized) with Western Culture. No longer a

[1] *Republic* VIII: 561, 564.

spirit of open inquiry and of pioneering for community, freedom simply becomes the American way of doing things, which is presumed good for everybody. Perhaps we are even ready to "make" peoples "free" against their own wishes if necessary because we know it is for their good!

Paul's letter to the Galatians is about freedom, the precious essence of Christianity, which was in his time endangered from the third source followed by a recoil to the first. There was the attempt of the Judaizers to identify Christianity with Jewish Culture—a genuine peril to Christian liberty which would have put an end to Christianity before it got out of the first century. But there was also the opposite danger which is shown in the libertine motto, "Anything goes, all things are lawful"—a peril which would have put an end to Christianity just as surely by dissolving it into anarchy. No topic is more in the headlines these days than freedom; Galatians is about freedom; therefore, no New Testament writing is more timely.

I. WORKING YOUR WAY INTO THE BOOK

JUDAIZERS

Omitting the customary thanksgiving and prayer with which he introduced his letters, Paul flies at once with some severity to his main concern:

Read Galations 1:6.

His readers were in danger of embracing a perversion of Christianity, mistaking it for the real article:

Read Galatians 3:1, 3; 4:9-11; 5:7.

Foolish, confused and bewitched, the readers were Paul's "dear idiots" who were "advancing to the rear" in their so-called Christian progress. Under Christian banners, they were retreating into Judaism. This had not been their own idea. Certain Jewish Christians, zealous for the Law of Moses, had come to bewitch them.

Read Galations 1:7; Acts 15:1b.

From what is said at various points in the letter it is clear that the Judaizers attacked Paul's apostolic authority. They claimed that he preached a gospel at variance with that of the "real" apostles. What is more, they said, Paul is not consistent; in some quarters at least, he still preaches circumcision:

Read Galatians 5:11.

Paul is harsh with them. He even curses them:

Read Galatians 1:8, 9; 5:8-12; 6:12, 13.

He mistrusted the motives of the Judaizers. They were looking for popularity and for power. Paul's answer took the form of a defense of his apostolic authority followed by an emphatic statement of the principle of justification by faith. We can follow the trail of his argument through certain key verses:

Read Galatians 1:11-12.

Here Paul asserts that his preaching in no way reflected tradition or mere human influence. It was a direct personal revelation from Christ himself. Moreover, though he had no opportunity to take his message from the other apostles, when he went up to Jerusalem several years later the apostles received him and ratified his commission to the Gentiles:

Read Galatians 2:1, 9.

So secure was Paul in his gospel that he did not hesitate even to rebuke Peter himself, the leader of the Jerusalem apostles, when the latter momentarily yielded to the Judaizers at Antioch. Peter knew that he stood self-condemned:

Read Galatians 2:11, 12, 14.

The Judaizers, calling themselves the only true Christians, really are enemies of Christianity.

LAW VERSUS GOSPEL

For if it is true that we are saved by works of the law, we do not need Christ. Why be Christians at all?

Read Galatians 2:21; 3:2, 3.

Salvation comes not through works of the law by way of what we *achieve* but through faith by way of what we *receive* from God. This way of faith is actually older than the law, and it is the men of faith who are the true children of Abraham:

Read Galatians 3:7.

The law can show us our sin but only faith can rescue us from that sin:

Read Galatians 3:10, 13.

Does this mean that the law has no function? On the contrary, it has a disciplinary and an educative function. It was a kind of parent or schoolteacher, bringing us up to our spiritual maturity:

Read Galatians 3:23, 24.

Christianity is the religion not of spiritual children or slaves but of mature, free men in Christ:

Read Galatians 4:7.

The Galatians had come out of a pagan form of religious bondage. They were now being enticed to retreat into a Jewish legalism just as enslaving:

Read Galatians 4:9.

Paul appeals to them on the strength of their first strong affection for him and of their early sense of freedom and joy in the gospel to reject such bondage and keep on growing toward their full freedom as sons:

Read Galatians 4:15, 19; 5:1.

It is not circumcision nor its absence that saves a man, but faith working in love:

Read Galatians 5:6.

A Christian is a free man, but this does not mean that he is a libertine or an anarchist:

Read Galatians 5:13, 16, 24.

On the contrary, Christian liberty means being inwardly compelled by the spirit of Christ to live a brotherly life:

Read Galatians 6:2, 9.

Such a life is not the root of salvation but its fruit. The root is faith in Christ by which the power of God is received in a life, and this power manifests itself by destroying pride and creating a new kind of person capable of love.

Read Galatians 6:14, 15.

This is to say that death lies at the beginning and not at the end of the Christian life. Of course, it is not the death of the body which is important, but rather the complete renunciation of selfish control over one's aims and actions. To acquire knowledge, power, possessions we must strive; but to become a self we must surrender. To have and to hold we must *achieve*; to be and to live we must *receive*.

Summary

A quick summary of Paul's thought in this letter may be found in the closing section which he appended in his own handwriting:

Read Galatians 6:11-18.

Let us paraphrase the section: "To sum up (in my own handwriting): The Judaizers are insincere. They want a form of Christianity that will be popular and easy; they want even more to crow over you because they have been able to sway you. They do not consistently keep the law. Really they are filled with pride. If I am a Christian my pride must die on Christ's cross and I must allow the spirit of Christ to make me into a new kind of person altogether. God's peace and love be upon all who live this way. Let me hear no more accusations against my own character! The proof of my loyalty to Christ is found in the scars which I have received in his service. May his blessings fill your hearts." In this closing paragraph we notice the elements prominent in the letter as a whole: (1) Paul's defense of his authority, (2) his attack upon the Judaizers, (3) his statement of the basic doctrine of salvation by faith in Christ, and

(4) his presentation of the responsible freedom which is fully implied.

If we ignore the element of personal justification which occupies so much space, another concentration of the message may be found in Galatians 2:15-21. Here it is in a nutshell.

SCHOLARLY QUESTIONS

There are a number of critical questions about this letter the solutions of which do not materially affect the message: Whether it was written to "South Galatia" or "North Galatia," whether the Jerusalem conference referred to in Galatians 2 is or is not identical with that in Acts 15; whether it was written early at Corinth or late in another city. The letter is undoubtedly Pauline and it is addressed to the problem of Judaizing which he met in many quarters. Since these questions need not be settled before the message of the letter is grasped we shall leave them open here. It has often been noticed that Galatians is "a little Romans," but there are an urgency and a severity here not found in Romans, as well as a personal note which is absent from the more formal epistle. In Galatia Paul and his Gospel were under attack; he felt that the very life of Christianity in that region was at stake, and he rushed upon the scene in battle dress. As in the controversial Corinthians, Paul reveals a good deal of himself here. There are a number of biographical details not found in Acts; some of these create unsolved perplexities for the scholars, but most of all they show us the personality of Paul.

The long allegory in 4:21-31 is an example of rabbinical reasoning which does not now sound as convincing as it did to Paul's Jewish readers. The point of the allegory is to prove the superiority of the gospel to the law from the law itself. It is a kind of logical *tour de force*, like catching a man in his own trap. Though we do not reason as Paul did here, we can see the validity of his conclusion and we can accept it.

OUTLINE OF THE LETTER

Introduction, 1:1-9
    A. Greetings, 1:1-5
    B. The problems: Judaizers in Galatia, 1:6-9
  I. Paul's defense of his apostolic authority, 1:10-2:21
    A. His motives, 1:10
    B. His personal call and revelation, 1:11-24
    C. The apostolic ratification of his call, 2:1-10
    D. His rebuke of Peter, 2:11-14
    E. The principle behind resistance to the Judaizers, 2:15-21
 II. Paul's offensive: the doctrine of salvation through faith, 3:1-5:12
    A. An appeal to the Galatians' own experience of the gospel, 3:1-5
    B. An argument from Abraham, 3:6-9
    C. The role of the Law, 3:10-4:7
        1. Its power to curse; Christ's power to save, 3:10-14
        2. Its temporary, educative function, 3:15-4:7
    D. An appeal to choose liberty over bondage, 4:8-20
    E. An allegory proving the superiority of faith to law from the
       Law itself, 4:21-31
    F. A further appeal to embrace liberty, 5:1-12
III. Paul's advice: ethical implications of Christian liberty, 5:13-6:10
    A. Not license but loving service, 5:13-15
    B. Outgrowth in Christlike behavior, 5:16-26
    C. Burden-sharing with Christian brothers, 6:1-5
    D. Seedtime and harvest of service, 6:6-10
Conclusion, in Paul's own hand, 6:11-18
    A. A summary of the letter, 6:11-17
    B. Benediction, 6:18

II. PREPARING YOUR BOOK SERMON

CARDINAL IDEA

*Nothing but bondage can result from the attempt to achieve
salvation by conformity to the outward demands of a culture or a
code, for one is then captive both to convention and to one's own
unregenerate self; but freedom comes when a man surrenders his
selfish pride to die on the cross with Christ and accepts the forgiving
love of God shown in Christ, for then he is emancipated from a*

false self; and, inwardly compelled by the Spirit of Christ, he will serve gladly as a responsible and creative member of society.

The above is a long statement which may be somewhat condensed by limiting oneself to the positive element: *Christian freedom begins in emancipation from one's own unregenerate self through the crucifixion of pride on the cross of Christ and the acceptance of the love of God shown in Christ.*

For Paul, salvation was not a matter of adding something to a man like money to a bank account, or like the giving of a prize for an achievement; it was a changing of the man himself into the image of Christ. Christ is the true norm for human life. When a man is unlike Christ he is living away from his own center; he is then the captive of a false self. In such a state, every achievement of his, even a moral achievement, tends but to increase his selfish pride and to insulate him against inward change. Moreover, since his goodness is nothing but conformity to cultural expectations, it is a form of slavery. Even if he rebels against convention, he cannot become free, however, for then he is but a slave to his own passions and whims. The only way he can achieve freedom is by giving up the life of the false, prideful self and in coming to his true norm who is Christ. Then the love of God will enter his life and begin to make him over into a man who is inwardly real and outwardly at home among his fellows. Freedom is faith in Christ working in love; it is love received from God expending itself in love toward men.

The accent upon *receiving* rather than *achieving*, upon what Luther called "passive righteousness" rather than "active righteousness," does not rule out Christian action. It merely means that a man must be reborn as a Christian personality before he can begin to live as one. It means also that by no amount of effort and good works done for duty's sake can a man become a Christlike self. That is the work of God's love in a human life which has unbarred the door and let Christ in.

SHAPING A PREACHING OUTLINE

The above discussion can be fashioned into a sermon outline as follows:

I. Enslaved
   A. To an unregenerate self, 4:3, 7
   B. To outward convention, or 3:10-12
   C. To our own desires, 5:13, 16b
II. Liberated
   A. By dying to self, 2:20
   B. By living to Christ, 2:20
   C. By inwardly fulfilling the law of love, 6:2

A second outline emerges from a consideration embracing such questions as the price of freedom, its perils, its denials and affirmations:

I. The price of freedom
   A. Daily crucifixion with Christ, 2:20
   B. Unbroken companionship with Christ's spirit, 5:24, 25
II. The peril of freedom
   A. Backsliding to prideful living, 5:1
   B. Changing one convention for another, 4:8, 9
III. The negations of freedom
   A. License, 5:13, 16b
   B. Authoritarian obedience, 3:10-12
IV. The affirmations of freedom
   A. The Law of Love 5:14; 6:2
   B. The fruits of the spirit, 5:18-23

It should be possible to follow the general outline of the letter itself, which means a sermon with three main points centering in (1) Paul's defense of his own apostolic authority, (2) his doctrine of justification by faith and (3) its ethical implications. The points, universalized and rephrased, would then be I. Not man's gospel, but God's; II. Salvation not by works but by faith; III. Christian freedom: living by the law of love.

A Modern Title

"Christian Liberty" has often been suggested as a good name for Galatians. Quite obviously the title for our second outline is "Freedom—Its Price and Peril." "The Plight of Freedom" is the title of a good book which might be borrowed for the purpose. Since, however, we have here the basis of all freedoms, including the famous four and all others, we have called it "The First Freedom."

13

THE GOAL OF HISTORY
The Letter of Paul to the Ephesians

Here is a book with many well-loved passages which lie lightly on the tongue of countless Christians. But, familiar as selected verses may be, the main theme is little understood. An honest report from most Chirstians might tell us, "I don't know what it's all about. I get lost in the long sentences and stumble over unfamiliar terms. The central message eludes me."

I. WORKING YOUR WAY INTO THE BOOK

If the above reaction is reported correctly, perhaps the best point at which to begin in the reading of Ephesians is with the purple patches. Refresh your memory of these most cherished passages; let them sing their song of faith as you begin to grasp this letter by relaxing to the call of beauty.

PURPLE PATCHES

Read Ephesians 2:19-22; 3:14-19, 20-21; 4:1-16, 22-24, 31-232; 6:10-17.

Having reread these familiar verses, your curiosity will be sharpened for the main questions: What is the message of the book as a whole? Before we can answer that question, we must inquire about a few other matters.

THE READERS OF THE LETTER

The original letter did not bear a title; that was supplied by a scribe sometime in the second century A.D. as he copied the book as part of a collection of Paul's letters. While we do not doubt that the readers included the Christians at Ephesus, there is a great deal of evidence to support the belief that the letter was addressed to many churches throughout the Roman province of Asia of which Ephesus was the capital, or even to a wider audience. In other words, it was either a circular letter or a general letter. Let us look very briefly at some of the reasons for this belief:

The words "in Ephesus" are included after "to the saints" in a very few Greek manuscripts of this letter, but in none earlier than the fourth century. Other manuscripts have no reference to Ephesus. A footnote at the beginning of the letter in the Revised Standard Version reads, "Some ancient authorities read *who are at Ephesus and faithful.*" These words are not in the most ancient of manuscripts.

Marcion, a chuch father who wrote about A.D. 140, regarded this letter as the one referred to in Colossians 4:16, "the letter from Laodicea," which was intended for reading in Colossae and perhaps in other churches as well. Unless Ephesians is that letter, it is lost.

There were a great many of the readers whom Paul had never met. (See Eph. 1:15 and 3:2.) If Paul had been writing directly to Ephesus where he had so recently spent three years, why should he say that he had "heard of them" and that doubtless they had "heard of" him? In the face of such a curious statement, only two solutions seem logical: (1) That the letter was not addressed to Ephesus primarily or even at all, but to a church or churches where Paul was not personally known by many of the members. (2) That the letter was written many years after Paul's death by a dedicated Paulinist; a generation had arise even in Ephesus which had never seen Paul. Equally competent New Testament scholars may be found in support of both points of view. This seems to be a question that can be resolved only by the experts when there is more evidence.

Likewise, there is in this letter a complete absence of Paul's usual greetings to individuals in the church. In view of the fact that Paul lived longer at Ephesus than with any other church, this omission of a practice so customary is alone almost completely convincing.

We conclude, then, that the present book was not Paul's usual kind of letter and that it was not addressed primarily to the church at Ephesus. It may have been a circular letter, in which case it may be the one or like the one referred to in Colossians 4:16; such a letter would probably circulate in the province of Asia. On the other hand, it may have been a general letter intended for the whole church, in which case its initial circulation would have been much wider.

The Writer

The letter itself tells us that the author was "an ambassador in chains" (Eph. 6:20). It has been assumed that Paul wrote Ephesians at the end of his life while he was imprisoned at Rome, awaiting his trial before Nero. Tychicus, who carried the letters to Colossae (Col 4:7), to Laodicea (Col 4:16), and to Philemon (Col 4:9; Philem. 9-14), is named as the bearer of this writing as well.

Many close students of the writing find it difficult to believe that Paul was the real author. Chief among their reasons are certain peculiarities of style. Paul, as seen in other letters, is an impetuous protagonist who is often controversial; in Ephesians we have a calm, meditative mind who looks quietly out upon the whole church in a perspective of devotion and prayer. Moreover, the vocabulary of this book is as different from Paul's usual choice of words as is the spirit of the letter; there are eighty-two words not found elsewhere in Paul's writings, thirty-eight not encountered elsewhere in all of the New Testament.

If not Paul's, the letter is nevertheless Pauline, being a kind of summary of Paul's teachings lifted into a philosophy of religion and of history. In it the church is seen, not as a collection of local congregations, but as a world society which is the key to human destiny for all society.

Edgar J. Goodspeed has an attractive theory about the writer of Ephesus. According to this theory, Onesimus, historically known to us in the early second century as Bishop of Ephesus, was truly Onesimus, the former slave of Philemon. Paul's convert and student, he rose to leadership in the church. In time he collected the scattered letters of Paul and published them as a unit, prefacing them with Ephesians, a general summary of the whole body of Paul's doctrines, which he wrote as a labor of love in a truly Pauline spirit. To most students, Goodspeed's theory seems too elaborate; and the assignment of authorship to Onesimus, while beautiful to contemplate, is really arbitrary.

Is it not possible that Paul himself wrote this letter, after all? Paul, the torrential writer, the fiery protagonist, was capable of the long look and of the meditative spirit, as of the poetic vision. What question would have been more natural to his mind within the shadow of his death than "How does it all fit together? How does it all add up in the end?"

THE STRUCTURE OF THE BOOK

Ephesians falls very neatly into two main sections, 1:1-3:20 and 4:1-6:24. The first is doctrinal; the second is practical. The first we might call "the Philosophy of the Church"; the second, "The Ethics of the Church." Moreover, the second part of the letter flows out of the first. It is because the church is of a certain nature that Christian practice within the church must be of a certain character.

It might be helpful to read these two sections in reverse order. Begin with Ephesians 4:1 and read to the end. This reading will give you the ethical practice of Christians in the church. Now, after such a reading you will have a question, "*Why* should Christian practice be like that?" The answer to your question will then be found in the first three chapters; there the author gives his philosophy of the church.

OUTLINE

Introduction: The greeting, 1:1, 2

I. Doctrine: The mystery of the ages unveiled, 1:3-3:20
   A. Praise of God for his great design from the beginning of the world until the present day, 1:3-14
      1. The Father's loving purpose to make us his sons, 1:3-6
      2. The purpose fulfilled in Christ, 1:7-12
      3. The work carried on by the Holy Spirit, 1:13, 14
   B. Prayer for the enlightenment of the readers, 1:15-2:10
      1. The resurrection and supreme lordship of Christ, 1:15-23
      2. The new spiritual life made possible by God's grace, 2:1-10
   C. Exposition, 2:11-3:13
      1. The spiritual unity of mankind in the church, 2:11-22
      2. Paul's Apostleship in relation to the unity, 3:1-13
   D. Prayer for the growth of the readers in the knowledge of God's work, 3:14-19
   E. Doxology, 3:20-21

II. Ethical and practical: The Christian society, 4:1-6:20
   A. First exhortation: Promote the unity of the church, 4:1-16
      1. Consecration, 4:1-6
      2. Enrichment of unity by diversity of gifts, 4:7-16
   B. Second exhortation: Cast off paganism, 4:17-5:20
      1. A general appeal, 4:17-24
      2. Some special injunctions, 4:25-5:2
      3. Light against darkness, 5:3-14
      4. A brief summary, 5:15-20
   C. Third exhortation: Love one another at home, 5:21-6:9
      1. Husbands and wives, 5:21-23
      2. Children and parents, 6:1-4
      3. Slaves and masters, 6:5-9
   D. Fourth Exhortation: Be the Church Militant, 6:10-18

Conclusion, 6:19-24
   A. An appeal for prayers, 6:10-20
   B. Commendation of the bearer of the letter, 6:21-22
   C. Benediction, 6:23-24

THE MESSAGE OF THE BOOK

Let us now try to formulate the message of the book in a few words of our own making: The plan of God for humanity was a mystery hidden for ages until it burst upon the world in Christ and his church. Now the plan is revealed, and it is this: The hostile sections of humanity can be reconciled and the world can become One World through the church. Has not the church already overcome the most violent hostility in the Roman world—that of Jew and Gentile? It will be equal to all other hostilities in time to come, and so long as its life is hid with Christ in God, it will lead the way for all the world from ethical darkness to light and from strife to peace.

Paul does not say this prosaically. He sings it ecstatically. He does not argue it. He chants it. His vehicles are hymns and prayers. The mystery of the ages has been revealed to us! Now, after all the groping of centuries, we can see where history is going. It is not "a tale told by an idiot full of sound and fury." It is a drama according to God's eternal design—and lo! we are at the very center of it!

KEY VERSES

At two points in the book we find the message of the whole concentrated into a few words. One of these is 1:9-10: "For he has made known to us in all wisdom and insight the mystery of his will, according to his purpose which he set forth in Christ as a plan for the fullness of time, to unite all things in him, things in heaven and things on earth." The paraphrase of these verses by J. B. Phillips is clarifying: "For God has allowed us to know the secret of His Plan, and it is this: He purposes in His sovereign will that all human history shall be consummated in Christ, that everything that exists in Heaven or earth shall find its perfection and fulfilment in Him."[1]

A second key passage is 2:14-16: "For he is our peace, who has made us both one, and has broken down the dividing wall of hos-

[1] Phillips, *Letters to Young Churches* (Macmillan, 1953).

tility . . . that he might create in himself one new man [humanity] in place of the two, so making peace, and might reconcile us both to God in one body through the cross, thereby bringing the hostility to an end."

II. PREPARING YOUR BOOK SERMON

THE CARDINAL IDEA

Adapted from *The Interpreter's Bible*, the cardinal idea of Ephesians can be expressed as follows: *Christ is the focal point of the universe, of all history, and of all beings; all things, as they are brought into their true relation to him, are also brought into their true relation to one another and so into an all-embracing harmony.* Phrased another way, the cardinal idea reads: *The goal of history is one world through the church universal.*

SHAPING A PREACHING OUTLINE

One approach to the book of Ephesians may be made through the second key passage. This may be called "Peace for a War-weary World." We begin with "the dividing wall of hostility" (2:14) as experienced in our own world. We currently refer to two of these, "the iron curtain," and "the bamboo curtain." There are others. Therefore, we have no difficulty in understanding the strife that troubled the ancient world; we ourselves feel the author's urgent quest for a way to peace.

The sermon will have three main divisions. The first will deal with the causes of strife; it may be called "The Two Alternatives: We or They," and it will have two subdivisions, "Man against Man" and "Man against God." This world of strife is a world without a cross, a world of selfish and unregenerate men who are at odds with each other because they are in rebellion against God. The second division will be called "The Third Alternative," and will deal with the new kind of humanity which is created when men are reconciled to God through Christ; they come into harmony with one another in the spiritual community of the church, not only ending the strife among themselves but indicating the track that history must take to its final destiny. The third division, dealing with practical implications of the third alternative, may be called "Walking the Ways of Peace." It will deal with the four main concerns of the practical section of the letter: a spirit of unity in the church, a high, individual Christian morality, Christian unity in the family, and the Church Militant, aggressively pushing its missionary program.

Much the same development of ideas, labeled differently, may result from the use of the words most frequently repeated in the letter: they are *in Christ*. They occur more than thirty times. The suggested outline runs as follows:

I. Out of Christ
   A. Selfish men
   B. Barriers
   C. Strife
II. In Christ
   A. New men
   B. Reconciliation
   C. Peace
III. Life in Christ
   A. Belonging to the new community, the church
   B. Living by the code of Christ
   C. Building Christian homes
   D. Working at the Christian mission to the world

A third approach to a book sermon on Ephesians will take its clue from "The Goal of History." This sermon will begin with "The Mystery of the Ages," a mystery without a key for long centuries. This permits us to open the sermon with questions about the futility of history. Is it "a tale told by an idiot" or is it going somewhere? The current rash of books on philosophies of history testify to the pertinence of the question. This sermon will have three points:

I. Christ the center of history; II. A new kind of humanity; III. The church as the forerunner of universal society.

A Modern Title

"God's Design for the World," "The Goal of History," and "Peace for a War-weary World" have all been mentioned. We could add "The Way to One World" and "Man's Disorder and God's Design."

14

JOY INDESTRUCTIBLE
The Letter of Paul to the Philippians

WE KNOW how Christianity began for Philippi—with a vision in the night at Troas, when Paul saw the man from Macedonia standing and pleading, "Come over to Macedonia and help us." Paul's historian-companion reports, "And when he had seen the vision, immediately we sought to go on into Macedonia, concluding that God had called us to preach the gospel to them.

"Setting sail therefore from Troas, we made a direct voyage to Samothrace, and the following day to Neapolis, and from there to Philippi, which is the leading city of the district of Macedonia, and a Roman colony" (Acts 16:9-12). The vision-born labor at Philippi prospered. Paul moved on. Years passed. But Philippi did not forget Paul, nor did Paul forget Philippi. The time came, a half-dozen or a dozen years after that response to the Macedonian call, when the Apostle wrote his letter to the Philippians.

I. WORKING YOUR WAY INTO THE BOOK

Our questions are ready: Where is Paul now? What are his circumstances? What prompts him to write this letter? What is the burden of his book?

AUTHOR'S CIRCUMSTANCES

Read Philippians 1:13, 19-26; 2:17, 23; 4:11-14.

These verses tell us that Paul is in trouble. In fact, he is in prison awaiting trial, the outcome of which could be his execution.

Read Philippians 4:22.

Paul's jailers are Romans, and it looks at first as if he were in Rome, but when we discover that each provincial capital had a "praetorian guard" and that the slaves of "Caesar's household" were dispersed to many important centers of the Empire, we learn merely that Paul was imprisoned in a prominent imperial city.

Read Philippians 2:19, 25-26; 4:18.

There was a great deal of coming and going between Paul's prison and Philippi. But Rome was 840 miles away and required perhaps a full month of travel. Ephesus, however, was little more than a hundred miles away and might be reached in four or five days.

Rear 2 Corinthians 1:8-9; 1 Corinthians 15:32a.

These verses point to imprisonment and trial at Ephesus, although no such imprisonment is mentioned in The Acts of the Apostles. (Many of Paul's hardships were passed over in silence by the author of Acts; 2 Corinthians 11:23-27 gives a formidable list of them.)

If Paul wrote from Ephesus, it is relatively easy to arrive at an approximate date for the letter. (See Acts 19:1-20:1.) Paul spent nearly three years there on this "third" missionary journey. The dates could be A.D. 53, 54 or 55. They might be a year or so later. In all probability, Paul would not have been imprisoned until the end of this period.

If Paul wrote from Rome, which is the more usual hypothesis, it was during the imprisonment mentioned at the end of Acts. (See Acts 28:14b-16, 30, 31.) The Roman imprisonment is variously dated by different biblical scholars; it was a two-year period lying sometime between A.D. 58 and A.D. 65. Fortunately, the exact date of writing and the city—whether Rome or Ephesus—do not affect the essential message of this particular letter; we can afford to leave date and place open. The circumstances remain the same.

Read Philippians 4:15-16; 2:25-29; 4:18 (in that order).

The Philippian Christians had sent gifts to Paul twice at Thessalonica, and during his present trouble they had sent gifts again. They had also dispatched one of their members, a man by the name of Epaphroditus, to serve Paul.

We also read between the lines. Philippians were proud of their city. Named for the father of Alexander the Great, it was a Roman colony, and the seat of a strong military post.

PAUL'S PURPOSE IN WRITING

What prompted Paul to write this letter? Apparently there were several reasons. To discover them, turn to the letter itself:

See again Philippians 4:14-19.

Paul wanted to thank the church at Philippi for its generosity in sending him money and in providing him a servant.

See again Philippians 2:25-29.

Epaphroditus had fallen ill, an illness incurred by overzealous service to Paul. The faithful servant needed care and comfort, circumstances more favorable to his convalescence; therefore Paul was sending him home. He wanted the Philippians to understand this, so he provided Epaphroditus with a letter to carry back.

See again Philippians 1:12-26.

The Philippian Christians were naturally anxious about Paul and wanted word from him. He wrote to tell them what was happening to him and of the spirit in which he was bearing it. (This spirit is an amazing display of Christian morale in the face of hardships and discouragements, perhaps even in the face of death itself.)

See again Philippians 2:19-23.

Paul wanted them to know that he was planning to send Timothy to them as soon as the trial was over.

See again Philippians 2:3-4; 3:2; 4:2.

Paul wanted to help the Philippian Christians to keep the bond of Christian unity and to walk in the Christian way. Therefore he gave them practical advice on general and specific problems of Christian living.

OUTLINE OF THE BOOK

I. Salutation, 1:1-2
II. Thanksgiving and prayer for the Philippians, 1:3-11
III. Paul's own situation, 1:12-2:29
    A. A report, 1:12-26
    B. His concern about their steadfastness, 1:27-2:18
    C. Plans for Timothy and Epaphroditus, 2:19-29
IV. Warnings and advice, 3:2-4:9
    A. Warnings against Christians with wrong motives, 3:2-4:1
    B. Various bits of advice
        1. Christian brotherhood, 4:2-3
        2. Christian joy and trust, 4:4-7
        3. Positive Christian living, 4:8-9
V. Paul's thanks for the gift from Philippi, 4:10-20
VI. Greetings and benediction, 4:21-23

Notice that the letter has the informality which we expect from writings of this kind. In 3:1, Paul is about to close, and then plunges suddenly into strong invective against Christians with wrong motives. There are some scholars who think that we have two letters here. Edgar J. Goodspeed even advises us to read the second of these first: 3:2-4:23 and then 1:1-3:1. Whether these changes of mood need such a drastic explanation or are to be accounted for by the informality of Paul's method in a letter, we cannot and need not decide.

SPECIAL POINTS OF INTEREST

1. *Paul's spirit under adversity.* Although he is in prison facing the prospect of death, Paul is brimful of joy. He is happy: that he is a Christian, that he had advanced the cause of Christ, that even his

hardship turn out for the prosperity of the gospel. Through every paragraph of the letter the note of joy sounds strong and clear. (See 1:18-19; 3:1; 4:1, 4, 10-13.)

2. *Purple passages.* There are many highly quotable passages in this brief letter. As always when he writes, Paul frequently rises to poetic eloquence. Look for these verses. Mark them. Perhaps you will include these: 2:1-11; 3:20-21; 4:8-9.

3. *Key passage.* Sometimes, as we have seen in previous chapters, a book contains a verse or brief passage which summarizes its own central message in its own words. In this light, study: 2:14-18 and 4:4-7.

It is now time to begin at the beginning and to read this letter as a whole. Since it is brief, it can be read in a few minutes. With the help of the background that we have just been sketching, such a reading should be enlightening and inspiring.

II. PREPARING YOUR BOOK SERMON

The Cardinal Idea

There are various ways of expressing this idea. It may be found in either of the key passages suggested above. A third passage also conveys it: See Philippians 4:12-13. The Phillips translation is rewarding: "I know now how to live when things are difficult and I know how to live when things are prosperous. In general and in particular I have learned the secret of facing either poverty or plenty. I am ready for anything through the strength of One Who lives within me."[1]

Let us attempt our own phrasing of the cardinal idea: *There are troubles aplenty to plunge a Christian into gloom, but he does not succumb to them if he is truly Christian; in fact, he rises through them to joy because his life is found not in his circumstances but*

[1] *Ibid.*

in the Christian ambitions and assurances which he brings to those circumstances.

SHAPING A PREACHING OUTLINE

The simplest approach to Paul's letter is to see his joy as a victory over a flock of troubles and discouragements. This gives us our first outline:

JOY THROUGH PAIN

Introduction
- A. One mark of genuine Christianity is the joy of the Christian
- B. The joy comes through no evasion of pain and trouble but by conquest of it
I. A Christian and his discouragements
- A. The trouble that Christianity gets us into
    1. Paul in prison "for the gospel"
    2. Our various Christian tensions with a pagan world
- B. An imperfect Church
    1. Jealousy among Christian leaders, 1:15a
    2. Quarreling Christians, 4:2, 3
    3. False teachers, 3:2-3
    4. Lukewarm Christians, 2:20, 21
- C. Frowning fortune
    1. Epaphroditus ill and "invalided home," 2:25-27
    2. When trouble is added to trouble, insult to injury and "everything" seems to go wrong.
II. A Christian finds the springs of joy.
- A. The progress of the Gospel, despite opposition and misrepresentation, 1:12, 14
- B. A cause worthy of any cost, 1:21
- C. The sense of working with God, 4:13
- D. Remembrance of Christians who are true and faithful, 1:3, 4
- E. Christian generosity and fellowship, 4:14, 18
- F. Broad horizons: the Christian hope, 3:20, 21
Conclusion—The cardinal idea restated

A second approach, somewhat allegorized, is suggested by the key passage 2:14-18:

BANISHING DARKNESS

I. Cursing the darkness, 2:14, 15a
II. Lighting a candle, 2:15b-17
III. Living in the light of joy, 2:18

The development of this second outline must be such that the text is expanded to include constant documentation from the whole book; thus the sermon draws upon a portion of the book but is the message of the whole.

A MODERN TITLE

The two titles already suggested have been "Joy Indestructible" and "Joy through Pain." "Christian Happiness" comes to mind as a direct topical statement, and "Whatever the Circumstances" as an indirect one. "When Things Are Difficult" is not too far afield. If you want a poetic title, how about "Highway to Happiness"? "The Odds against Us and the Spirit within Us" and "Christian Morale" are two additional phrasings of the central message of this amazing book. But whatever the topic, let the preacher not fail to convey the idea that a Christian is a person who knows how to be deeply and infectiously happy.

15

CHRIST OVER ALL
The Letter of Paul to the Colossians

"CHRISTIANS only, but not the only Christians," is a slogan of some Protestant bodies. It is a noble ideal. Consider the first phrase, "Christians only." It sets a high goal of pure Christian loyalty seldom attained on land or sea. For most of us a more descriptive label would be "Christians also." To our pagan loyalties we add Christ. He is one among many.

In Japan recently an American missionary, after telling me that less than 1 per cent of the Japanese people are Christians, went on to say, "We have no doubt that millions of them would become Christians if they could do so without giving up Shinto and Buddhism." The Nipponese are willing to become "Christians also" but not "Christians only." While the deities of Shinto and Buddhism are not in our Western pantheon, we have other gods aplenty to take their places. We are about as reluctant as the Japanese to let "Christ be all and in all," as Paul instructed in his letter of Colossae (Col. 3:11). It is this modern problem which was also the Colossian problem.

I. WORKING YOUR WAY INTO THE BOOK

Colossae was a city about one hundred miles east of Ephesus, in the Roman province of Asia. Situated in the Lycus river valley, it straddled the east-west trade route connecting Ephesus with Mesopotamia. There a polyglot population dwelt and a pandemonium of faiths and philosophies clamored for Colossian ears. Streaming in with the traders came teachers of Stoicism and Epicureanism, of the mystery religions, of Judaism, and of Christianity. It is not surprising that someone, in the interest of peace and harmony, should attempt to combine these rival faiths in a kind of universal religion—a religious patchwork quilt with something from everywhere and for everybody. Actually such *eclecticism* could not produce a living faith but only a "philosophistry" not unlike modern Theosophy. Hierapolis and Laodicea were sister towns located nearby in the same Lycus valley.

To this valley, probably sometime during Paul's long residence at Ephesus, there came the Christian missionary, Epaphras, who organized churches in all three cities:

Read Acts 19:10; Colossians 1:7; 4:12-13.

The church at Colossae met in the home of the wealthy Philemon, whose son or kinsman, Archippus, was also an industrious Christian missionary:

Read Philemon 2, 23; Colossians 4:7-9, 17, 1:7-8 (in that order).

Epaphras not only had brought news to Paul concerning the church at Colossae but was at the time of Paul's writing a fellow prisoner with him. Paul had been keenly interested in the Colossian Christians from the beginning, but he had never visited Colossae and was personally unknown to most of the members of the congregation:

Read Colossians 1:9; 2:1.

The bearers of Paul's Letter to the Colossians also carried letters to Philemon and the Laodiceans, possibly to the Ephesians as well. The Colossians were requested to exchange letters with the Laodiceans. Unless the letter to the Laodiceans is our present canonical Letter of Paul to the Ephesians as Marcion suggested, it is lost.

Read Colossians 4:15, 16.

Paul refers several times to the fact that he is a prisoner. It is usually assumed that the imprisonment was the one at Rome pictured at the end of The Acts of the Apostles. But since Paul in his stormy career saw the inside of a good many prisons, we cannot be certain that he wrote from Rome rather than Caesarea, Ephesus or even elsewhere. Fortunately the message of the letter is not at stake:

Read Colossians 1:24; 4:10, 18.

The Reason for the Letter

Paul did not write this letter merely to express his interest in the Colossian Christians. From Epaphras he had learned that they were in danger of capitulating to the allurements of a "philosophistry" then making its appeal among them:

Read Colossians 2:8; 1:23 (in that order).

They were in danger of "shifting from the hope of the gospel." When we inquire into the nature of the enticing heresy, it appears as a hodgepodge of elements from Greek, Oriental and Jewish sources:

Read Colossians 2:8-21.

1. It contained a sophisticated system of thought characterized by Paul as "empty deceit," "human tradition," "puffed up without reason by his sensuous mind," "human precepts and doctrines," and "an appearance of wisdom."

2. It contained also certain rites of initiation including circumcision and "self-abasement." These initiatory rites were, of course, added to baptism.

3. Moreover, festivals of new moon and sabbath were added to the usual observances of the church, and other regulations and observances were practiced.

4. Asceticism was made mandatory. There were some food and drink concerning which the rule said "Do not handle. Do not taste. Do not touch."

5. Worship was accorded to angels and spirits, sometimes called "principalities and powers," "elements," "thrones" and "dominions." These were supposedly supernatural forces—spirits and demons. As one scholar has explained, beings corresponding to polytheistic gods are arranged in an ascending series of supernatural intermediaries connecting the Absolute God and lowly man imprisoned in evil matter. Christ, of course, was given a niche within this hierarchy, one spirit among many.

Call this heresy "incipient gnosticism" and we have a label fairly to stifle thought. It is not important to affix the proper label. What is important to see is that the uniqueness of Christ is lost and he is made one power among many instead of King of kings and Lord of lords. The result is a religion that is little more than a welter of superstitions without the power of revelation or redemption. At base this religious hodgepodge is a speculative and ritualistic dogma, highly intellectualized and sophisticated. Outgrowth in moral action and Christian character was not deemed necessary; in fact, the new teaching was consistent with the basest forms of immorality:

Read Colossians 3:5-10.

Paul's answer was an assertion of the unique lordship of Christ and a reiteration of Christ as revealer of truth and Redeemer of men. As in 1 Corinthians 8:5-6 he asserts: "For there are many so-called gods in heaven or on earth—as indeed there are many 'gods' and many 'lords'—yet for us there is one God, the Father, from whom are all things and for whom we exist, and one Lord, Jesus Christ, through whom are all things and through whom all exist." This is Paul's positive teaching in Colossians:

Read Colossians 1:15-20.

In these verses Christ is assigned not only a human but a cosmic significance. He is genuine Truth and real Power; he is Life and the Way; in short, he is the Saviour of men. He is Lord of Creation and of our Re-creation.

The results of trusting Christ as Lord are two in number: (1) rebirth of persons and (2) personal moral behavior:

Read Colossians 3:3, 17.

Whether a man really accepts the sole lordship of Christ, then, can be determined by two simple tests: has he yielded himself in complete surrender to be remade by Christ, and does he do everything, whether word or act, in the spirit of Christ? He does not need to be able to present his faith in skillful words like some brilliant professor of philosophy; he merely demonstrates it by what he is and does.

Perhaps the closest single approach to a key verse is a fraction of 3:11—"Christ is all, and in all."

OUTLINE OF THE LETTER

Introduction, 1:1-12
- A. Greetings, 1:1-2
- B. Thanksgiving for the Colossians, 1:3-8
- C. Prayer for their Christian steadfastness, 1:9-12

I. Christ as Lord and Saviour 1:13-23
- A. Their experience of deliverance by Christ's power, 1:13-14
- B. Christ as Lord of lords, 1:15-17
- C. Christ as Redeemer, 1:18-20
- D. The experienced redemption of the Colossians, 1:21-23

II. Paul's concern as God's messenger 1:24-2:7
- A. His message and concern for all Gentiles, 1:24-29
- B. His present concern about the Colossians, 2:1-7

III. Warning against false pholosophies 2:8-3:4
- A. Christian experience itself as a safeguard, 2:8-15
- B. True religion as new life, 2:16-23
- C. New life expressed in Christian behavior, 3:1-4

IV. Practical applications
- A. Christian ethics in general, 3:5-7
  - 1. Putting off pagan ways, 3:5-11
  - 2. Putting on Christian ways, 3:12-17
- B. Christian ethics in the home, 3:18-4:1
- C. Prayer, 4:2-4
- D. Behavior toward outsiders, 4:5-6

V. News and greetings, 4:7-18

Points of Interest

1. Paul's tone in this letter is gentle and conciliatory. Since he is not personally acquainted with the Colossians, he dare not be severe, as he could be when occasion demanded among those who knew and loved him well, as with Corinth.

2. The heart of Paul's appeal to the Colossians is not theoretical but empirical. He argues from the Christian experience of his readers. Once "estranged and hostile in mind, doing evil deeds," they had been made into *a new kind of persons* solely by the power of Christ working in and through them. They had experienced the saviorhood of Christ and accepted his lordship. Therefore, when Paul went on to discuss these things they knew him to be dealing not with speculations but with tested realities. That is how true Christianity deals with perversions of Christianity; it refutes a speculation, not by opposing it with another speculation but by crowding it out with facts, the facts of regenerate human nature and Christian character.

II. PREPARING YOUR BOOK SERMON

The Cardinal Idea

Christ is not one lord and saviour among many; he is supreme Lord, Revealer and Redeemer, whom to accept is to be born anew and to live anew.

Shaping Your Preaching Outline

One way to shape a sermon outline is to work through key passages which represent the principal stages of thought in the letter. Such a treatment of Colossians would begin with 2:8-23 where the false philosophy is presented; the essence of this "empty deceit" is that sophisticated thinking makes Christ one among many—that Christ gets only a fraction of our life and that he permeates very little of it. This is practical polytheism. The moral outgrowth of this practical polytheism is ethically negative, as shown by the key section 3:5-11. The vices detailed there are of three general kinds: sensualism, pride and unbrotherly division. Having looked at the nature and moral outgrowth of practical polytheism we are then ready to consider the balancing Christian realities, these are: first, Christ as Lord, Revealer and Redeemer, 1:15-20; second, the moral regeneration of men accepting Christ over all, 3:1-4; and third, the outgrowth of this new birth in Christian behavior, 3:12-17. The resulting outline would be:

I. Christ among many lords and saviours
    A. Practical polytheism
        1. The spirits and powers worshiped in Colossae
        2. Competing loyalties served by us today
    B. The moral results
II. Christ over all and in all
    A. Practical Christian monotheism
    B. Persons made new in Christ's image
    C. Persons living in Christ's way

A second approach could be made from the text, 1 Corinthians 8:5-6, which so well summarizes the Colossian letter. The two main points of the sermon are phrased for us: (1) Many "gods" and "lords." (2) One God, the Father, and one Lord, Jesus Christ. Under the second point there are three subpoints: (a) creation, (b) providence and (c) personal redemption, these suggested by the phrases, "from whom are all things and for whom we exist" and "through whom we exist."

A topical treatment of the book might be developed to begin with Colossian and American superstitions which divide and dissipate the power of Christ. It is instructive to notice that the superstitions of the first century had to do principally with supernatural demons and spirits, while those of the twentieth century are mostly materialistic—science, military might, technological production, this-worldly utopianism, and the like. Within these superstitions there is no redemption; we worship and we are not saved, we are not changed, and from them we cannot do that which is good. When Christ is only one power among many we do not accept him as Saviour; instead we try to make him our servant to do our unregenerate bidding. When we do this we go on calling ourselves and our way of life "Christian" but the label is specious, for we have really done nothing more than add Christian sanctions to a pagan life. Turning the shield, we see our acceptance of the sole lordship of Christ beginning in our own selfish moral and spiritual death (3:4); we give up our sovereignty and let Christ reign. We let him be "all," and our service to him is in all that we do; there are no secular interests and activities for everything has been sanctified by our response to Christ in the common life. Thus we determine whether Christ is really our Master by a change from pride and self-righteousness, from the rebellion and resentment of self-made and self-controlled men; this change is not wrought in us by our own moral achievement but by our surrender of sovereignty to the true king. And we test it also by daily Christian behavior, such behavior is not the reason why we are changed persons but a simple outgrowth in humility and gratitude of the redemption that Christ has wrought in us.

A Modern Title

Thinking of the danger in the Colossian and American superstitions we might accept the negative title, "Practical Polytheism." "If Not One God, How Many?" has the value of an implicit denial that atheism is a live option, while at the same time it represents the positive interests of the letter. "Faiths that Compete for My Loyalty" is the title of my study book on modern secular substitutes and rival faiths, but it could also serve for this sermon. Perhaps "Christ over All" will appeal to most readers as a simple description of the main positive message of the Colossian letter. So be it.

16

FAITH'S CONTAGION
The First Letter of Paul to the Thessalonians

IT IS TRUE that all men, as Men, walk more by faith than by sight— be that faith noble, ignoble or mediocre. But it is also true that a faith seldom comes to a man out of his own solitary thought, unaided by the thought and lives of his fellows. More often it is communicated from another person or other persons; and the charged wire over which it is transmitted is personal concern. A faith is communicated only when there is an investment of a life in lives, as with Paul and the Thessalonians: "So, being affectionately desirous of you, we were ready to share with you not only the gospel of God but also our own selves, because you had become very dear to us" (1 Thess. 2:8). It is hard to escape the faith of a person who loves us.

But, turn the shield over; there is a reciprocal action in such communication. Do you think that Paul received nothing from the Thessalonians? Let him tell it: "I feel encouraged, brothers . . . at your faith, for now I can really live, since you are standing firm in the Lord" (1 Thess. 3:7, Goodspeed). Paul was no spiritual Atlas supporting the world upon his lonely shoulders; he gained strength from the touch of brotherhood.

Yes we walk by faith, but the faith in whose light we walk is cast by other lives. I am unyielding under temptation, for example, not because I have firmed up my will in Stoic solitude, but because I remember you and "the good news of your faith and love." You are the light of faith in which I walk, and it is a little sobering to realize it, but perhaps I am yours.

I. WORKING YOUR WAY INTO THE BOOK

Paul came to Thessalonica directly from the prison experience in Philippi:

Read Acts 17:1-10.

He was accompanied by Silas and Timothy. Working in their accustomed manner through the synagogue, the three missionaries were soon successful, especially among "the devout Greeks" or God-fearers. These "proselytes of the threshold" who were drawn to Judaism by its monotheism and its lofty morality, but not yet into it in full communion, constituted a ripe harvest field to the Christian mission. After only a few weeks, however, hostile Jews motivated by jealousy incited a mob against Jason, the chief Thessalonian convert, and a number of his fellows. Paul's mission in Thessalonica, for the time being, was ended, but not without important results. For it was in Thessalonica that the revolutionary character of Christianity was so clearly attested: "These men who have turned the world upside down have come here also" (Acts 17:6).

Thessalonica, so named about 300 B.C. in honor of the sister of Alexander the Great, was the capital of the Roman province of Macedonia. Known in ancient times as Therme, for its hot springs, it eventually became a city of 200,000. Situated on the main trade route between the Far East and Rome, it was a city of importance. A Roman "free city"—ungarrisoned—it was to rival Constantinople as a possible capital of the Empire.

Paul's visit to this Macedonian capital may be dated about A.D. 49.

From Thessalonica, he and his companions passed on to Berea, where the hostility encountered in other Macedonian cities reappeared. But at Berea it was Paul himself who was the chief object of attack. So he went on to Athens alone, leaving Silas and Timothy to follow only after the situations at Thessalonica and Berea had been somewhat stabilized.

Read Acts 17:14, 16a.

Paul waited for them at Athens. The book of Acts indicates that Timothy and Silas rejoined Paul at Corinth (Acts 18:5), the implication being that Paul was in Athens the whole time alone. But 1 Thessalonians 3:1-2 indicates that Timothy may have rejoined him at Athens, only to be dispatched almost at once on a special mission to Thessalonica. The reason for this was Paul's anxiety about the Macedonian Christians. He had left them under fire. He wanted himself to return:

Read 1 Thessalonians 2:17, 18; 3:5.

His special mission accomplished, Timothy rejoined Paul at Corinth (Acts 18:5), in company with Silas. The news he brought from Thessalonica was more than reassuring:

Read 1 Thessalonians 3:6-9.

So, in the name of the three of them, Paul wrote at once a letter of overflowing thankfulness. New Testament scholars are fairly well agreed that this was the first of Paul's New Testament letters. He had met with so much opposition and discouragement at Philippi, in Thessalonica itself, at Berea, and even in Athens, that his own morale was exceedingly low when he arrived at Corinth:

Read 1 Corinthians 2:1-3.

The news from Thessalonica gave him heart again. They were standing the test. His labor had not been in vain. From them his faith took fire again. It was out of such feelings that he wrote our present letter.

TEMPTATIONS AT THESSALONICA

The pressures at Thessalonica were severe. Notice how frequently Paul referred to persecutions which the Thessalonian Christians had endured and were experiencing:

Read 1 Thessalonians 1:6; 2:2, 14-16; 3:3, 4.

Such persecution arose from the Jews. But there were other pressures, among them the low moral practices of the pagan community.

Read 1 Thessalonians 4:3-7.

Paul was enough of a psychologist to know that the hunger of the Thessalonian Christians for acceptance and belonging could drive them from the arms of the Jews, who now persecuted them, to the Greeks whose blood kinsmen they were. If they were to remain Christian they would have to establish and maintain their own community. There was no indication that any Thessalonian Christian had succumbed, but Paul knew the pressures and he wanted to forearm by forewarning them. His fears for the Thessalonians were later abundantly fulfilled in kind at Corinth, proving that he was dealing with no imaginary danger (see 1 Corinthians 5:1, 2). Thus Paul emphasizes the importance of reinforcing their own sense of togetherness, not only locally but with the entire Christian brotherhood in Macedonia:

Read 1 Thessalonians 4:9-10a; 5:12-13.

But there must be no abuse of family togetherness by lazy members whose aversion to work might make them a charge upon the community:

Read 1 Thessalonians 4:11, 12; 5:14a.

Paul had noticed a tendency in this direction on the part of some converts while he was still with them. Timothy must have reported that the tendency continued. And he brought other reports as well. Some members had died, and there was concern about them. Would they share in the imminent messianic kingdom?

Read 1 Thessalonians 4:13, 14.

Once launched upon this theme of Christ's second coming and the "last things" of history Paul could not restrain himself. This note had been sounded in his preaching among them. It was then that he had taught them "to wait for [God's] Son from heaven" (1 Thess. 1:10). Now he embellished the same theme:

Read 1 Thessalonians 4:13-5:11.

How could he foresee that the Thessalonians were to seize upon this "eschatalogical passage" and magnify it out of its proper proportion? He sought to conquer their sorrow, to strengthen their Christian steadfastness and make them equal to their trials and temptations. His motives in writing it were more practical than theological. He wrote so that they could "encourage one another and build one another up" (5:11).

ACHIEVEMENTS

The Thessalonians repaid Paul's belief in them. When Paul made his collection for the poor saints of Jerusalem, these same Christians were so generous that "their extreme poverty overflowed in a wealth of liberality" (2 Cor. 8:1-4). This was only because they had so completely given themselves first (2 Cor. 8:5). Three members of this church attached themselves to Paul as a part of his itinerant retinue: Aristarchus, Secundus and Demas (Acts 19:29; 20:4; 27:2; 2 Tim. 4:10). Paul revisited them at least twice (Acts 20:2, 3). And Timothy was also sent back to them on at least one other occasion (Acts 19:22). Apostle and church were mutually strengthened on many occasions.

In the background of this letter there lies the elementary gospel which Paul preached everywhere, which, indeed, the whole apostolic company proclaimed. We have set this forth above in our general introduction to the Four Gospels. Nothing less would have been able to work "in power and in the Holy Spirit and with full conviction" (1 Thess. 1:5).

SUMMARY

We are now ready to review the whole, connected message of the letter: In the first chapter Paul exults over the wholehearted acceptance of the gospel by the Thessalonians and praises them for their steadfastness in it. The second and third chapters are obviously Paul's personal answer to what his enemies were whispering into the ears of the Thessalonian Christians. We hear their insinuations coming through: "Where is your Paul now? He quit when persecution started! Could it be that he came only for what he could get out of you—your flattery and your money?" Paul's readers know how thoroughly the facts refute such insinuations, but nonetheless Paul reminds them of some of the facts: He did not live at their expense, but supported himself at his trade. He did not exploit them but loved them and served them, "like a nurse taking care of her children" (2:7). And, far from deserting them in danger, he had made several attempts to return (2:17-18; 3:1, 2). In the third chapter Paul tells of his concern for them, his dispatching of Timothy, and his joy over Timothy's glowing report about them. The fourth and fifth chapters contain several items of practical advice about the Christian life: Keep sexually pure, work hard, don't grieve about your recent dead as those who have no hope. Neither be alarmed over the imminent end of history. For the wicked only is it Doomsday; for you it is Sunrise. Respect your leaders. Help those in trouble and build the brotherhood. Keep praying. Trust the Spirit.

OUTLINE OF FIRST THESSALONIANS

Introduction: Salutation, 1:1
  I. Thanksgiving for their acceptance of, and progress in, the Gospel, 1:2-10
 II. Paul's defense of his Thessalonian mission against Jewish insinuations, 2:1-16
III. An account of events since leaving Thessalonica, 2:17-3:10
    A. His desire to return, 2:17-20

    B. His sending of Timothy, 3:1-5
    C. Timothy's glowing report, 3:6-10
IV. Paul's prayer for them, 3:11-13
 V. Practical advice on problems, 4:1-5:22
    A. Moral instructions, 4:1-12
    B. The second coming, 4:13-5:11
    C. Church life and conduct, 5:12-22
Conclusion: Final prayer and benediction, 5:23-28

KEY PASSAGE

"You know what kind of men we proved to be among you for your sake. And you became imitators of us and of the Lord, for you received the word in much affliction, with joy inspired by the Holy Spirit; so that you became an example to all believers in Macedonia and in Achaia" (1:5b-7).

Also 1 Thessalonians 2:8 coupled with 3:7, 8.

II. PREPARING YOUR BOOK SERMON

CARDINAL IDEA

Contagious Christian faith rooted in the gospel, communicated through loving personal concern and incarnate in a community of Christian brothers, overcomes opposition, temptation and bereavement, and encourages the faithful everywhere.

SHAPING A PREACHING OUTLINE

Using a narrative topical approach, one finds the thought of First Thessalonians moving through three phases: (1) The revolutionary gospel, (2) the hostile world and (3) the triumphant church. For the first division we take our clues from Acts 17:6b; 1 Thessalonians 1:5; 2:7, 8. Thus the gospel which overturns the secular order is not merely words but the power of God in Christ and the Holy Spirit—God's deed proclaimed in the *kerygma*. And it is transmitted by persons who care deeply enough to share themselves. The hostile world in this letter shows itself as active persecution and as a cultural climate of anti-Christian values. The pressure from this world is severe and unrelenting. The triumphant church is "all the time getting into trouble, and it is absurdly happy." It rises above opposition; it breaks with pagan morality; it is undismayed by bereavement; and it practices brotherhood while building up a new kind of human community. The faith in this church is contagious and inspiring. It encourages the apostle who planted it; it becomes "an example to all believers."

A second topical organization may be derived from the cardinal idea, as phrased above. We have (1) the marks of contagious Christian faith and (2) the achievements of contagious Christian faith. The marks include (a) a Gospel of God, (b) a sharing of human life with other lives, (c) the creation of a fellowship of faith. The achievements are (a) a new morality, (b) a new expectation (4:13-11), (c) victory over oppositions and (d) the inspiring of others to like faith.

A textual organization of the key passage will yield a usable outline. Paul appeared among the Thessalonians as a messenger and example of the gospel. The Thessalonians imitated him. Even under much affliction they discovered a new joy—from God himself. And they became an inspiring example to others, including Paul himself. We have then: Demonstration, Imitation, Inspiration.

A MODERN TITLE

"For Now We Live" is a biblical topic from 3:8: "For now we live, if you stand fast in the Lord." We have already suggested "Faith's Contagion" by selecting it as the title of this chapter. The kind of faith that the critics of Christianity saw in Thessalonica is reported in Acts 17:6b: "A Faith that Overturns the World."

17

BLUEPRINT FOR DOOMSDAY
The Second Letter of Paul to the Thessalonians

SECULARISM is a pseudo-religion which makes this world absolute; it aims to create heaven on earth, of, by and for the earthly. Its ultimate expression is not the human paradise sought for, but a totalitarian "animal farm." Recent history has shown us this. Despite the disastrous outcome of triumphant secularism, however, otherworldliness has few attractions for most of us. We associate it with queer people who placard the highways with signs warning that "Jesus Is Coming Soon," or with anchorite monks who abandon the world to the devil. The truth of the matter is that we are not safe citizens of either world when that world is cut off from the other. We, who are taken from the ground and into whose nostrils God himself breathed the breath of life, are created to be citizens of two worlds at the same time. We are in the world but not wholly of it; we are in the world, but as pilgrims and sojourners.

No one ever wrote more tellingly of the balance or tension of these two worlds within our human heritage than the unknown third-century author who penned the *Address to Diognetus:*

For Christians are not distinguished from the rest of mankind in country or speech or customs. . . . Though they live in Greek or barbarian cities, as each man's lot is cast, and follow the local customs in dress and food and the rest of their living, their own way of life which they display is wonderful and admittedly strange. They live in their native lands, but like foreigners. They take part in everything like citizens, and endure everything like aliens. Every foreign country is their native land, and every native land a foreign country. . . . They find themselves in the flesh, but they do not live after the flesh. They remain on earth, but they are citizens of heaven.[1]

It would seem, then, that our Creator intended us to have one foot solidly planted on earth but the other in heaven. That was Paul's problem among the Thessalonian Christians: They were trying to plant both feet in heaven. The Thessalonian problem was exactly opposite to that of Corinth, where the world was too much with them and the Corinthians were all but submerged in it.

I. WORKING YOUR WAY INTO THE BOOK

The problem at Thessalonica was an excessive and excited preoccupation with the Lord's Second Coming:

Read 2 Thessalonians 2:1-2.

In his first letter to them Paul had dwelt upon this theme for the purpose of comforting those whose loved ones had died, that they might "not grieve as others do who have no hope" (1 Thess. 4:13). Paul had expressed himself strongly on the subject, but the topic of the Second Coming was not new to them. It had been a part of his oral message to them. (See 2 Thess. 2:5.) Possibly Paul's strong statements in the first letter were misconstrued. Yet this would hardly account for Paul's allusion to "a letter purporting to be from us, to the effect that the day of the Lord has come." Nothing in the first letter can be construed to have that meaning. Moreover, Paul would hardly repudiate his own letter because it had been misread; rather he would repudiate the misinterpretation of the letter. We are left, then, with the probability that the Thessalonians were cherishing as Paul's a forged letter which supported the extreme millennialism of

---

[1] *Address to Diognetus* 5:1, 4-6, 9, 10. *The Apostolic Fathers, an American Translation*, by Edgar J. Goodspeed (Harper, 1950).

some members. What messenger brought this news to Paul's ears, we cannot guess, but however it came, the news was sufficient to provoke a letter from Paul repudiating the forgery and its distorted teaching.

IDLENESS

But there was more. The tendency toward idleness, which Paul had detected while still among them and to which he alluded in his first letter, was now greatly aggravated. Paul felt called upon not only to speak sternly against such idleness, but to advise the excommunication of idlers:

Read 2 Thessalonians 3:6-14.

It seems clear that the offending idleness was caused by exaggerated notions about last things. In America in the middle of the nineteenth century the Millerite movement exhibited the same symptoms when hundreds of people abandoned their callings, sold their possessions, robed themselves in white and waited on hilltops for the coming of the Lord. Nearly every generation produces an excitement like this. In 1954, for instance, a small group of disciples attached to a Chicago prophetess set a date for the arrival of a space ship which would inaugurate the Last Days—a modernized, mechanized version of the millennial hope. The day came and went; a second, revised schedule failed. There will be other movements like these, as there have been throughout the history of Christendom, for distortions of the doctrine of the Second Coming are as persistent as the doctrine is real. The temptation to deny the doctrine in order to eliminate the distortions is very attractive, but we are beginning to see that no amount of rationalization can justify such elimination. The doctrine is in the New Testament. It was a part of the primitive *kerygma*. Moreover, if we follow the clue of the Thessalonian correspondence, we will see that abuse and distortion attached to the doctrine from the first.

SPECULATION

Idleness was only one of the fruits of exaggerated millennialism at Thessalonica. Another was speculation. The idlers became metaphysical busybodies. If we may impute to them the vices noticed in their spiritual descendants down the ages, we will suspect them of studying the scripture in the light of the calendar as a literal map of the future. How many times has the date for the end of the world been set? How much misguided energy has been spent, how much paper and ink have been wasted in calculating "the day and the hour"! And all of this has flourished in the face of the express words of Jesus: "But of that day and hour no one knows, not even the angels of heaven, nor the Son, but the Father only" (Matt. 24:36).

These words from Matthew's Gospel seem to convey Paul's own attitude. He undeniably felt that the last days were near, but they were still future and no man could predict them. The practical implication was, "Brethren, do not be weary in well doing" (3:13). Life on earth continues in its multiform relationships and responsibilities, but it moves in the light of a transcendent destiny and an immortal hope.

ESCHATOLOGY

The details of Paul's eschatology in this letter have baffled scholars, causing some to declare that the letter could not have been Paul's because it reflects a historical situation which applied only after the death of Nero, it being supposed that "the man of lawlessness" was *Nero redivivus*. In recent years this opinion has subsided, and Paul's eschatology is seen as a reflection of the refined Jewish hope which early Christians had lifted out of the Old Testament and to which they had added elements which came naturally from the death and resurrection of Jesus.

Now look at some of the elements in Paul's eschatology:

1. The first coming of Jesus, the Messiah, is assumed. With this

coming the age to come had dawned. But it had not been fully realized.

2. Before Jesus comes again to complete his work and bring the age to come to its consummation, evil will rise to its crescendo. There will be "rebellion." "The man of lawlessness" ruling from the temple itself will appear (2:3, 4). The big lie will pass for the truth. Wrong will masquerade as right (2:11-12).

3. Then Jesus will come and slay the lawless one with the breath of his mouth (2.8), and inflict vengeance upon those who do not know God (1:8, 9). This is the day of the Lord.

4. The time of fire for the ungodly will be the day of redemption for the faithful (1:10; 2:13). Such is the last judgment.

The reaction of liberal Christians is to understand Paul literally, which leads to the observation that what he expected did not happen, and that in consequence the whole eschatological element in New Testament Christianity is to be rejected. Such a rejection—sometimes by means of pretending that it was not there—has been tried and found wanting. We are beginning now to look beyond the literal and chronological meanings to the essence of the eschatological hope. It is not even clear that Paul, being an Oriental, was meant to be taken literally; it is clear that, as an articulate representative of the early Christian mind, he is to be taken seriously. E. J. Bicknell, in the *Westminster Commentaries*, has pointed us to four permanent values in Apocalyptic, which are:

1. It is God, not human progress, who stands at the center of history.

2. The givenness of God's grace. This means that men do not and cannot build the kingdom of heaven. It is *God's* kingdom. The conditions for belonging to it are moral and spiritual conditions, for the kingdom is not an engineering operation.

3. The real and vital difference between good and evil. To this we may add the subtlety and power of evil. It is not simply that evil

opposes good but that it masquerades as the highest good in doing so. (The man of lawlessness enthrones himself in the temple.) Moreover, this evil, while subtly infused into every human life, suffers a kind of polarity, manifests itself in increasing demonic strength as it is incarnate more and more in personalities and institutions. The earth is the scene of a moral struggle.

4. Far from invalidating the reality of life on this earth, apocalyptic intensifies it. For this life has all its own inherent significance plus its meaning as a testing ground for the life to come.

Wherever man may be collectively in relation to the *finis* of history, each human individual is close to it. Death is not to be denied. But the *finis* is not the *end*. It supplies the urgency within which the true end of man—his goal and crown—is to be achieved. This end is supplied by God, who reveals himself in Christ our Lord, presides over a moral universe, brings evil to judgment, and by whose grace we are saved. We have the end of history in view when we look to Jesus as Lord of life and death. But it is not necessary to wait for the *finis* to begin to realize the *end* of history. The *end* broods over the *process*, eternity hovers over time; whatever meaning there is in this world escapes and eludes us without the other world. The two belong together and we must live in both.

Second Thessalonians is a slight epistle of three chapters, but what towering implications it invokes! It points beyond the three- or four-dimensional world to a world of six dimensions, because to the four dimensions of *space* and *time* it weds *life* and *spirit*, and it makes them presently real.

OUTLINE OF SECOND THESSALONIANS

Introduction: Greeting, 1:1-2
  I. Thanksgiving and prayer for the Thessalonians, 1:3-12
      A. Thanks for their growth in faith and love under affliction, 1:3-5
      B. Thanks that they are prepared by Christ's coming to punish sinners and reward believers, 1:6-10

      C. Prayer that they may attain this reward, 1:11-12
II. Errors about the Second Coming corrected, 2:1-17
    A. The day of the Lord as still future, 2:1-2
    B. The day will be preceded by rebellion, which Christ will over-
       throw, 2:3-12
    C. God's election of the faithful as their reassurance, 2:13-15
    D. A prayer for their encouragement, 2:16-17
III. Practical instructions and warnings, 3:1-15
    A. Paul's request for their prayers for his work, 3:1-5
    B. Injunction against idlers, 3:6-15
Conclusion: Prayer, greeting, blessing, 3:16-18

This letter does not seem to yield a key passage.

II. PREPARING YOUR BOOK SERMON

CARDINAL IDEA

As long as we are on this earth we will accept it as real and carry our full responsibilities here, but we will do so in the light of goals and principles which come to us from God through Christ our Lord. We will live on earth in the light of Eternity.

SHAPING A PREACHING OUTLINE

The Thessalonian problem which provoked Paul's letter was a minimizing of earth and an exaggerating of heaven. His readers were unduly preoccupied with last things. This same preoccupation with the *finis* of history shows itself today in the road sign "Jesus Is Coming Soon" and equally in the wholly unreligious predictions of atomic doom. In either case normal human living is abrogated in terms of emergency behavior which gets us all out of focus as to life's meanings and our normal responsibilities of holding things together. This is what a blueprint for Doomsday does to us. That was the unhappy predicament of the Thessalonians.

The corrective is a moral view of history and faithfulness to responsibilities in the light of God's sovereignty. The moral view of history does not glance off the problem of evil; indeed it takes evil far more seriously than most of us do. Evil is no cultural lag, no absence of good; it is a demonic force, subtle, endowed with the capacity to disguise itself. And the world—the soul of a man—is a mortal battleground upon whose outcome cosmic issues hang. The end of history is Christ as Lord judging and ruling, but we do not have to wait for *finis* to know this *end*. We can live now in the light of it. The practical outcome is Christian work and growing love and faith. Thus we move through three phases: the error of doomsday-ism; the corrective, a moral view of history; the practical implications for our way of life. These are the principal phases in the thought of the letter itself. We have omitted only the note of thanks for the growing faith and love of the Thessalonian Christians. That can be included easily under the practical implications.

Since the Corinthian and Thessalonian problems are opposite in nature, one is tempted to discuss the two letters together. In Corinth the imbalance was a case of "two feet on earth"; in Thessalonica the temptation was "two feet in heaven." The cure for both situations is one foot on earth, one foot in heaven. This joining of Corinth and Thessalonica is all the more attractive when it is recalled that the Thessalonian correspondence was written from Corinth.

Bicknell's construction of the permanent significance of apocalyptic, referred to above, yields a four-point outline on the central message of the book. It even carries the implication against idleness. If this outline were prefaced by a presentation of the Thessalonian heresy and its modern counterparts, the picture would seem to be complete.

The contrast between end as *finis* and end as *goal* has already been used, but it could be made central to the sermon. The preoccupation of much fear of atomic annihilation is focused on the wrong questions: "*When* will the end come?" "*How* will the end come?" These both deal with *finis*. The proper question is, "*What* is the end (goal) of history?" When we see this in the light of the

Christian revelation we will go back to our deserted posts and leave the outcome to God, who is Lord of history. There is entirely too much of this managing of the future in contemporary psychology; at bottom it is faithlessness.

A MODERN TITLE

"One Foot in Heaven," reflecting the book and movie of the same title, may be thought a little light for so serious a subject. Perhaps it is, but it does come naturally to mind. Some men may want to use it. "Blueprint for Doomsday" aims at the error which Paul was attacking and it has a certain dramatic quality which is appealing. "The End of History" is literal, but not without interest. Even more literal is "The Second Coming" but most men will want to avoid it because of its many misleading implications.

From our present discussion one thing should have become clear; Second Thessalonians does have a vital, neglected message for our day.

18

THE CHRISTIAN PASTOR
The Letters of Paul to Timothy and Titus

SINCE 1726, when Paul Anton of Halle so labeled them, the three letters of Paul to Timothy and Titus have been known as "the Pastoral Epistles." The reason is simple: they deal with the work of the Christian pastor. That pastor is a leader within a movement which has several generations of history, a movement whose members regard Christianity as a heritage and who are in danger of slipping away from its radiant core into some twilight land of faith and morality. The task confronted by the Christian pastor, as we see him through these letters, is not that of pioneer but that of homesteader, gradually establishing the secure ways of a settled community life. He is not so much a creator of new spiritual values as a conserver of an old and cherished faith which must be renewed for each generation and safeguarded against decline and loss. Though not as heroic as the apostle or the evangelist breaking new territory for his faith, the pastor is just as essential to an ongoing movement perpetuating itself in history. Whether the lamp of faith flickers or flames in any Christian community in any generation will depend upon the kind of leadership the Christian pastor brings to his flock. That is the concern of these letters.

I. WORKING YOUR WAY INTO THE PASTORAL EPISTLES

It is possible to deal with each letter separately, since it may be argued that each has a slightly different emphasis. Subjects can be assigned to them in the following manner: First Timothy—*Church Administration*; Second Timothy—*Christian Life and Character*; Titus—*Right Belief*. But such a classification will not satisfy the student for long; it is too rigid for the fluid material under study, and it is obviously imposed for an analytical mind impatient to turn everything into categories.

The Pastoral Epistles are better studied as a group. Moreover, it is best to approach them in the order of their own developing thought. Thus, one will begin with Second Timothy, the most personal and the least ecclesiastical; he will pass on to Titus, in which the needs of the organized church are somewhat clearer; and he will end with First Timothy in which many organizational directions become clear and explicit. Why not read them now, and in that order?

Read Second Timothy; Titus; First Timothy.

No discussion of these letters can get far without confronting the question of authorship. Most students see the difficulties: the biographical details do not fit into anything that we know about Paul from the book of Acts or from his previous letters. The whole atmosphere of the churches addressed has changed from that of the Pauline era; it is a church with some years of heritage, a church with waning fervor and consequently more concerned with organization and discipline than with spirit and gospel. The vocabulary and the style are different; even in English it is apparent that this is not Paul's usual writing style, and it can be established by a simple census of words that this is not Paul's vocabulary. Certainly it is not Paul's zealous, pioneering spirit.

Scholars are led by these facts to conclude that the Pastoral Epistles almost certainly come from a time late in the first century, say A.D. 90 to 95; and that at the very most they contain only a few fragments from some of Paul's personal notes not previously published. The effort to secure apostolic authorship for them by positing a fourth missionary journey, predicated upon Paul's trial and release by Nero after Acts 28, looks less and less credible. In any case, we need to remember that it is not the individual author in isolation who writes scripture; it is the Holy Spirit through the church as Christian community which does so. There can be no doubt that the Pastoral Epistles are the product of the Christian community and that they reflect the life and need of that community at one stage in its development. As such they are scripture, whether Paul wrote them or any part of them. No question of forgery is involved; pseudonymous writings were well known and perfectly respectable in that day before copyright laws.

It is clear, however, that the writer of the letters was appealing to the immense prestige of the apostle Paul, that he was using the letters and teachings of the great missionary as normative of the life and faith of the Christian community in his own later generation. In this there was a stroke of genius. To set Paul the person in the midst of church life as a dynamic norm was obviously more vital than a manual of right beliefs and sound organizational practices.

We shall lay to one side the question of Pauline authorship, therefore, and address ourselves to the message of the maturing New Testament church to its pastors.

Problems of a Maturing Church

A Christian heresy plagued the church whose maturing life we glimpse through these letters. Notice the reiterated references to *speculations, vain discussions, myths, godless chatter:*

Read *1 Timothy 1:3-7, 4:1-4, 7, 6:3-10, 20; Titus 1:10-12, 14, 16, 3:9-11; 2 Timothy 2:14, 16-18, 23-26, 3:13, 4:3-4.*

Clearly we do detect the signs of Christian heresy or heresies aggressively pushed by certain teachers within the church. The exact outlines of that heresy or of the heresies do not appear, though they seem to be compounded from elements of Jewish legalism and Greek dualism. One definite item in the creed taught by these "deceivers" is that the resurrection had already taken place. Another was a severe asceticism of the body. Demons were included, and genealogies. The growing picture points toward certain varieties of gnosticism, an esoteric knowledge of God based largely upon Greek dualism but with some elements from Jewish legalism. What it amounted to in the eyes of the writer of the letters was a religion which had degenerated into speculation and discussion, with frequent outbursts into quarreling and wrangling. The faith and love which ought to characterize Christians was lost in these hot contentions.

While many of the heretical teachers were undoubtedly sincere —for not only were they deceivers, they were also themselves deceived—others were insincere. They were in the game for money:

Read 1 Timothy 6:5; Titus 1:11; 2 Timothy 3:2.

The tendency for religion to get into side eddies of speculation does not rest upon the leaders alone. There are always people in the rank and file who have itching ears and who thus wander into myths:

Read 2 Timothy 4:3-4.

In all of this the danger is that of holding to the form of religion while denying its power (2 Tim. 3:5), thus changing the essence of Christianity.

There was also the danger of moral lapses. Sometimes these lapses were associated with, and even encouraged by, the false teaching. Sometimes they were a simple matter of succumbing to the surrounding pagan social pressures:

Read 1 Timothy 1:19b-20, 4:2; Titus 1:12, 13; 2 Timothy 1:15, 3:1-9.

The Pastoral Epistles are not concerned to answer the heretics directly. The answer given does not lie in an argument but in positive teaching of sound faith and in a disciplined community life led by a conscientious pastor. Nevertheless, the pastor must deal with the heretics. This he is to do with gentleness and patience, and in a democratic manner—as a pastor and not as an autocrat. But there are times when the only cure is excommunication:

Read 1 Timothy 5:1-2, 19; 2 Timothy 2:24-25; Titus 3:10-11.

To characterize the problems in a few words, we may say that the Christian pastor was faced by perils to the ongoing Christian movement by: (1) speculative perversions of the Christian faith, (2) by misguided and sometimes unscrupulous Christian leaders, (3) by the moral lapses of members and (4) by the pagan pressures of the surrounding society. With these he was constrained to deal in the spirit of a shepherd concerned with some sheep who were going astray and with the whole flock which need to be kept safe.

SUMMARIES OF SOUND DOCTRINE

We have in these letters a number of summaries of doctrine which must have been fashioned to conteract the threatening heresies. They have what appears to be a liturgical structure which makes them suitable for use in corporate worship. As such they look toward the formulation of the early creeds:

Read 1 Timothy 3:16, 6:11-16; 2 Timothy 1:8-10, 2:11-14; Titus 2:11-14, 3:5-7.

These early formulations of Christian belief were safeguards for the Christian heritage, to keep the faithful from wandering after myths.

OTHER SAFEGUARDS

There were other safeguards. One of these was the selection and training of good leaders for the local congregations:

Read 1 Timothy 3:1-7.

First were the elders, also called bishops. Notice the emphasis upon the moral character of these men. Nothing is said of their precise ecclesiastical status or their duties. The important thing is what kind of men they are; even outsiders must concede that they are above moral reproach.

Read 1 Timothy 3:8-10, 12-13.

Deacons constitute another group of local officers, with secondary duties, we may surmise, but with no secondary moral standards.

Read 1 Timothy 3:11; 5:3-16.

These verses point, somewhat ambiguously, to an order of "widows" who were enrolled and paid as regular workers for the church. Again, we learn little of their duties but much of the exacting moral demands resting upon them.

Read Titus 1:5-10.

Church leaders are to be men of genuine Christian character, but they are also to have authority and they are to exert it.

Still another safeguard of the faith was the integrity and industry of the Christian pastor. Through public teaching and preaching, and by constant pastoral care, he is to be a spiritual father to his children. There are a number of passages which are gems of concentrated instruction for Christian pastors. Notice some of them:

Read 1 Timothy 4:11-16, 6:11-16; 2 Timothy 4:1-5.

Though lacking the venerable authority of the apostles, the Christian pastor is to be a firm leader. His authority lies in his own disciplined Christian life, in his personal example, and in his knowledge of the faith. He is to preach, teach, read and explain the scriptures in season and out of season. He is to work tirelessly among his people as their moral mentor, seeking to achieve sound doctrine and right morals. To his ministry he is to bring a quality of consecration which amounts to a constant rekindling of his ordination (2 Timothy 1:6). And in all of this he is to look back for inspiration and guidance to the ideal Christian pastor, the apostle Paul:

Read 2 Timothy 1:13-14; 3:10-11; 4:6-8.

Paul's reward can also be his, if he brings to his work the same kind of consecration and industry.

It remains to mention two other safeguards. One is the high moral quality of life of Christians within the secular community. While we today may not agree with the code in every particular, especially on the items of womanly behavior, we can see the importance of noble Christian behavior in a pagan setting:

Read 1 Timothy 2:1-4, 8-15.

The aim here is not a rigid code for women, but a standard of public behavior on the part of Christians which will make them true light in the world.

There was also the safeguard of prayer, to melt the shell of quarreling hearts and open closed, dogmatic minds to Christian teachings.

THE LETTERS IN OUTLINE

1 Timothy
Introduction, 1:1-2
The Charges to Timothy
   I. Resist heresy; promote love and faith, 1:3-20
  II. Teach prayer and intercession, 2:1-8
 III. Encourage womanly behavior, 2:9-15
 IV. See that elders are qualified, 3:1-7
  V. Set similar standards for deacons and "widows," 3:8-13
 VI. Square your personal life with your faith, 4:11-16
VII. Be careful about enrolling "widows," 5:3-16
VIII. Keep slaves within bounds, 6:1-2
 IX. Shun the pull of money, 6:3-19
Conclusion, 6:20-21
2 Timothy
Introduction, 1:1-2
  I. The tradition defined and guarded, 1:3-2:13
 II. The perils of nominal Christianity, 2:14-4:8
    A. The passion for wild speculations, 2:14-16
    B. Selfish perversions of Christianity, 3:1-9
    C. Some norms, 3:10-17

Key Verses

Key verses are to be found in the concentrations of pastoral instruction already cited above, and in the following: "Follow the pattern of sound words which you have heard from me, in the faith and love which are in Christ Jesus; guard the truth that has been entrusted to you, by the Holy Spirit who dwells within us" (2 Tim. 1:13, 14). "You then, my son, be strong in the grace that is in Christ Jesus, and what you have heard from me before many witnesses entrust to faithful men who will be able to teach others also" (2 Tim. 2:1, 2).

Some Leading Ideas

As listed in the *Abingdon Bible Commentary*, here are some of the implications and emphases of the Pastoral Letters which are worth statement:

1. God's work will be best served and advanced by orderly, careful methods.
2. The disciplined life and the disciplined church furnish the finest medium for transmitting the power of the Spirit.
3. The supreme qualifications for any Christian worker is character.
4. The greatest service one can render the cause of Christ is personal influence and holy example.
5. The sins that break down the cause and shipwreck faith are the ordinary sins.
6. Pagans or outsiders will never respect a faith with lower standards of living than their own.
7. The Church may rightly be described as a school for character.

8. The one all-inclusive work of the church is to build lives after the pattern of Christ. Living is the final test of all religion.[1]

II. PREPARING YOUR BOOK SERMON

We are not here suggesting a separate sermon on each of the Pastoral Epistles, though such would be possible, using the outlines of the books given above. It would seem wiser to approach the letters as a unit and to present their message at one hearing. At least, that is the pattern we shall follow here.

CARDINAL IDEA

To the Christian pastor belongs the task of safeguarding and transmitting the faith in loyalty to its apostolic pattern and purity. The vitality and transmission of the Christian faith depends upon devoted, insightful and industrious Christian pastors.

SHAPING A PREACHING OUTLINE

One approach which will readily yield an outline is to think of the classifications of pastoral work called for in these letters. They are much like the ones listed today in a book on the ministry. They include: preaching and teaching, the selection and training of others who will also teach; the selection and spiritual guidance of church administrators; and the exercising of pastoral discipline. The motivation for these activities of the Christian pastor supplies the beginning of the sermon; it lies in the peril under which Christianity always lives in history, that is the peril of being perverted, adulterated or even lost as it passes from one generation to another. It may be dissipated in talk, caricatured by wild speculations, annulled by the low morality of church members, swallowed up in paganism, discredited by the disorder or the ignorance of undisciplined and untaught congregations. These perils supply the urgency behind an adequate Christian ministry for the churches.

[1] Abingdon Press, 1929, pp. 1278-79.

It is certain that good sermons can be based upon the key passages. For example 2 Timothy 2:1, 2 yields a two-point outline under which may be subsumed the corresponding duties found throughout all the letters. Each man will have to fulfill his own ministry; he will also need to provide for its perpetuation.

The leading ideas quoted from the *Abingdon Bible Commentary* might easily become the basis of a typical approach to the letters. Rephrased and slightly expanded so as to be more inclusive of all teachings within the letters, they might be made the basis of two or three sermons on the task of the Christian ministry in perpetuating the faith.

The nine charges to Timothy listed in our outline of the first letter suggest a sermon with a slightly different grouping of duties but still couched in the language of a charge. Nine charges are too many to remember, but we do not need that many, since the separate charges for the various church officers may be gathered under one heading.

Whatever the approach, we want to make sure that the central reason behind the letters becomes central in the concern of our hearers: Christianity is a heritage; we do not want it to become a declining or a vanishing heritage.

A Modern Title

"The Christian Pastor," which stands at the head of this chapter, may not be a good title for a sermon on the Pastoral Epistles. Popular interest in the ministry as a calling is not particularly feverish just at present. "Conserving the Christian Heritage" is accurate but rather prosaic. "Faith of Our Fathers Living Still" makes use of a good hymn to good purpose. "Inheritors of Faith" may be used since the privileges of inheritance entail certain duties and responsibilities, namely those of preserving and transmitting the inheritance.

It has often been noted that the Pastoral Epistles lack the fire and the fervor of first generation Christian writings, that they have a commonplaceness which is anticlimactic after the rapture of the first surge of missionary advance. Perhaps this is true, but they are not less Christian for it. The explorer and the pioneer are ever more appealing to imagination than the homesteader and the settler, whose success depends upon a number of prosaic tasks faithfully performed through days and years of drudgery. A healthy congregation of Christian people is made so by a great deal of attention to commonplace tasks, just as it can be weakened by commonplace failures. There is courage for the exceptional, for the heroic call to high adventure—and let us never underestimate it. But there is also courage for the long haul, courage for the commonplace which holds life steady and passes it as a sound capital to coming generations.

19

HOW TO BEGIN A REVOLUTION
The Letter of Paul to Philemon

Reading time for this slight epistle tucked away between Titus and Hebrews is one minute and thirty seconds. Philemon is deceptively small, like a three-inch cube of uranium small enough to be held in one hand, powerful enough to change the course of civilization.

I. WORKING YOUR WAY INTO THE BOOK
The Setting

To understand this letter it is necessary to know something about the background. Roman society was divided into two great classes, "bond and free." Slaves made up from one-half to two-thirds of the Empire's population; in many places they far outnumbered their masters. We have records of patricians who owned as many as eight thousand slaves apiece! These bondsmen had no civil rights; before the law they were not persons but property. Their masters had absolute authority over them in all matters of life and death. At court, a slave's testimony could not be admitted as evidence unless it was extracted from him under torture. The Emperor Augustus crucified one of his slaves for the simple offense of eating a quail intended for the royal table! It was common to kill slaves for theft or for attempted escape, as it was common to mutilate them for petty offenses.

Roman slaves were often more learned and more cultured than their masters. Among them there were philosophers and deposed aristocrats. Their only inferiority to free men and citizens consisted in their bondage itself. Most slaves were prisoners of Rome's imperial wars and their children, or debtors whom greedy creditors had sold in much the same way as a real estate broker today forecloses a mortgage.

Everywhere throughout Roman society masters feared their slaves. They were always sitting upon the lid of a social explosion. They knew it, and were driven by their knowledge to measures which became increasingly cruel and oppressive. A limited number of slaves were allowed to buy their freedom, it is true, but the idea of universal emancipation was not even thought of. The ruling idea was to "keep the slaves in their place" with an iron hand, to give them scant justice and mercy, and to strike them down like beasts if they threatened to get out of hand.

The Writer

The apostle Paul wrote this letter while he was in prison:
Read Philemon, vv. 1, 13, 22, 23.

No less than four times within the short space of twenty-five verses he refers to his imprisonment. He is not cast down about it, however, for he expects an early release which will enable him shortly to come to Colossae as Philemon's house guest.

As he wrote, Paul was surrounded by certain men who shared his imprisonment and from whom he sent greetings to Philemon. These were Epaphras, Mark, Aristarchus, Demas and Luke:
Read Philemon, vv. 23-24.

Paul dictated both Philemon and Colossians to Timothy:
Read Colossians 1:1; Philemon, v. 1.

To both of these letters Paul added a personal note in his own handwriting:

Read Colossians 4:18; Philemon, vv. 18-20.

No one of the letters, including Ephesians, tells us where Paul was imprisoned. When, however, we learn from Acts 28:16, 30 that Paul was imprisoned in Rome and that Luke was most probably with him at that time, we can make one reasonable supposition that Paul wrote Philemon, together with Colossians, Ephesians and/or Laodiceans (see Colossians 4:15) while he was held captive in Rome. This must have been about A.D. 63.

THE RECEIVER

Philemon, to whom the letter is addressed, was a prosperous citizen of Colossae and an active Christian. Paul calls him "our beloved fellow worker." The church of his city met in Philemon's house:

Read Philemon, vv. 1, 2.

Moreover, Archippus, who was probably Philemon's son, was a fellow campaigner of Paul's; the apostle addresses him as "our fellow soldier," and again reminds him in the Colossian letter that he must fulfill his ministry:

Read Colossians 4:17.

Philemon was Paul's personal convert to Christianity. He must have met the apostle at Ephesus, for Paul seems not to have visited Colossae:

Read Colossians 2:1.

"Apphia our sister" is without much doubt to be identified as Philemon's wife:

Read Philemon, v. 2.

This wealthy Christian was, like other men of position in his day, a slave owner:

Read Philemon, v. 16.

THE BEARER

It seems likely that Paul entrusted our present letter to Onesimus, whose cause it pleads:

Read Philemon, v. 10.

Onesimus, in turn, was the traveling companion of Tychicus, the courier charged with delivering the letters to Colossae and Ephesus:

Read Colossians 4:7-9; Ephesus 6:21.

Onesimus was a slave, bearing a common name for men in such a station. *Onesimus* means *useful.* Formerly, while he was still in Philemon's household, he had not lived up to his name. At that time it would have been more appropriate to call him *useless.* Onesimus had run away from his master, and he may even have robbed him:

Read Philemon, vv. 11, 12, 18.

Paul soon came to feel that it was wrong for Onesimus to remain with him without Philemon's knowledge and consent. Therefore, he persuaded Onesimus to return to Colossae, give himself up, and throw himself upon the Christian mercy of his master. Such a return required a high order of moral courage on the part of Onesimus, and a staggering faith in the Christian integrity of Philemon.

THE PURPOSE

The purpose of this letter was to persuade Philemon to take Onesimus back, not only accepting him without the customary punishments, but welcoming him into the church as a Christian brother.

Notice how Paul applies pressure to Philemon as he pleads his case: "... for love's sake I prefer to appeal to you." "I am sending him back to you, sending my very heart." "So if you consider me your partner, receive him as you would receive me." "If he has wronged you at all, or owes you anything, charge that to my account." "Refresh my heart in Christ." "Confident of your obedience, I write to you knowing that you will do even more than I say." Then Paul adds the most subtle and devastating pressure of all. He tells Philemon that he will visit him shortly (when he is released from prison). Paul also commended Onesimus in the highest terms to the Colossian church, which met in Philemon's house: "Onesimus, the faithful and beloved brother, who is one of yourselves" (Col. 4:9).

The heart of Paul's appeal is found in the new relationship between Philemon and Onesimus through their conversion to Christianity. Since both are in Christ, they are brothers. Paul sends Onesimus back "no longer as a slave, but more than a slave, as a beloved brother. . . ." This new relationship in Christ leveled all pagan barriers:

Read 1 Corinthians 7:20-24, 12:13; Galatians 3:28; Colossians 3:11.

Paul was not striking directly at the institution of slavery, but it would be difficult to devise a method that would prove more deadly to it in the long run. If there could be no bond or free in Christ because all were one in him, as Christianity swept on its conquering way, there would ultimately be no slaves. This was the way to begin a revolution.

OUTLINE OF THE LETTER

   I. Greeting, vv. 1-3
  II. Prayer and thanksgiving for Philemon, vv. 4-7
 III. The request on behalf of Onesimus, vv. 8-21
 IV. Paul's plan to visit Colossae, v. 22
  V. Salutations from Paul's fellow prisoners, vv. 23-24
 VI. Farewell and benediction, v. 25

READING THE LETTER

Having prepared yourself by this brief glance at the circumstances under which Paul's letter to Philemon was written and having in mind an outline of its contents, now turn to read it for yourself as an organic whole. Try to imagine what Paul felt as he wrote it, how Onesimus felt as he neared Colossae with it, and what Philemon's reaction was when he received it.

II. PREPARING YOUR BOOK SERMON

The Cardinal Idea

When men come into Christ, though they spring from the farthest social extremes, they enter a new relationship to one another which nullifies the old barriers. To restate the theme: *Men naturally at odds are transformed into brothers when they are individually drawn into the body of Christ.*

This cardinal idea is contained, as nearly as possible, in vv. 15 and 16: "Perhaps this is why he was parted from you for a while, that you might have him back forever, no longer as a slave but more than a slave, as a beloved brother, especially to me but how much more to you, both in the flesh and in the Lord."

Shaping a Preaching Outline

One good approach toward an outline is through a division of incidents and attitudes *before* and *after* Paul's conversion of Onesimus. Such a *before* and *after* outline would be easily interlaced with modern parallels of human barriers—color lines, iron curtains and bamboo curtains. Suppose we righteous Philemons within the church begin to act toward fellow Christians on the other side of these curtains as Philemon was urged to act toward Onesimus, what changes would that require in us?

Following such an approach, the outline itself might shape up something like this:

I. Before men are in Christ
   A. They are divided against one another
      1. Onesimus, slave, against Philemon, master

      2. Modern parallels, or one modern parallel
  B. The source of this outer division is within them
      1. Wrong attitudes of the exploited
         a. Onesimus
         b. Modern "forgotten men"
      2. Wrong attitudes of the exploiter
         a. Philemon, as Paul feared he might be
         b. We modern men of privilege
II. After men are in Christ
  A. They are united as brothers in a family
      1. The nullification of barriers between Onesimus and Philemon
      2. The goal of tumbled barriers between modern men in the church
  B. They undergo inward changes to make this brotherhood possible
      1. Changes in the exploited
         a. Onesimus
         b. Modern "forgotten men"
      2. Changes in the erstwhile exploiter
         a. Philemon
         b. Modern men of privilege

Another approach may be made through the three terms to be found in the letter: *master, slave* and *brother*. This sermon would proclaim that the way to a new world is through a third alternative; and it could shape up something like this:

Introduction: The need for social revolution
  A. In the modern world: our barriers
  B. In the ancient world: as seen in the book of Philemon
 I. The way of two alternatives: slaves or masters
  A. Hostility indefinitely extended and wrong increased
  B. Mutual privation: the gain of one must be the loss of the other
II. The way of the third alternative: slaves and masters become brothers
  A. Hostility ended and wrong redressed
  B. Mutual enrichment: the gain of each is the gain of both

Second treatment of the same approach yields still another outline:

Introduction: How can we start a much needed revolution?
    I. Change a sinner (slave into brother)
    II. Change a saint (master into brother)
    III. And you will change society

A MODERN TITLE

No one way of phrasing the title for a book sermon on Philemon can be insisted upon. There are several possibilities, among which these may be mentioned: "How to Begin a Revolution," "Resolving Our Differences" and "When Men Are At Odds."

20

A KINGDOM THAT CANNOT BE SHAKEN
The Letter to the Hebrews

WE OF THE generation now living do not need to read history to know that "crowns and thrones may perish, kingdoms rise and wane." We have seen them do just that within a brief span of years. Eight great powers entered World War II; two emerged. The rest came out as dwarfs, even imperial Britain and once-mighty France. World politics seem to be dissolving into a sea of change which engulfs every familiar object in our social landscape—segregation, colonialism, triumphant, world-conquering capitalism. Into this same dissolving sea sink also classical mechanics and the unsplit atom. This last change seems to be changing everything else from fuel to military strategy, from scientific theory to world diplomacy. The brooding cloud under which we wake and sleep these days and nights is mushroom-shaped.

The world is being shaken—"not only the earth but also the heaven" (Heb. 12:26). It would be a blind man who did not see it. But not all who see are able to perceive that it is God who is doing the shaking. Not all who see the turbulence understand it as cosmic action to sift the perishing from the eternal, "the removal of what is shaken . . . in order that what cannot be shaken may remain" (Heb. 12:27). But the Christian, seeing history as "his story," will so understand it. Having found the unshaken rock, he "will not fear though the earth should change, though the mountains shake in the heart of the sea; though its waters roar and foam, though the mountains tremble with its tumult" (Ps. 46:2, 3).

This is the theme of The Letter to the Hebrews. What could be more contemporary, more timely?

I. WORKING YOUR WAY INTO THE BOOK

There are a great many things that we do not know about this eloquent writing. We do not know the name of the man who wrote it, nor do we know to what churches it was directed. From the nature of the book, though, we are able to infer some things: It was written by a Christian Jew who had grown up outside Palestine under the strong influence of Greek philosophy—probably at Alexandria, Egypt, which was the stronghold of Hellenistic Judaism. He was a master of the Greek language. It was directed late in the first century to the Jewish members of certain unspecified Christian churches, probably outside Palestine. The readers of the letter were the converts of the first disciples, but did not themselves belong to the first generation:

Read Hebrews 2:3.

Shortly after their conversion they had suffered some well-remembered persecution or series of persecutions:

Read Hebrews 10:32-33.

Now, the early leaders of the Christian movement had died:

Read Hebrews 13:7.

And these converts, having lost the keen edge of their enthusiasm, were in danger of abandoning the Christian faith altogether:

Read Hebrews 5:11-12; 6:4-6; 10:23-25.

Starting from this problem, which is always in the background of the letter, the author proceeds to compare Christianity with its nearest rival, Judaism, showing how it is in every way superior, and, consequently, worth living and dying for. To this task the writer brings the gift of an extraordinary eloquence. He has a passionate will to persuade and exercises no little skill of logic in doing so. Writing to Jews born and reared in the Greek world, he casts his argument in the mold of Greek philosophy.

GREEK THOUGHT

At the very beginning of the book we see Alexandrian influence in a free quotation from the Old Testament apocryphal book, The Wisdom of Solomon:

Read Hebrews 1:3.

This looks very much like Wisdom 7:26: "For she [wisdom] is a reflection of the everlasting light, And a spotless mirror of the activity of God, And a likeness of his goodness."[1] It is the same kind of idea. The apocryphal book of Wisdom is a product of a considerable industry which over a number of decades labored at Alexandria to win a Greek hearing for Judaism. As late as A.D. 50, the greatest Jewish-Hellenist of them all, Philo, had elaborated a whole new philosophy of religion for exactly such a purpose.

Nevertheless, the dependence of The Letter to the Hebrews upon Greek thought goes considerably beyond any quotation from the Apocrypha. The mental world of the book is that of Platonism plus that of Judaism. To see the Platonic element, we must take a brief look at some of the features of Platonism. Plato taught that reality is a two-story affair made up of the eternal and the temporal. Not only was the eternal above the temporal, but it was the source of the temporal. The eternal was reality itself; the temporal was only the shadow or mirrored image of this reality. The eternal was perfect; the temporal was imperfect. The eternal was unified; the temporal was multiform and divided into "the many." The eternal always had existed and would continue to exist forever; the temporal is mortal.

[1] Goodspeed, *The Apocrypha: An American Translation* (University of Chicago, 1938).

When we turn to Hebrews with such a background in mind, we find the letter filled with these contrasts between the heavenly and the earthly, the reality and its shadow; the one and the many. The line of argument is that through Christ men may move from the shadow world of the Jewish sacrificial system into the reality of God. The Mosaic law was only the shadow of the true law which was revealed in Christ:

Read Hebrews 10:1.

This means that the new covenant superseded the old, that, as Paul had said, the law was nailed to the cross and died with Christ in order that new life might come through faith.

In place of many mortal high priests in the Jewish system, Christianity gives us Christ, the one, eternal High Priest:

Read Hebrews 7:23-25.

This High Priest did not need to make a yearly atonement, as the mortal high priests were compelled to do. The very fact that the Day of Atonement had to be repeated showed how imperfect it was. But for the true High Priest there was only one Atonement Day; his sacrifice, being perfect, was "once and for all":

Read Hebrews 9:12-14, 24-26.

The inference to be drawn from all this is that the whole Mosaic structure is obsolete, it being nothing better than a shadow of the "tabernacle" which through Christ has now taken its place:

Read Hebrews 8:1-7, 13.

Jewish Background

To understand this letter a reader must know something about three thought worlds: Jewish, Greek and Christian. The original readers fulfilled this threefold requirement. There were Hellenistic Jews who had become Christians. The modern reader will have more difficulty, for, although he is in debt to all three traditions, he does not now think of Judaism in terms of its temple ritual, centering in animal sacrifice. Judaism for him means the ethical teachings of Moses and the prophets. But the thought of this book turns upon the temple ritual; more especially it centers in the ceremonies of the Day of Atonement, when the high priest entered the Holy of Holies and made a blood sacrifice for the sins of the whole people. We are far more ready than the original readers to grant that this whole sacrificial system is obsolete. In fact, it is so remote and foreign to us and our way of thinking that we are not easily drawn to a book that starts with it and reasons from it. Thus, the Jewish sacrificial system, which was the greatest attraction to the original readers, proves to be the greatest obstacle to us.

It is not necessary for us to accept the details, however, in order to see and assent to the author's basic assumptions: That man is a sinner who needs a mediator, and that reconciliation between man the sinner and God his Creator and Father cannot be accomplished without suffering and sacrifice. Still more basic to the whole presentation is the covenant relationship between God and his people; God deals not with an individual alone but with that individual as a member of a people who are called out by God, bound to his service and sustained by his fellowship. The thought of the letter about the covenant turns on the pivotal passage of the Prophet Jeremiah who looks forward to the new covenant written on the hearts of men: *Read Hebrews 8:6-11.*

It remains only to accept the author's further argument that all human mediators are inferior to Christ who supersedes them, that he is the one supreme reconciler, the perfect and final sacrifice, the lone pioneer of God's new people. In other words, The Letter to the Hebrews presents Christianity as the final religion. But Christianity is not without its forerunner; it does not annul Judaism but fulfills it:

Read Hebrews 11:39, 40.

Nevertheless, this demonstration of the superiority of Christianity to Judaism (and, by inference, to all other religions) was no merely academic exercise. The purpose was practical: to stop the drift toward apostasy:

Read Hebrews 2:1-3; 3:12, 14; 4:11; 6:4-6; 10:23-25, 28-29.

STRUCTURE OF LETTER

Someone has said that Hebrews "begins like a treatise, proceeds like a sermon and ends like a letter." This is a helpful observation. Certainly Hebrews is unlike Paul's letters in which are discerned two distinct divisions: teaching and ethics. In Hebrews the two are interlaced throughout the letter. Thus, the main theological argument of the book may be read in the following passages:

Hebrews 1:1-14; 3:1-6; 5:1-10; 7:1-10:18.

In these passages we see the reasoned demonstration of the supremacy of Christ, the high priesthood of Christ, the new covenant, and the finality and complete effectiveness of Christ's sacrifice.

But we are never permitted to forget that the supremacy of Christ has immediate, practical bearings for Christians. Consider the practical implications of Christ's sufferings:

Read Hebrews 2.

Attaining the promised "rest":

Read Hebrews 3:7-4:16.

Warning against relapse:

Read Hebrews 5:11-6:20; 10:18-39.

A final challenge based upon the heroism of martyrs for the faith:

Read Hebrews 11 and 12.

In these two chapters there is an inspiring roll call of heroes, all of whom believed in and hoped for the unseen and invisible, and looked upon suffering as a heavenly discipline.

The letter ends with final injunctions and personal messages:

Read Hebrews 13.

These two strands, theological and ethical, are woven together in a unified whole, which may be outlined as follows:

Introduction: Contrasting revelations, 1:1-3

I. The supremacy of Christ, 1:4-4:13
II. The high priesthood of Christ, 5:1-7:10
III. The new covenant, 7:11-8:13
IV. The sacrifice of Christ, 9:1-10:39
V. The achievements of faith, 11:1-39
VI. Encouragements and warnings, 12:1-13:19
Conclusion: Benediction and greetings, 13:20-25

KEY PASSAGES

In no one passage do we find the thought of Hebrews summarized, but a selection of passages can be made which will serve the purpose fairly well: Hebrews 1:1-4 plus 2:1-3a. Or Hebrews 4:14-16. Or Hebrews 10:19-25. Or Hebrews 13:8 plus 12:28-29.

Joseph F. McFadyen speaks for every careful student of Hebrews when he says, "In this epistle, as hardly anywhere else even in the New Testament, do we feel ourselves lifted above ourselves, out of the sphere of the sensuous, the petty, the passing, into the realm of the timeless, the unseen things that abide."[2]

II. PREPARING YOUR BOOK SERMON

CARDINAL IDEA

Since Christ is the supreme and final mediator between God and man, and in him we have found the eternal in the midst of the passing, let us fix our loyalties on him through every changing circumstance; thus are we assured of a kingdom that cannot be shaken.

SHAPING A PREACHING OUTLINE

One sermon outline will begin with the tendencies toward apostasy found in our contemporary church which may also be paralleled in The Letter to the Hebrews. There is drift into apostasy, and there is outright desertion. Both are known today as they were among the letter's first readers. But there is no use in attempting to pull ourselves back into ardent faith; we must be drawn by looking

[2] McFadyen, *Through Eternal Spirit* (George H. Doran Co. n.d.), p. 34.

to Jesus the "pioneer and perfecter of our faith." We see him under two aspects: in terms of his supremacy and his eternity. To whom is he supreme? To angels, to Moses, to Joshua, to the Levitical priests. We will scarcely know what to do with the modern meaning of Jesus' superiority to the angels, but the meaning of the others is clear: Moses represents moral law; Joshua symbolizes leadership, both military and political; the priests represent the human striving for forgiveness through confession and penance. Jesus is clearly more than lawgiver, leader or confessor. In what, then, does his supremacy consist? In his sharing in both the divine and the human nature through the incarnation, thus making him the God-Man, the perfect mediator, through the completeness of his entrance into the very presence of God; in the union in his own person of mediation and sacrifice—he did not offer the sacrifice; he was the sacrifice—and in his pioneering of the new covenant. We are led naturally to see this same Jesus as eternal, the one sure, unchanging point in all the shifting temporal scene.

Looking to Jesus who is both supreme and eternal, we are empowered for our own part, which is the constancy of the Christian. Here we must first see what is at stake if we fail and drift away from our Lord: (1) The perfecting of the heritage handed down to us from the long past, and (2) our own salvation. To drift away from the Eternal One is to be engulfed in the changing sea. Second, we must go on to the action of persevering Christians; these acts involve conscientious participation in the life of the church including regular attendance, the practice of Christian brotherhood, the withstanding of temptation and the willingness to suffer. Thus do we become anchored to the eternal, and the flux of a turbulent, changing world holds no terrors for us.

A second outline may result from the use of scintillating quotable passages, in which the book abounds. The method is to go through the book underlining the passages in a reading at one sitting, and then to arrange them in appropriate order for the framework of the sermon. One may follow the arrangement of the book, in which case Christian truth will be interlaced with the responsibilities of Christians throughout. Or one may separate the doctrinal from the ethical and arrange it topically with a view to the best psychological approach. If one is gifted enough as to cast the modern applications in the same literary style, he may well create a sermon of almost unimagined spiritual power. Since the arrangement of passages in their present order needs no comment, we shall here explore the possibility of a different arrangement:

Introduction: Change and decay
    A. The transient world, 13:14a
    B. The inconstant Christian, 3:12
    C. The judgment of inconstancy, 10:26; 4:11-13; 10:31
  I. Jesus Christ, the same yesterday, today and forever, 13:8
    A. God's Last Word, 1:1-4
    B. Jesus' complete humanity, 2:18; 4:15; 5:8
    C. The mediator, 6:19-20; 7:25; 9:24
    D. The sacrifice, 9:26b; 10:12-14
    E. Pioneer of a new people, 8:6, 13
  II. Unwavering Christians, 10:22-25
    A. Enduring Christians, 10:36, 39; 6:11-12; 3:14; 12:12; 12:4, 7, 11
    B. Growing Christians, 6:1a
    C. Hoping and believing Christians, 11:1-3
    D. Loving Christians, 13:1-4a
Conclusion: Experiencing eternity, 12:28; 13:20-21

A third outline may be developed along textual lines upon the passage 10:19-25, which is the most complete of the various key passages cited above. The main elements of the book are found here.

A MODERN TITLE

Beside the title of the present chapter, "A Kingdom That Cannot Be Shaken," which is a direct quotation from 12:28, we may offer two others also taken from the book itself: "Jesus Christ the Same, Yesterday, Today and Forever" (which may be shortened to "Yesterday, Today and Forever") and "Things That Cannot Be Shaken."

21

THE UNDIVIDED LIFE
The Letter of James

Many a "Christian" man is a house divided against himself: creed against deed, ideals against impulses, altruism against ambition. When we come upon such a man with a civil war seething inside him we frequently find him to be a generating source of social strife; his war within leads naturally to conflict without. It is not that he possesses no Christian convictions; it is, rather, that his Christian convictions do not completely possess him. He has been evangelized but not Christianized. He believes, but he has not learned to trust his belief to the uttermost. Someone has recently suggested that some of us have been inoculated with a mild form of Christianity which makes us immune to a severe dose. That is the problem. But it is not our problem alone; it has belonged to the church since New Testament days, and the book that deals with it is The Letter of James.

I. WORKING YOUR WAY INTO THE BOOK

Together with First and Second Peter and Jude, The Letter of James forms "The General Epistles," so called because they are addressed to no one specific, local situation but to the church in general. From the address of our present letter it might be supposed that it was sent to the Jews of the dispersion, but, though references to Christ are few, they are sharp enough to assure us that the letter was written to those who "hold the faith of our Lord Jesus Christ" (Jas. 2:1). These appear to have been scattered Jewish Christians in and beyond Palestine. The conditions for such a letter were supplied as early as the martyrdom of Stephen (Acts 8:1-4). Another scattering took place in A.D. 44 when Herod killed the Apostle James (Acts 12:1-2). It may be that the circuit of the letter did not extend very far beyond Judea. Certainly the few local references we have— those to the neighboring sea, figs, olives, grapes, salt and bitter springs, and the earlier and later rains—are Palestinian. The author, at least, is living there.

AUTHOR

We should like to know the identity of this author. He calls himself "James." The most prominent man of that name among Jewish Christians in the early church was James the brother of Jesus. Early church fathers believed that he was the author, but they also tell us that many considered the letter spurious and that the letter was for a long time excluded from the New Testament canon. Thus the church historian Eusebius gave his opinion that James the brother of the Lord wrote it, but went on to admit, "I must observe that it is considered spurious. Certainly not many writers of antiquity have mentioned it."[1] Jerome, translator of the Latin Vulgate who did his work in Bethlehem as the fourth century turned into the fifth, reflected the same opinions: "James who is called the brother of the Lord, known also as the Just, wrote one Epistle only, which is one of the seven Catholic Epistles. Yet that too is said to have been set forth by someone else in his name, though gradually, as time went on, it gained authority."[2] Modern scholars have gone no

---

[1] *Hist. Eccles.* III. 25.
[2] *Catalog. Script. Eccles.*

further in resolving the question. Why a letter attributed to the most influential leader in the Jerusalem church should have been barred from the Canon baffles complete explanation, but there are some reasons: (1) The church early became a predominantly Gentile community. James, as the leader of the Jewish Christians, would decline in authority as his constituency declined in numbers. (2) The supposed opposition between Paul and James meant that Paul's prestige worked against James. The wording of sections on faith and works are superficially in contradiction, though a careful reading will show that the differences are largely verbal. Nevertheless no less a personage than Martin Luther called James "a right strawy Epistle"; as a partisan of Paul he had little tolerance for James. Perhaps a similar attitude in the earliest days accounts for the situation reported by Eusebius and Jerome. At any rate, we can say this much: The Letter of James is such a writing as James the brother of the Lord might have composed. It fits what we know about him from the New Testament and from Christian tradition. (Biblical references to James include: Matt. 12:46-50, 13:55; Mark 3:31-35; Luke 8:19-21; John 7:3-5; Acts 1:14, 12:17, 15:19-21, 21:18-25; 1 Cor. 9:5, 15:7.)

Eusebius gives a long account of James' manner of life and his martyrdom.[3] Much embellished with legend, this account tells us that James was "consecrated from his mother's womb. He drank neither wine nor fermented liquors, and abstained from animal food. A razor never came upon his head, he never anointed with oil, and never used a bath. . . . He used to enter the temple alone, and was often found upon his bended knees, interceding for the forgiveness of the people, so that his knees became as hard as camels' through his habitual supplication and kneeling before God." James was killed by his fellow Jews, like Stephen, because of his power as a Christian evangelist. They placed him on the pinnacle of the temple,

[3] *Hist. Eccles.* II. 23.

demanded of him a public denial of Jesus' messiahship; when he refused, they cast him down and began to stone him. He knelt and
prayed for his murderers as Stephen had done. Then a fuller beat
him to death with the club that he used to beat out his clothes. This
martyrdom took place only a few years before the Jewish-Roman
wars; some devout Jews even attributed the subsequent siege of
Jerusalem to this cause.

SIMILARITIES TO SERMON ON THE MOUNT

We have called the book of James a letter. It has also been called
a homily or sermon. Indeed, it looks like nothing so much as a collection of preachers' texts. The style is pithy and epigrammatic,
similar to that of the Sermon on the Mount. In fact there are a
number of striking parallels. Compare:

JAMES	MATTHEW
1:2	5:10-12
1:4	5:48
1:5; 5:15	7:7-12
1:9	5:3
2:13	5:7; 6:14, 15
2:14	7:21-23
3:17, 18	5:9
4:4	6:24
4:10	5:3, 4
4:11	7:1-5
5:2	6:19
5:10	5:12
5:12	5:33-37

WISDOM LITERATURE

James has also been classed as wisdom literature. Such a label is
justified not only because of its pithy, proverbial style, but also because of its close parallels with passages in two wisdom books, The

Wisdom of Jesus Ben Sirach and The Wisdom of Solomon, from which notice the following quotations:[4]

> Say not: "From God is my transgression,"
> For that which He hateth made He not.
> [Sirach 15:11]

Read James 1:13.

> Be swift to hear,
> But with patience make reply
> [Sirach 5:11]
> The wise man is silent until the (proper) time,
> But the arrogant and the scorner take no note of the time.
> [Sirach 20:7]

Read James 1:19.

> Strife begun in haste kindleth fire,
> And a hasty quarrel leadeth to bloodshed.
> If thou blow a spark it burneth, and if thou spit
> upon it it is quenched;
> And both come out of thy mouth.
> [Sirach 28:10-12]

Read James 3:5-6.

> Let us crown ourselves with rosebuds before they wither.
> [Solomon 2:8]

Read James 1:11.

Those things all passed away as a shadow,
And as a message that runneth by:
As a ship passeth through the billowy water,
Whereof, when it is gone by, there is no trace to be found,
Neither pathway of its keel in the billows:
Or as when a bird flieth through the air,
No token of *her* passage is found,
But the light wind, lashed with the stroke of her pinions,
And rent asunder with the violent rush of the moving wings, is passed
through,

[4] R. H. Charles (ed.), *The Apocrypha and Pseudepigrapha of the Old Testament in English* (Clarendon Press, 1913).

And afterwards no sound of her coming is found therein.
Or as when an arrow is shot at a mark,
The air disparted closeth up again immediately,
So that men know not where it passed through:
So we also, as soon as we are born, cease to be;
And of virtue we have no sign to show;
But were utterly consumed in our wickedness.
Because the hope of the ungodly is like chaff carried off by the wind,
And like a thin spider's web driven away by a tempest.
And like smoke which is scattered by the wind,
And passeth away is the remembrance of a guest that tarrieth but a day.

[Solomon 5:9-14]

Read James 4:14.

CIRCUMSTANCES

Only from internal evidence are we able to tell about the circumstances in the churches to which The Letter of James was addressed. Many of these conditions argue for a church of the second generation and later when a settled congregational life can be assumed and the first fervor is waning:

Read James 2:14-16.

First-generation Christianity had been distinguished by radical benevolence. No one then thought of himself as owning anything; what was his belonged to the whole fellowship. In the churches addressed by James love and good works had fallen into decline. Love, which had been an unsophisticated deed of sharing, had degenerated into high-flown language about "love" and "brotherhood." Fellow Christians were left in want, side by side with those who had an abundance. James attacked this condition with heavy sarcasm, "Can the naked clothe themselves with words? Can the hungry eat words?"

Social caste with its jealousy and strife had also crept into the church:

Read James 2:1-5; 3:13-16; 4:1-2; 5:9.

The time was when the church had been recruited almost exclusively from the poor and outcast. (See 1 Cor. 1:26-28.) By the time James was written, this condition seems to have changed. It was not so much that wealthy Christians arrogated privileges to themselves as that the poor kowtowed to them.

Wordliness began to be a problem:

Read James 4:4, 13-16; 5:1-6; 1:21 (in that order).

Formerly the church had invaded the pagan world; now the world began to invade the church. Greed for profit actuated some to conduct their businesses as though economic concerns were outside the providence of God. This same greed drove others into actual exploitation. Certain areas of conduct began to approximate pagan morality. For this reason James urged loyalty to Christian standards amid the trials of a downward dragging paganism.

But the most tragic loss was the decline of *faith* into mere *belief*. For Paul and earlier Christians, faith had meant full personal commitment to Christ. Faith had been compounded of belief, plus trust, plus commitment of life and conduct. Now it became creed, intellectual belief:

Read James 2:14-20, 26.

James' sarcastic identification of orthodoxy with demons was reflected by Alexander Campbell, pioneer of the Disciples of Christ, who once said, "Satan is as orthodox as Paul, or Peter, or John. And yet he is the adversary of God, of holy angels and of all good men. But truths and truisms never saved or damned a human being. They are the pastimes of knaves and simpletons."

"Excess of words is as fatal as lack of deeds," said James Moffatt. Christianity cannot be taken out in talk, but some make the attempt:

Read James 3:1-5; 9; 12; 5:12.

Great damage can be done by the tongue alone, to be sure, but the tongue by itself is an inadequate instrument of good. It is easy for Christian teachers and preachers to confuse words with deeds.

They come unwittingly to believe that because they have said something about Christianity they have done something about it. The word comes to be a substitute for the deed. There is a kind of self-hypnotism here which James is quick to recognize. The Christian teacher or preacher, therefore, must acknowledge that talking about religion places upon him the added weighty responsibility of practicing it even more conscientiously than those who say little about it.

THE UNITY OF THE LETTER

The unity of James is not immediately apparent. The book looks like a collection of aphorisms on many subjects. And yet there is a ruling passion; this is the appeal for Christian consistency. Here were Christians with deep inconsistencies: trying to serve God *and* mammon; Christians in ritual, in speech and in belief but pagans in business, in social practice and in charity; men claiming a common membership in Christ, dismembering Christ by their unbrotherly behavior. The positive antidote of James is a wholehearted religion rooted in Jesus' summary of the Mosaic law: "You shall love the Lord your God with all your heart, and with all your soul, and with all your mind. . . . You shall love your neighbor as yourself" (Matt. 22:37, 39, based on Deut. 6:5 and Lev. 19:18).

THE LETTER IN OUTLINE

Introduction: Salutation, 1:1
    I. Trial and temptation, 1:2-18
       A. As discipline of character, 1:2-4
       B. Wisdom for this through prayer, 1:5-8
       C. The impermanence of trial as reassurance, 1:9-11
       D. The source of temptations, 1:12-18
    II. Christian Consistency, 1:19-5:6
       A. The unity of hearing, speaking and doing, 1:19-27
       B. Social unity in the church: no caste, 2:1-13
       C. Faith expressed in works, 2:14-26

D. Control of the tongue, 3:1-12
  1. Excessive talking; ambitious talkers, 3:1-5
  2. Evil speech, 3:6-12
E. Inward and outward peace, 3:13-4:12
  1. Godly wisdom *versus* devilish wisdom, 3:13-18
  2. The inner sources of strife: greed and ambition, 4:1-10
  3. Censoriousness as impiety, 4:11-12
F. Secular interests in a religious framework, 4:13-5:6
  1. Recognizing God's providence, 4:13-17
  2. Sins of the rich, 5:1-6
III. The duty and reward of endurance, 5:7-11
IV. Miscellaneous exhortations
  A. Oaths, 5:12
  B. Prayers for the sick, 5:13-18
  C. Restoration of a fallen brother, 5:19, 20

Key Verses

Several verses come close to gathering up the emphasis of the whole letter: "The man who trusts God, but with inward reservations, is like a wave of the sea, carried forward by the wind one moment and driven back the next. That sort of man cannot hope to receive anything from God, and the life of a man of divided loyalty will reveal instability at every turn" (1:6b-8, Phillips). "But be doers of the word, and not hearers only, deceiving yourselves" (1:22). "So faith by itself, if it has no works, is dead" (2:17). "Show me your faith apart from your works, and I by my works will show you my faith" (2:18). "If you really fulfill the royal law, according to scripture, 'You shall love your neighbor as yourself,' you do well" (2:8).

II. PREPARING YOUR BOOK SERMON

Cardinal Idea

The Christian religion calls for a radical consistency of conviction, speech and action together with a radical practice of Christian brotherhood.

SHAPING A PREACHING OUTLINE

Let us begin by categorizing the cardinal idea; this will yield a good outline. There are really two aspects of Christian consistency treated in the letter; one is individual, the other is communal. Breaches of Christian consistency appear in the divided self and the broken community. It will be possible to assign the ills mentioned in the letter to one or the other of these classifications. Since the aim of the writer is the restoration of lost wholeness in these two areas, we shall state the two divisions positively: I. The Undivided Self; II. The Unbroken Christian Community.

Our next avenue to an outline is through the key passages which may be taken together to give us a progressive development: I. Without inward reservations; II. Beyond the hearing of the gospel; III. From creed to deed; IV. To the building of the brotherhood. The third division is actually a little too narrow; it should include all kinds of talking as well as verbal expressions of faith. Perhaps one might rephrase it: "From talking about Christ to walking as he walked."

The outline of the letter itself in its major features ought to be a good way of organizing the sermon. It begins with the down-dragging pressures that a Christian experiences when he tries to live according to God's will in a world geared to a lower purpose. The trial and temptations felt and yielded to become "the world's slow stain" gradually despoiling Christian character and the Christian witness. This is a good introduction. The unity of hearing, speaking and doing (II. A in "The Letter in Outline" above) then becomes the basic positive principle of the sermon. This is set forth as the first main point. Thereafter, using the jewel sermon type, the preacher will show how this principle of Christian consistency should work out in several areas such as belief and practice, talking, communal life, business. It is clear that several topics now scattered in the book will be grouped; i.e., under "talking" there will fall the section on oaths (III. A) as well as the longer passage in 3:1-12 (II. D). Similarly, "communal life" will couple the section on inward and outward peace (II. E) with prayers for the sick (IV. B) and restoration of a fallen brother (IV. C). The duty and reward of endurance, returning as it does to the introductory topic of trials and temptations, is perfectly suited as a conclusion.

Modern Title

We have used the words "Christian consistency" several times in this chapter. They would make a good title. "The House Divided" suggests itself as quickly; and it recommends, further, the use of Jesus' original saying as the text for the sermon. "The Undivided Life," chosen as the name of the chapter, also has much to commend it.

22

HIGHWAY TO HOPE
The First Letter of Peter

FRIGHTENED by communism and H-bombs, we moderns are accurately described by Scripture as "men fainting with fear and foreboding of what is coming on the world . . ." (Luke 21:26). No part of the human race ever "had it so good," no people has had so much of comfort and so little of hardship, was less ravaged by disease, less burdened with toil for daily bread, less bayed by the wolf of poverty. And no people has lived in such an atmosphere of chronic fear as now envelops us. "The mind of modern man," as Philip Wylie put it, "is in a murderous and hysterical condition." And all of this in the midst of ease and plenty, because of what *might* be. Approaching the world through our unprecedented physical comforts we have anything but comfort in our minds.

If ours is the way that leads to fear, perhaps hope has another highway. The First Letter of Peter signposts that road: "By his great mercy we have been born anew to a living hope through the resurrection of Jesus Christ from the dead" (1 Pet. 1:3). These words about human rebirth to a living hope were spoken to Christians undergoing or about to undergo "the fiery ordeal" of persecution. With scant comforts to hug to their breasts but with bold convictions to suffer for and a risen Lord to serve they found the hope that eludes us.

Since The First Letter of Peter contains this message of living, triumphant hope, it is assuredly relevant to our time.

I. WORKING YOUR WAY INTO THE BOOK

The letter is addressed to the scattered Christians in the whole of Asia Minor north and west of the Taurus Mountains:
Read 1 Peter 1:1.
How Christianity came to all these Roman provinces, we do not know. Paul introduced it to Galatia and Asia, but he was prevented from entering Bithynia (Acts 16:7, 8). Neither, so far as we know, did he ever reach Pontus or Cappadocia. Since the Pentecostal crowd at Jerusalem contained residents of "Cappadocia, Pontus and Asia" (Acts 2:9), it is by no means impossible that some of the churches in these regions were planted by no apostle but by residents who had witnessed the great events at Jerusalem in which the church began. Perhaps Peter preached in these provinces; we do not know.

AUTHOR

When we ask about the author we are answered by the letter's opening words: "Peter, an apostle of Jesus Christ." This, plus the fact that the book was readily received into the New Testament canon, has led many scholars to conclude that the letter was indeed written by Peter and not merely in his name. In other words, though they think Second Peter is pseudepigraphic, they believe that First Peter is not.

There are some obstacles to belief in Petrine authorship. Some of these are easily disposed of, such as the fact that the letter is written in excellent Greek, an achievement hardly to be expected of a rough, unlettered Galilean fisherman such as Peter had been. The Greek Old Testament, or Septuagint, moreover, is freely quoted as by one who is fully at home in it. Both of these objections are overruled by 1 Peter 5:12; Silvanus is the actual writer of the letter, and to him we may ascribe its literary form.

But there are more serious objections to Petrine authorship. The tradition that Peter died a martyr in the Neronian persecution in Rome about A.D. 64 has never been disputed. How is it, then, that the letter can refer to a general persecution of Christians that has spread as far as Asia Minor? The Neronian persecution was localized in Rome; a general persecution of Christians by the Roman government did not arise until the latter part of Domitian's reign, about A.D. 96. Two answers may be urged against this objection: (1) It appears that the persecutions mentioned in the letter are expected for the near future; it is not clear that they are already happening. Peter may have reasoned that the Neronian terror might be expected to spread to the whole Empire. (2) While it appears that the persecutions referred to in the letter are of state-origin, it is not certain that they are. Persecutions of Christians did not have to wait upon Rome; they had existed from the beginning. Paul's very first letter, First Thessalonians, shows the vigor and venom of the attacks upon the church both from Jewish and from pagan quarters. (3) Moreover, the "fiery ordeal" of First Peter does not seem to be quite as extreme as the actual pogrom of Domitian who made an issue of emperor worship. In the light of such idolatry, it would not be easy to say, "Honor the emperor" (1 Pet. 2:17). The book of Revelation, which came out of the Domitian persecutions, spoke in no such terms.

Another obstacle to Petrine authorship remains. The eldership, as revealed in 1 Peter 5:1-5, seems to be rather fully developed. Could it have advanced this far by A.D. 64? A paid eldership with younger leaders subject to them more accurately reflects conditions late in the first century, so far as we know them. But we cannot be sure. It is still possible that such conditions did exist by A.D. 64. Peter the apostle could have been the author. If he was not, Silvanus may have been, writing much as Mark later did, reflecting the message of Peter although he couched it in his own language. Silvanus was a member of the mother church at Jerusalem who joined Paul at Antioch, accompanied him on his second journey, and may have acted as amanuensis in the writing of several Pauline letters (Acts 15:22, 40; 1 Thess. 1:1).

One remarkable thing about First Peter is the absence of any reference to Peter's own suffering or the sufferings of other Christians in Rome. He calls Rome "Babylon" as Revelation was to do later (Rev. 14:8; 18:2), but he says nothing of the suffering he was undergoing or that he had witnessed. He seems rather to think only of the moral fortification of his readers against their own hour of suffering. This sounds like the Peter we have met in The Gospel according to Mark, and like Peter who asked to be crucified upside down because he was unworthy to imitate his Lord's death. Peter had learned to exalt his Lord; he tended to belittle himself. He was not writing to get sympathy for himself or his companions but to nerve his readers for their own testing time. So it would seem.

PERSECUTION

Suffering because of persecution is in the background of the letter from beginning to end, and it breaks into the focus of attention again and again.

Read 1 Peter 4:12-19; 5:9.

This persecution looks world-wide. Other references to the suffering may be noticed:

Read 1 Peter 1:7; 2:21-25; 3:8-9; 14-18; 4:1.

Suffering is set forth in these passages as something more than an evil to be endured. Moffatt is suggestive when he translates suffering as the normal tax of citizenship in the kingdom: ". . . learn to pay the same tax of suffering as the rest of your brotherhood throughout the world" (5:9). It is not only to be endured; it is also to be expected, and that largely upon the basis of the pattern of Christ. In Christ's experience the glory of Easter grew out of the shame and agony of the cross; crucifixion and resurrection were welded together. A disciple is not above his Lord; what is true for Christ must be true for the Christian. When he suffers for righteousness' sake and without retaliation, the Christian is following in the steps of Christ. Moreover, when he is upon his cross he may be certain of his Easter, because of his Christ. Beyond this, suffering for righteousness' sake is of a very different order than suffering justly for one's crimes. It is redemptive, both of self and of others. Such suffering lies beyond the realm of justice in the domain of conquering love. By it the moral power of God is revealed.

ETHICS

Martyrdom is made no substitute for morality; it is not conscience money for moral failure. Quite the contrary, the willingness to suffer as a Christian is the very core of Christian morale and morality, which is the willingness to stand and be counted for Christ at all times. The ethical passages of the letter are as numerous and as urgent as the passages on suffering:

Read 1 Peter 4:1.

Here is the core idea. It is the same as Paul's picture of a Christian as one who has died to sin on the cross, and risen in baptism to a new kind of life (Rom. 6:1-7). In fact, the letter says specifically the same thing. "You have been born anew" (1 Pet. 1:23).

We can classify the kinds of moral behavior demanded under five headings:

1. Putting away paganism with its vices:

Read 1 Peter 4:2-5; 2:1; 1:14-16 (in that order).

2. Living as Christians before pagan eyes. This includes private morality and constructive citizenship:

Read 1 Peter 2:11-17.

This is no monastic withdrawal from society; neither is it abdication of moral judgment to the authority of the state. The emperor is due his *honor* but not *worship*. Christians are responsible and public-spirited citizens, but their morals come from Christ not from the state.

3. Demonstrating a new community life through their churches:
Read 1 Peter 1:22; 2:4-9; 3:8; 4:7-11; 5:1-5.

Taken together these passages can only mean that Christians were to think of themselves collectively as a covenant people, the new Israel, demonstrating a new humanity at work. This church is a functioning "brotherhood."

4. Showing a new order of life in family life:
Read 1 Peter 2:18; 3:1-7.

The details are not as important as the spirit. Christian family life is a more radical demonstration of love than pagan family life can ever be. It roots in genuine respect for persons and in simple virtue. Any legalism that would perpetuate slavery, or patriarchal authority, or stereotyped dress for women on the basis of these verses is a misconstruction of their spirit. The main message is: Christ lives in genuine families.

5. Trusting and watching:
Read 1 Peter 5:6-9; 3:9, 15 (in that order).

Christian vigilance is not fearful but ready. Trusting in God, true Christians are also alert to temptation and ready to witness to their faiths. And the whole ethical enterprise is bathed in prayer.

THE GOOD NEWS

But, why suffer as a Christian; why live as one? The whole thought of the letter rests upon the good news of God in Christ:
Read 1 Peter 1:3-5, 8-12, 17-21.

The outline of the familiar *kerygma* lies here. The expectation of the ages is reality; the time is fulfilled in the historical Christ. From the earthly life of Jesus two pre-eminent facts are chosen: his crucifixion and resurrection. His return is expected: history moves to divine judgment which will be the vindication of the faithful. Those addressed in the letter have long since responded to the final part of the *kerygma* as Peter preached it on Pentecost: "Repent and be baptized . . . for the remission of your sins; and ye shall receive the gift of the holy spirit" (Acts 2:38). Thus the whole Christian enterprise rests upon the mighty acts of God in history through Jesus Christ.

Few of the readers had met Jesus in the flesh, therefore the same conditions of faith that were open to them are open to us, so that the writer can say directly to us as well: "Without having seen him you love him; though you do not now see him you believe in him and rejoice with unutterable and exalted joy. As the outcome of your faith you obtain the salvation of your souls" (1 Pet. 1:8, 9).

The historical life of Christ was no remote event; it was brought psychologically near through the resurrection experience of each Christian who had died to an old order of life and risen to a new. It was this experienced resurrection, this known salvation, that served as base of all else. It explains how those holding it were able to go through suffering. Because they *knew* the resurrection they were willing to face the crucifixion. Having started with Easter they were not afraid to move back to Good Friday. This, in fact, seems to be the implied rhythm of reality: crucifixions lead to resurrections, but resurrections lead us back again to the cross, from which new resurrections are born.

OUTLINE OF THE LETTER

Introduction: Address, 1:1, 2
 I. The Christian hope through the resurrection, 1:3-2:10
   A. Security for persecution, 1:4-12
   B. Lives worthy of the hope, 1:13-2:3
   C. The church that results, 2:4-12
 II. Some directions for Christian conduct, 2:13-4:6
   A. In the state, 2:13-17
   B. In society at large, 2:18-25

KEY VERSE

The whole of the letter is happily summarized in one verse: "Therefore let those who suffer according to God's will do right and entrust their souls to a faithful creator" (1 Pet. 4:19).

II. PREPARING YOUR BOOK SERMON

CARDINAL IDEA

Those who have experienced the new life that Jesus can give from God will be willing to live upright lives and even to suffer for their faith.

SHAPING A PREACHING OUTLINE

There is little in First Peter about hoping; there is a great deal that produces hope. A sermon that starts with the current hopelessness might follow the discussion just completed, moving through: (1) Suffering as a Christian, for convictions and for an antipagan life, (2) living as members of a new covenant people with all the ethical implications of such membership, and (3) an examination of the good news upon which such startling behavior rests. Such a treatment assumes that today we have little Christian hope because we have ventured so little for our faith, and that the timidity of our venture implies little faith in, or knowledge of, our gospel; but a reversal is possible all down the line. To stand up for one's faith, to live it day by day before pagan eyes, even to suffer for it—and always to be willing to suffer—will deepen our sense of its reality and power. What is more, it will lead us back to hope, for this way is the highway to hope.

A textual outline based on the key verse, 4:19, will follow these same three steps in the same order: (1) those who suffer according to God's will, (2) do right, (3) entrust their souls to a faithful creator.

The contrasting kinds of suffering mentioned in the letter may be used to good effect for a third approach to preaching outline. The key verses for it are: "But let none suffer as . . . a wrongdoer . . . yet if one suffers as a Christian, let him not be ashamed, but under that name let him glorify God" (4:15, 16). The two points suggested by these verses are (1) suffering as wrongdoers and (2) suffering as Christians. Wrongdoing is not confined to outright criminals but to those who give consent to a pagan order by benefiting from it without protesting. This letter has nothing to say about the innocent victims of evil; though there are such, many who loudly acclaim their innocence are deeply implicated in wrong. Our hopelessness may be a measure of our working commitment to a decaying paganism. For example, a church member who owns a large block of substandard houses in a city slum may have little social hope; he is so committed to the wrong by which he lives day by day that he cannot believe in the right which he holds as an abstract ideal. This sermon development cannot be completed within the thought of the two verses which gave us the germinal idea. For the third point, we shall have to go beyond them to the ground of courage in the facts of the gospel.

Modern Title

The title of this chapter is recommended, but it may disappoint some because it says nothing about suffering or persecution, so important to the thought of the letter. Therefore we offer "Suffering in the Light of the Resurrection" and "The Easter Cross."

23

THE RAMPARTS OF CHRISTIAN LIBERTY
The Second Letter of Peter

LIBERTY and license are really opposites. "Liberty is doing what I like," someone says. He is not describing liberty at all, but license. He may imagine himself to be free, but he will not be free for long; he will soon be the slave of his own passions, or the minion of the latest fad or changing fashion. Self-expressionists, priding themselves on being emancipated, may "promise freedom, but they themselves are slaves of corruption; for whatever overcomes a man, to that he is enslaved" (2 Pet. 2:19). Liberty, far from being a life of whim, is one of principle, inwardly controlled by purpose. The free man is not undetermined, uncontrolled, but is self-determined and self-controlled, harmonious with truth. He has inward reality. He follows the law of his own higher nature. He has free will because he earnestly seeks the will of God. Such is the paradox of freedom and slavery, so nobly stated by George Matheson in the hymn:

> Make me a captive, Lord
> And then I shall be free;
> Force me to render up my sword,
> And I shall conqu'ror be.

The problem at the back of Second Peter is the doctrine and practice of a group of Christian subversives who sought emancipation from all moral law. The author called upon the rest of the church to man the ramparts of genuine liberty. The task of this writer is only slightly different from that of The Letter of Jude, upon which his second chapter largely depends. The heresies of the libertines are the same in Second Peter as those indicated in Jude, with a single addition—the denial of the Second Coming of Christ. In the light of this fact, it would seem wise to turn to the chapter on Jude before studying this one, and to prepare a book sermon on Jude before attempting one on Second Peter. Some preachers may want to choose between the two books. For them we would advocate the use of Second Peter for this reason: Second Peter spends a great deal of time upon the Christian antidote to the libertine heresy, whereas Jude is content with denunciation and very little more.

Thus, even if you plan to go on at this time with the preparation of a sermon on Second Peter, take time now to read the chapter on Jude.

I. WORKING YOUR WAY INTO THE BOOK

RELATION TO JUDE

As we have just noticed, the problem confronting the biblical writer in our present letter is all but identical with that previously faced by The Letter of Jude—antinomianism or libertinism, a sophisticated doctrine which allowed certain "spiritual" Christians to flout the moral law.

Read The Letter of Jude. Follow it by reading 2 Peter 2:1-22; 3:3, 4.

The literary dependence of Second Peter upon Jude is evident, but it is also clear that Peter enlarged upon Jude's treatment, principally by adding the positive sections on Noah and Lot. Then, too, Peter called attention to one offense of the false teachers which had not yet arisen for Jude; this was the scorn of the Second Coming: "Where is the promise of his coming? For ever since the fathers fell asleep, all things have continued as they were from the beginning of creation" (2 Pet. 3:4). Such a piece of ridicule must presuppose a date relatively late in the New Testament period. It seems not at all unlikely, in fact, that Second Peter is the latest of the canonical books of the Bible.

A LATE BOOK

Other evidence supports the lateness of the book: The letters of Paul had been collected and were known as a group (2 Pet. 3:15, 16). The prediction of Peter's death at the end of the Fourth Gospel is alluded to in 2 Peter 1:14, 15. And a knowledge of the tranfiguration story of the Synoptics lies at the background of 2 Peter 1:17-18. This characteristic association of the Transfiguration and the Ascension is also found in the New Testament apocryphal writing, The Apocalypse of Peter, a known late writing. Second Peter is obviously pseudepigraphic.

Origen was the first church father to mention the book, and he expressed doubts about its acceptability as scripture. Eusebius of Caesarea said that of the writings under the name of Peter he recognized "only one epistle as genuine." This would be our present First Letter of Peter. "As for the current Second Epistle, it has not come down to us as canonical, though it has been studied along with the rest of the scriptures, since it has been useful to many people." Jerome later reasoned that the letter had not been generally received as scripture because it so obviously disagreed in style with the First Letter. Nevertheless, the church finally accepted it as scripture, and it is in that confident light that we may study it. It is expressive of an inspired Christian norm—Christian liberty expresses itself in a lofty morality and not in a self-indulgent throwing off of restraint.

UNIQUE FEATURE

The unique contribution of The Second Letter of Peter lies in its positive moral teaching. Jude was content to attack error. Peter sought to counteract it, and to place the weight of apostolic authority and Christian tradition behind his positive witness. The core of this positive teaching lies in the first chapter:

   Read 2 Peter 1:3-11.

Here we recognize the view which Paul had advocated earlier, namely, that if anyone is in Christ he is a new creature. But this newness is not, as the antinomians taught, a new metaphysical nature lifting one above the ordinary demands of human life; it was a new moral nature, ending human rebelliousness against God. It was a new responsiveness to divine grace shown in Christ, a responsiveness which begins at once to show itself through growth of moral character.

The seven graces of Christian living here listed are worthy of careful attention: *Faith* is fundamental personal belief in, and commitment to, Christ. *Virtue* is a healthy, virile goodness. The Greek term carries the implication of prowess. *Knowledge* was a favorite word with the false teachers who meant by it a speculative flight into a secret philosophy or mysticism. Second Peter uses it to mean practical wisdom, intelligence and insight. *Self-control* stands in obvious contrast to the self-indulgence advocated by the errorists. *Steadfastness* was the simple ability to endure; this had special significance in the light of the long delay in Christ's return (3:3, 4). *Godliness* is real trust in God; this lifts the preceding steadfastness out of stoical grimness and makes it something more than dogged determination; godly endurance is reverent, not defiant. *Brotherly affection* supplies the social context of virtue which lifts it out of priggishness. *Love* here is Christian love, a deepening of brotherliness into the unselfishness of Christ. The entire list forms an interlocking system of moral checks and balances; and it is not static but dynamic. It is the positive core of genuine Christian liberty which will withstand every attack of the libertines.

The rest of the first chapter centers in two objectives: To back the positive teaching just given with apostolic authority and Christian tradition, and to puncture the fantastic interpretations of scripture being used by the false teachers:

Read 2 Peter 1:12-21.

Note especially the beauty of Christian tradition as a "lamp shining in a dark place," and the inwardness of the Christian truth as a day that dawns and a morning star that rises in the heart. Tradition may in certain times and circumstances be the dead hand of the past, but not here. It is one of the guarantees that the light which shone in Jesus will keep on shining and that the darkness will not overcome it.

The second chapter deals directly with the errors of the false teachers. These are treated rather fully in our chapter on The Letter of Jude, to which we have referred you.

The third chapter is largely concerned with the doubt and moral indifferentism arising from the delay of the Second Coming. The answer of the letter is a stirring reaffirmation of the hope. Jesus may be delayed, but he assuredly is coming. Judgment may be postponed, but it is not abrogated. God does not count time as men do: "The Lord is not slow about his promise as some count slowness. . . ."

Read 2 Peter 3:1-13.

The judgment of God through water and then through fire mirrors the flood in the time of Noah and the later destruction of Sodom and Gomorrah. But a cosmic conflagration was also expected beyond Hebrew sources; it was a common Stoic doctrine too. For our purpose, it is not the literal fire that matters—though certainly fire on the earth has become reality through modern mechanized warfare; what matters is the certainty of divine judgment.

The certainty that the life of Christian integrity is not merely a human tale with a mortal ending but a divine drama with eternal significance is not the least of the secrets of Christian morale.

OUTLINE OF SECOND PETER

Introduction: Salutation, 1:1, 2

    I. The positive Christian life, chapter 1

    A. Growth in grace, 1:3-11
    B. Assurance of Christian salvation, 1:12-21
      1. Through the teaching of the Apostles, 1:12-18
      2. Through scripture, 1:19-21
  II. The negative life of false teachers, 2:1-22
 III. The certainty of Christ's return, 3:1-13
 IV. Expectant, faithful Christian waiting, 3:14-18
    A. A pure life, 3:14
    B. Correct interpretation of doctrine, 3:15, 16
    C. Resisting false teachers, 3:17
    D. Growing in grace and knowledge of Christ, 3:18

Key Passage

The whole message of the letter is summarized in the two last verses: "You therefore, beloved . . . beware lest you be carried away with the error of lawless men and lose your own stability. But grow in the grace and knowledge of our Lord and Savior Jesus Christ. To him be the glory both now and to the day of eternity. Amen."

II. PREPARING YOUR BOOK SERMON

Cardinal Idea

A Christian, to be truly free, must be inwardly controlled by the law of Christ and he must grow in Christian character and in Christian insight; liberty which is mere license is slavery.

Shaping Your Preaching Outline

Sermon outlines may be derived directly from the biblical material in any one of three immediate ways: (1) From the key passage, which suggests a two-point textual development; (2) from the outline of the whole book; or (3) from the outline of 3:14-18, which also carries the letter in a nutshell. For psychological impact, the textual organization may prove to be the most effective of these three. In using the outline of the whole book for the sermon itself, it would seem that a more dramatic arrangement would result from transposing the first and second main divisions, "The Negative Life of False Teachers," coming before "The Positive Christian Life." A rephrasing of both these divisions in terms of Christian liberty is recommended: I. Liberty Runs to License; II. Morality Builds True Liberty.

Topically considered, there are three movements of thought in this letter. One deals with the antinomian threat to the faith. A second is a positive presentation of some of the leading aspects of true Christian living. The third is the mention of various safeguards and incentives, of which there are two: Christian tradition and the certainty of judgment.

In all these developments the place of Christian growth should be stressed. The life that is growing is seldom in danger, whereas a life that has a static, defensive faith is certain to decline or sour. As presented in Second Peter, the Christian life is securely rooted in tradition; it goes back through the apostles and through scripture to Jesus himself. But it also has its own live, growing response to the grace of God transmitted through these channels. There is a kind of defense of the faith "once for all delivered to the saints," which is a betrayal. The true defense that works is a company of people living by the gospel and growing toward Christlikeness. One of the apostolic fathers in the period after the New Testament clearly saw this: "When pagans hear from our lips the oracles of God, they marvel at their beauty and greatness; but afterwards, when they discover that our deeds are unworthy of our words, they turn to malign the faith, declaring that it is a fake and a delusion."[1]

A MODERN TITLE

The affinities of this letter with Galatians may throw us back to some of the titles considered for that book. "The Law of Liberty"

---

[1] *Second Clement 13.* Goodspeed, *The Apostolic Fathers: An American Translation.*

might be borrowed for our present purpose. "Guarding the Faith" is certainly in order, though the implication of a static position must be corrected through proper emphasis upon growing in grace. The same is true for the title chosen for this chapter, "The Ramparts of Christian Liberty."

24

TRUE CHRISTIANITY
The First Letter of John

THE First Letter of John might easily bear the title, "Against Heretics." We have chosen to call it "True Christianity" because its author is concerned with combating heresy only to make room for a positive Christianity of the right sort.

I. WORKING YOUR WAY INTO THE BOOK

ENEMIES IN THE HOUSE

In every chapter and in almost every paragraph, the letter bears evidence of a threatening heresy. "What heresy?" you will ask. Let us see what the letter itself can tell us:

Read 1 John 4:1, 5; 3:7; 2:26; 2:19 (in that order).

These verses tell us that there were in the churches to which this letter was addressed a group of false prophets or teachers who were receiving a wide hearing and leading many members astray. They appeared to be the true friends of Christianity instead of its enemies, and they were deceiving many, who had in turn no test with which to tell true from perverted faith. The heretical group had, in fact, grown so powerful that a large portion of it had pulled off from the church and formed a separate sect of its own. There was apparently grave danger that the heretics would gain more converts and produce an even deeper schism. The unity and peace of the church was threatened.

What were these false prophets teaching that they were able to produce such a serious disturbance in the church?

Read 1 John 1:6, 10; 2:4, 9, 22; 5:6; 4:20 (in that order).

These heretics apparently had certain pet phrases which they kept repeating: "We have fellowship with God." "We have not sinned." "We know God." "We are in the light." "We love God." There seems to be a kind of spiritual arrogance here and a claim to special status with God. We surmise that this special status was based upon a secret "knowledge" involving a peculiar mystical experience of its own. Clearly it ridiculed and discounted morality as the distinguishing mark of Christianity and did not hesitate to break the fellowship of the church over its dogmas. In fact, the controversy over doctrine seems to have grown so fervent that actual hatred was felt for those who would not see the light as taught by the prophets of this new knowledge.

The doctrine of the group quite obviously had something to say about the nature of Christ: "Jesus is not the Christ." This was not what it appears to be on the surface, a complete denial of the central truth of Christianity; it was rather a distortion. From sources outside the Bible we know that there was a group which taught that since matter was evil and hence foreign to God, that the Christ, the divine Son of God, could not have been identified with Jesus of Nazareth, a mortal living in a material body. Christ the Son only seemed to be Jesus the Man. Christ came upon Jesus at the baptism but departed before the crucifixion. This is probably the meaning of the rather obscure verse, 5:6; John's denial of the heresy says strongly that Jesus who was also the Christ came not only in the water of baptism but also in the blood of the cross, thus being identified completely with mortal suffering in the body.

What, then, were the heresies of the false prophets?

Distorting Christianity into a special kind of knowledge, a particular brand of theology or doctrine.

Lifting mystical experience above moral living.

Uncharitable, unbrotherly behavior.

The denial of the full humanity of Christ.

From outside the New Testament, through the early church fathers, we are able to learn a good deal about these heretics and their teaching. They were called *Gnostics*, a word based on the Greek root meaning *knowledge*. Gnostics were therefore those who claimed a special, mystical knowledge. They thrived between A.D. 95 and 150, although they may have made some headway even before this. They taught that *reason* and *matter* were the two poles of the universe, reason being divine, good and full of light; and matter being demonic, evil and full of darkness. A human being was a divine soul imprisoned in an evil body. By cultivating reason through special knowledge, the human soul might break its prison house and make communion with the divine. Such a metaphysics had no room for the usual view of the incarnation of God in Jesus of Nazareth; for how could divine light lie in a body of demonic darkness? Plainly salvation was for a few highly skilled philosophers and mystics who could retreat into their own inner minds and soar "from the alone to the Alone."

Thus we piece together the heresy which the author of our letter confronted. What had he to say to the Gnostics?

THE ACID TEST OF FAITH

"Beloved, do not believe every spirit, but test the spirits to see whether they are of God" (4:1). But *what* tests were Christians to apply?

Read 1 John 2:4-6; 1:7; 2:23; 3:7b, 10, 14, 17, 24; 4:2, 7, 15, 19; 5:3, 12 (in that order).

These verses give us no systematic arrangement of the tests of true Christianity, but a study of them will show at least three separate standards:

1. *Moral living.* Such phrases as "walk in the light," "obey his commandments," "walk as he walked," and "do right" carry this one idea. Genuine Christianity makes a moral difference in those who adhere to it.

2. *Love of the brethren.* John is so sure of this that he even says that no one can love God unless he loves his brethren. God, in fact, is found by men in their love toward other men! Failure to love, talking about loving men instead of performing the deeds of love, or placing something else above love, are practical atheism. Christian love is not mere sentiment. It involves the action of sharing. Whatever else the Christian faith is, it is a "faith that works in love." A faith that works toward suspicion and hate is a perversion.

3. *Acceptance of Jesus as the Christ.* Obviously this is more than belief. It is devotion. It is a personal surrender to Christ, in whom is found the clue to what is highest in spirit and deepest in nature. This is a revelation, an initiative which God took in history, for "we love him because he first loved us."

Now that we have these three tests before us, we see that they are not three but one: Christians who accept Jesus as Christ, must walk as he walked—in the way of love, which sets for them a high moral program. Therefore, the acid test of Christianity is love, rooted in the love of Christ. This is a high orthodoxy, one very remote from the doctrinal orthodoxies that have often masqueraded in its name.

AUTHOR AND READERS

This book has the informality of a letter, while omitting the salutation and benediction which we usually find in such communications. It tells us nothing directly of its author or its readers. What we have to go upon here must come largely from sources outside the New Testament—from the early church fathers; and this is meager. Possibilities and probabilities are the best we can now achieve. Without detailed arguments, here are some tentative conclusions:

1. The author was probably John the Elder, a venerated leader of the Ephesian church who lived and worked about A.D. 100. He was probably not the Apostle John, although we cannot be at all certain about this.

2. The readers were probably the churches of the Roman province of Asia, perhaps the same congregations to whom Paul's Letter to the Ephesians was addressed at an earlier date.

OUTLINE

As to the structure of the book, we have here something very informal. It is quite impossible to make an outline upon which there will be no disagreement. In fact, the thought seems to be like the turning of a giant diamond in the sunlight. A central truth is stated and then that truth is turned before the eyes until its several facets are revealed. If an outline is demanded, that of C. H. Dodd of Cambridge University will perhaps be as satisfactory as any:

Introduction, 1:1-4
   I. What is Christianity? 1:5-2:28
   II. Life in the family of God, 2:29-4:12
   III. The certainty of the Faith, 4:13-5:13
Postscript, 5:14-21

PURPLE PATCHES

The First Letter of John contains some of the most striking literary gems in the whole Bible. Many of them are familiar to all Christians. While reading the book, do not fail to mark them. See if you agree that these should be included:

1 John 1:1-3, 6, 9; 2:9-10, 16; 3:1, 2, 14, 17-18; 4:7-12, 16, 18, 10, 20, 21.

The light cast by these gemlike passages shines in three colors, as it were: Life, light and love. These colors interpenetrate—the life of love is life indeed; to walk in it is to walk in light.

A key passage is difficult to select. Nevertheless try your hand at it. We suggest 4:19-5:5. Another, briefer, key passage is 3:23.

Now you have come to the time for a reading and rereading of The First Letter of John as a unit. Saturate your mind in it. Then you will be ready to begin work on your sermon.

II. PREPARING YOUR BOOK SERMON

The Cardinal Idea

True Christianity finds its light in the historical career of Jesus of Nazareth and its life in active love toward God shown through brotherly service of men.

Shaping a Preaching Outline

First John is a study in contrasts between false and true Christianity as it was experienced near the end of the first century. It would seem, therefore, that the best way of outlining the message of the book for modern ears will be through contrasts, such as *false* and *true* or *death* and *life*.

Following the treatment in the two sections above, "Enemies in the House" and "The Acid Test of Faith," one might derive an outline with the following points:

I. Christians go astray
   A. When they identify Christianity with a special kind of knowledge, creed or doctrine
   B. When they lift mystical experience above moral living
   C. When they are unloving, and schismatical
   D. When they make Jesus foreign to human needs and problems
II. Christians keep the faith
   A. When they find their light in Jesus of Nazareth
   B. When, motivated by Jesus' love, they live a life of love
   C. When they test the mental creed by the moral deed

The three cardinal words of the book, *light*, *life* and *love*, fairly demand recognition in the main divisions of an outline. In practice, however, these terms interpenetrated one another so as to make an outline based upon them very difficult to construct. The light seen in Jesus is love, and love is life. *Light,* moreover, has the double meaning of truth and virtue, as darkness has the double connotation of falsehood and sin. *Life* is not so much a member of the triad as the product of the other two: whoever would have *Life,* let him find the *light* of truth in Jesus and let him live a life of *love* toward the brethren, being motivated by the *love* of God seen in Jesus. The contrasting attitudes of the heretics will suggest themselves at every point and will there receive treatment. The presence of the negative along with the positive will serve to make the positive appeal all the more persuasive. To avoid anticlimax, construct this sermon with the points in this order: Life, Light and Love.

Although the arrangement of First John is not in logical sequence, it would be possible to use the three main headings of C. H. Dodd's outline of the book, given above. Even here, transposing the second and third divisions will make the development of thought more progressive, as below:

I. What is Christianity? 1:5-2:28
II. The certainty of the faith, 4:13-5:13 (add 1:1-4)
III. Life in the family of God, 2:29-4:12 (add 5:14-21)

A careful organization of the material in each of these sections should produce an effective sermon.

Chapter three, verse fourteen, offers itself as a suggestive basis for a two-point division: "We know that we have passed out of death into life, because we love the brethren. He who does not love remains in death."

A MODERN TITLE

The title of this chapter would make a good sermon topic: "True Christianity." Other possibilties look equally inviting: "From Death to Life," "The Acid Test of Your Christianity," "Are You a Heretic?" "The Deeper Orthodoxy."

25

CHRISTIAN INTOLERANCE
The Second Letter of John

How far should Christian tolerance go? Is it ever Christian to be intolerant? If so, upon what grounds? These are some of the vexing questions which confront a reader of this short New Testament letter.

I. WORKING YOUR WAY INTO THE LETTER

HERETICS

A consecutive reading of The First and Second Letters of John will show that the underlying problems of the two writings is similar and that their teaching is the same. Both are concerned with infractions of Christian fellowship caused by active propagandists of a heretical "Christian" teaching; both aim to eliminate the heresy from the life of the church. The First Letter seems to have been addressed to several churches, presumably in the Roman province of Asia; The Second Letter was sent to a single congregation. That congregation was bedeviled by aggressive missionaries who professed to carry an "advanced" Christian view.

Read 2 John 7-11.

These verses make several things clear. (1) There were groups of active propagandists itinerating among the churches. (2) They advertised their doctrine as an "advance" upon Christian insight. (3) They discounted the Incarnation. (4) They were presuming upon and exploiting the hospitality of Christian homes and a friendly hearing in the congregations. (5) They threatened to divide the church.

The writer pens a harsh judgment against them: (1) They may have called themselves "advanced Christians," but they had "progressed" beyond Christ himself and were really enemies of Christ; (2) their so-called "truth" was a lie; (3) and so dire was their threat to genuine Christianity, they were to be refused all marks of Christian hospitality. They were to be given no lodging nor meals in homes; this would deprive them of a means of livelihood. They were to be refused the fellowship of the church; this would deprive them of a base of operations. No one was to greet them nor pass the time of day with them; this would deprive them of all moral support from within the church community.

During the early centuries when the destruction of Christianity by internal heresies was no academic question but a real possibility, even the most irenic Christian leaders made short shift of heretics. Polycarp, who has been described as "saintly," was met in the street one day by Marcion, a Christian gnostic. Marcion said, "Do you recognize me?" "I recognized Satan's first-born," was Polycarp's reply. A similar story is told of "John, the disciple of the Lord" who was one day in an Ephesian public bath when Cerinthus, another gnostic, entered. John leaped out of the bath immediately, declaring as he did so, "Let us hurry away lest the building collapse on us, because Cerinthus, the enemy of truth, is here!" We are able to understand these stories about men of such noble Christian character only when we see them against a background of extreme danger to the church.

The problem of itinerating teachers continued for several decades. In spite of safeguards, some of these traveling teachers were dissenters from true Christianity and others were outright impostors who were "milking" the churches for food, lodging and money. They were able to do this only because of the remarkable hospitality of Christians toward their fellow believers. The fraud highlights the spontaneous outreach of Christian togetherness across the Mediterranean world. By the middle of the second century a method of detecting impostors had been devised. We find it in The Didache: "Let every apostle who comes to you be welcomed as the Lord. But he shall not stay more than one day, and if it is necessary, the next day also. But if he stays three days, he is a false prophet. And when an apostle leaves, let him take nothing except bread to last until he finds his next lodging. But if he asks for money, he is a false prophet."[1]

Nature of Heresy

For the nature of "the lie" refer in this book to the chapter on The First Letter of John or to a good discussion of "Gnosticism." Cerinthus, for example, taught that Jesus the man was as physical and as sinful as any man but that the divine Logos entered the earthy Jesus at the baptism and continued as the second spirit within the same body until the crucifixion, when the Logos cast off the flesh and again became pure spirit. Such dualism was based on the belief that the created physical world, including human bodies, is evil; as applied to Christianity it was an effort to deliver Jesus from all evil; to do so it denied the Incarnation. It was not really Jesus who revealed God, therefore. Other gnostics, called Docetists, were even more severe; they maintained that Jesus had no physical body at all; he appeared to come in the flesh, but did not actually do so. He was too high and holy, too far above "evil matter" to do that. Christian leaders like the writer of our Second Letter saw in such teachings a complete perversion of historically rooted Christianity which would quickly disfigure it out of all recognition.

---

[1] III. 5, 6; Goodspeed, *The Apostolic Fathers, an American Translation.*

AUTHOR

The author of our letter is anonymous; he calls himself "The Presbyter" which is the same as "The Elder" or "The Old Man." He introduces The Third Letter in the same way. It is obvious that he is a person of some authority in a neighboring church and probably over more than one church. Some scholars see "the presbyters" as a class of leaders intermediate between the apostles and the monarchial bishops of the second century. Evidence is still too scanty for an assured conclusion.

Although there has been a good deal of speculation about "the elect lady and her children," it seems wisest to assume that this was a euphemism for a local church and its members. A similar reference to a church as a woman is found in 1 Peter 5:13.

A PARAPHRASE OF SECOND JOHN

Vv. 1-3. "The old Man, to a certain local church and her members, whom I love as only Christians can love one another, with a love that is based not on mere affection but on reality as seen in Christ. The favor of God, the Father of Jesus Christ, keep you close to that reality, which is a way of love. Vv. 4-6. "I am glad to see some of your members keeping the faith. I want to remind you of our distinctive Christian commandment, the law of love. Hold on to it.

Vv. 7-11. "For a widespread movement of heretical propaganda is afoot. It denies the Incarnation. Its adherents consider themselves to be Christian missionaries, but they are really enemies of Christ. Don't listen to them! Don't lodge them in your homes. Don't even say 'Hello' to them in the street, lest you seem to be giving them your moral support.

Vv. 12-13. "I have a great deal more to say, but I don't want to write it. I prefer to talk it out with you in person shortly when we may experience the deep pleasure of Christian fellowship.

"The members of the church where I write ask to be remembered to you."

OUTLINE OF THE LETTER

I. Truth and love, 1-6
    A. The greeting, 1-3
    B. Keeping the truth, 4
    C. Abiding in love, 5-6
II. The lie and disfellowship, 7-11
    A. Propagandists, enemies of Christ, denying the Incarnation, 7
    B. Their dangerous persuasiveness, 8, 9
    C. The refusal of all fellowship to them, 10, 11
Conclusion: Plans and greetings, 12, 13

POINTS OF INTEREST

1. The special emphasis upon *truth* gives this term a meaning closely analogous to the Christian title "Those of the Way" which was used by the disciples in the early church. It means loyalty to the historical person of Christ as the revelation of God; it is truth as incarnate, together with the claim which the incarnate Person makes upon those who believe. This term dominates the first four verses of the letter; it finds many parallels in The First Letter:

Read 1 John 2:21; 3:19; 4:6; 5:7.

2. *Love* is intimately related to *the truth;* it is, in fact, a force which derives from *the truth.* Thus we must not confuse it with *affection* nor with human *brotherliness* in general. The *love* in question springs from, and centers in, the historical Christ. It is the togetherness which results from membership in Christ, such as Paul described through his figure of the body of Christ. Therefore, we are not talking about love as an attribute of individuals; we are really talking about a community centering in the person of Christ. The love we are dealing with is *life in a family of faith.*

All of this adds up to a rather impressive demonstration of the necessity of a core of agreement at the heart of Christian fellowship.

That core is not a doctrine but a basic confidence that the Son of God appeared fully in the historical Jesus who was completely human, but no less completely divine. Thus, the historical person of Jesus stands at the center of Christianity; this is its *truth*. But the essence of Jesus' life was outgoing love; and thus, love is grounded in the truth.

Read *1 John 2:7, 8; 3:1a; 4:9-11.*

3. The *deceivers* who are to be treated so harshly are not misguided members of the church who are willing to submit to instruction. They are self-conceited, self-styled teachers who are presuming to instruct the church in a dissenting doctrine. We must believe that many of these men were sincere—just as Paul's enemies, the Judaizers, were sincere. Nevertheless, the success of their teaching would have spelled the end of the Christian Church. It is because of this danger through the usurpation of spiritual authority that the heretical teachers were to be excluded from Christian fellowship. A man who presumes to teach Christianity is under a severe responsibility toward the truth of Chirstianity, and he should expect to incur the penalties of defection from that truth if ever his mind is bewitched by a different gospel.

We are hesitant to grant the correctness of Christian intolerance in any case lest it run wild, creating a spirit of censure and heretic hunting far beyond the limited area in which The Second Letter of John applies it. For the letter of John advises it only when two conditions are found together: (1) When men have deserted the historical rootage of faith in the human life of Jesus and (2) when they set themselves up as teachers to lead the whole church astray to their speculative version of the truth.

KEY VERSES

Second John 9 and 10 come as close as any to bearing the concentrated message of this already compact letter.

II. PREPARING YOUR BOOK SERMON

CARDINAL IDEA

Any teacher who presumes to teach a version of Christianity which dispenses with the historical life of Jesus as the revelation of God, and who persists in doing so, should be barred from Christian fellowship.

It should be pointed out that such a cardinal idea establishes the central creed of Christianity but that the intolerance counseled by it does not extend beyond this central creed and that it is not to be applied except against those who actively advocate a propaganda in opposition to the central creed.

SHAPING A PREACHING OUTLINE

The outline of the letter itself as given above would seem to be one fruitful way of outlining the sermon. Under I. "Truth and love," it will be shown that Christian community roots in Christ as incarnate truth. Under II. "The lie and disfellowship," the line of development will show the nature of the "lie" which concerned the biblical writer, pointing out how it threatened the very life of the Christian community, and going on to demonstrate the logical necessity of disfellowship.

The life situation to which the sermon may be oriented is a dual one: (1) An easy tolerance which is largely indifference to Christian truth, and (2) a dogmatic intolerance which results in division over many points of doctrine beyond the central one. In the light of this dual contemporary situation the book sermon might aim to show that there is a kind of intolerance that is a proper expression of Christian faith but that this intolerance must be conscientiously limited to its proper sphere.

Another organization of the sermon, adhering to the teaching of the Second Letter but not following its structure, may be more topical. I. When should a Christian church be intolerant? The answers are: (A) When Christian truth is threatened by rejection of the Christian faith in Jesus as the Christ; (B) When members of the church persist in setting themselves up as authorities to teach this rejection as an enlightened form of Christianity. II. How shall a Christian church implement its intolerance? The answer is: (A) Through disfellowship in the church. It might be added: (B) Not by general persecution, and certainly not in bitterness.

It is not easy to foresee a situation in modern Christendom where the harsh action advocated by Second John may be necessary. The harshness has all the marks of an emergency measure.

Modern Title

"Dealing with Christian Subversives" is a grandiose title with a contemporary flavor. It may not be as appealing as the more paradoxical "Christian Intolerance," or the question, "When Does Christian Tolerance End?"

26

A BIG MAN IN A LITTLE CHURCH
The Third Letter of John

"FOR ME to live is to make myself important." There is something wrong with this quotation. It is a reversal of Paul's guiding motto, "For me to live is Christ." But many of us could not fly Paul's banner without gross hypocrisy. Let us be honest: Christ is seldom in the picture, we do not live for him. We live for ourselves, we "look out for Number One" even, in church. If we are leaders we want to be considered "big wheels" and even if we don't lead we make ourselves big in a kind of church life whose basic question is, "What's in it for me?" Men who are all the time striving to make themselves big create "little" churches, churches little in vision, little in love, little in power. Such was the problem faced by the Elder John in his Third Letter.

I. WORKING YOUR WAY INTO THE BOOK

Begin by reading The Second and Third Letters of John. Scholars assure us that in form and in length Third John is fairly typical of the personal letters of the Roman world in the first century. Many of the phrases are standard: "to beloved," "I pray that you may keep well," "greet you. Greet." Like Paul's Letter to Philemon, this one is written to an individual Christian.

Read 3 John 1; Acts 19:29; 20:4; Romans 16:23; 1 Corinthians 1:14.

The letter is addressed to Gaius. The name occurs five times in the New Testament. Whether the Gaius of our letter is to be identified with any of these cannot be known, though the generous hospitality mirrored in Romans 16:23 is exactly what we would expect of the Gaius of Third John.

At first reading it may seem that Second and Third John are companion letters sent to the same community at the same time, one to the whole church, the other to an individual member of the congregation.

Read 3 John 9a.

HOSPITALITY

But this first impression will not bear scrutiny. Though both letters touch on the matter of hospitality to traveling missionaries, Second John is written to close the door of a generous hospitality which had proved ruinous to the church because it had encouraged "deceivers," whereas Third John has the opposite problem in view: hospitality has been refused to accredited missionaries bearing the proper letters of recommendation. In Third John there is no mention of heresy in any form; Second John is written to combat the spread of heresy.

The central concern in Third John is the officiousness of a local church leader, Diotrephes.

Read 3 John 9b-10.

(1) The officious Diotrephes had blocked communication between "The Elder" and the church; this seems to mean that Diotrephes had received the Elder's letter for the church but had refused to read or have it read to the church. He exercised a pocket veto upon the letter. (2) Diotrephes was exercising monarchial control over the local church; he loved to show his power. It was a daring, rebellious kind of leadership because it rejected the authority of the venerable

Elder who apparently exercised pastoral oversight over a whole region containing many churches. Diotrephes was so drunk with his own power that he was insubordinate. (3) To insubordination, Diotrephes added insult. He spoke out against the Elder "with evil words" abusing the venerable leader and undermining his authority. (4) Diotrephes was blocking the missionary enterprise of the whole region by a refusal of the usual courtesies of Christian hospitality to traveling missionaries. Diotrephes, as leader of the church, was the logical man to play host to the itinerants. He had refused to do so. What is more, he had forbidden any member of the church to entertain them, on pain of excommunication.

CHURCH ADMINISTRATION

Much has been written about the light which this letter throws on the history of church administration. Unfortunately the evidence is somewhat equivocal. It does seem that "the Elder" represents the small group of Presbyters each of whom acts as successors to an apostle in exercising pastoral care over a number of churches. But what about Diotrephes? (1) Is he a properly constituted ruling bishop of his local church? If so, we have within the New Testament one of the earliest records of the monarchial bishopric, which came to be the church polity of the early second century. (We know about the early development of the monarchial bishopric from the letters of Polycarp written on his way to martyrdom at Rome about A.D. 120.) (2) Or is Diotrephes a highhanded member of the church who has usurped leadership without authorization of the congregation itself or of the Elder? Was he simply an officious individual who was "throwing his weight around?" In either case we have an example of wrongheaded leadership which was doing the church more harm than good. It was isolating a local church from its natural intercourse with the universal church; and it was creating a spirit of division and bitterness.

Read 3 John 5, 6.

Gaius had done what Diotrephes had both forbidden and refused to do. The report of Gaius' hospitality and of the moral courage required to exercise it under the circumstances had come to the Elder by word of several of the traveling brethren whom Gaius had befriended. In fact, these brethren had sung Gaius' praise before the congregation in the Elder's city.

Read 3 John 7-8; Mark 6:8-9.

From these verses we get a rather clear picture of traveling evangelists or missionaries who were following out as literally as possible the instruction of Jesus to his immediate disciples. They carried no wallet or collecting bag as did many of the non-Christian traveling teachers who were familiar sights in that time; they avoided all appearances of being professional beggars who were more interested in what they could get than in what they were trying to give. We have a contemporary record of one pagan teacher of a Syrian goddess who returned from a journey with seventy bags which he had collected. For this reason Christian missionaries made it their policy to refuse hospitality from non-Christians and to accept nothing but what was given in Christian fellowship.

"To support such men" meant providing their financial needs along the way. Gaius had been doing that. It was living link missions of the most personal sort.

Read 3 John 12.

Demetrius may have been the bearer of this letter. If so, the letter was, in part, a certificate for him as a traveling missionary. Letters of recommendation were quite familiar among the churches.

Read 2 Corinthians 3:1a-3; Romans 16:1-3.

Such letters bear witness to the unity of the early church which gathered the members of local congregations into a universal solidarity.

Outline of the Letter

Introduction, vv. 1-2
  A. Greeting to Gaius, v. 1
  B. Prayer for Gaius' physical and spiritual prosperity, v. 2
    I. Gaius' support of traveling missionaries, vv. 3-8
      A. Gaius' reputation as a sincere Christian, vv. 3, 4
      B. Gaius' support of the missionaries, vv. 5-8
    II. The obstruction of missionaries by Diotrephes, vv. 9-11
      A. His repudiation of the Elder's authority, v. 9
      B. His verbal abuse of the Elder, v. 10a
      C. His refusal of hospitality for missionaries, v. 10b
      D. His blocking of hospitality, v. 10c
      E. His bad example and its opposite, v. 11
    III. A certificate for Demetrius, v. 12
Conclusion, vv. 13-15
  A. Plans for an immediate visit, vv. 13-14
  B. Greetings, v. 15

Points of Interest

1. *Truth* is a favorite word which appears again several times in this Third Letter. It is a synonym for Christianity itself; it means loyalty to Christian faith and living in the Christian way.

2. The greeting at the close of the letter contains a famous New Testament title for Christians which has been adopted by the Society of Friends: "The friends greet you. Greet the friends." Thus the members of one local church say hello to the members of another local congregation, testifying as they do so to the intimacy of fellowship which early Christians felt for one another within the whole church. This friendship was more fundamental than acquaintanceship, for even strangers were embraced by it (see v. 5).

Any view of the Christian movement which sees local churches in the New Testament but fails to see the whole church as an intercongregational community is superficial. In the same way anyone who sees the missionary enterprise as something added to the life of the church has never really seen the New Testament church as it was, for world-mission was of its essence.

II. PREPARING YOUR BOOK SERMON

CARDINAL IDEA

An individual Christian who uses the church as an arena for the display of his own power over people is an obstruction to the advance of the church universal in the world at large; whereas an individual who is bent upon being genuinely Christian will be concerned to exercise the duties of brotherliness and will give substantially to the support of the Christian world mission.

It would be easy for us to get sidetracked from the central message of Third John by the word *hospitality* or by the concept of *administration,* both of which play roles in this letter. But the hospitality of Third John is a means to the advancement of the Christian mission; in the strictest sense it is missionary giving. And bad administration appears here as an obstruction to the unity and the growth of the church universal. By making himself big Diotrephes made his church local and little; by making himself the servant of Christ, brother to his fellows and steward of his possessions, Gaius made his church big, kept it universal, and advanced its world-wide expansion.

SHAPING A PREACHING OUTLINE

The persons in Third John fall into four categories: (1) the author, who is the embodiment of the apostolic passion for the spread of the gospel all over the world and for the unity and fellowship of the church throughout the whole of its life; (2) the traveling brethren, who are the working missionaries busily engaged in the expansion of the church and needing the generous support of local churches to do their work; (3) Diotrephes, a leader who is an obstructionist more interested in recognition and power for himself than in the gospel or the church; (4) Gaius, a consecrated Christian whose primary loyalty is to Christ and who in consequence has moral courage and displays brotherliness and generosity, making of him a very effective missionary expediter. These four categories of the letter might easily serve as the principal points of the book sermon, the introduction of which could emphasize two points: First, the fact that Christianity is not a limited, provincial concern but a world enterprise. Second, the fact that all of us Christians are involved and will play our roles either as obstructionists or as expediters.

It might be suggested that the Diotrephes of the New Testament has at least two kinds of offspring: (1) the active leader who leads for the sake of the power he wields, (2) the inactive member who merely attends church for reasons of social recognition and of personal satisfaction. The controlling motive in a Christian of Diotrephes' stamp, in other words, is self-interest: "What's in it for me?" The result of the Diotrephes life in a church is localism, bitterness and stagnation. Gaius is the opposite of Diotrephes; as such he is the epitome of the right sort of church leadership. His life was genuinely Christian; he was fully committed to the Christian faith and way. He had moral courage. He was brotherly. And he supported the universal mission of the church with his own money.

Such a contrast of Diotrephes with Gaius is a natural basis for a sermon outline. The master motive of Diotrephes, "What's in it for me?" makes himself big and his Christ nonexistent for him, and his church little. As a result of that littleness Diotrephes repudiates the Elder who is the voice of the church universal, subverts Christian missions by refusing to support the missionaries, and sows the local church with bitterness and division. The master motive of Gaius is "to follow the truth." For him to live is Christ. The resultant magnifying of Christ does not make Gaius little, in opposition to Diotrephes who wants to be "a big man in the church"; rather it makes him great, and it aligns him with a great cause.

The above suggestions yield two possible outlines, one with four main points, the other with two points. Both sermons will make liberal use of quotations from Third John, but both will attempt to set forth the essential and timeless message.

A MODERN TITLE

"Making Our Churches Little" is a negative statement but it does convey the essential dangers in the Diotrephes' state of mind. "Missionary Expediters *versus* Missionary Dynamiters" is tempting but is a title that borders on sensationalism and is cheap poetry; perhaps it could be shortened to read, "Missionary Expediters or Obstructionists?" Probably any title containing the word *Missionary* will be rejected, however, because of the emotional resistance which it induces in so many hearers. We, therefore, offer one more suggestion: "A Big Man in a Little Church."

27

CHRISTIANITY AND MORAL RIOT
The Letter of Jude

Religion is not morality tinged with emotion. Some religions give rise to immorality, as in the case of Baalism with its cultic prostitution and human sacrifice. Nevertheless, it is impossible for us to think about Christianity without thinking about a noble ethic. Christianity expresses itself in a high moral standard. Both Jesus and Paul indicate that the Christian ethic is the fruit on a healthy, well-rooted tree of the spirit, and Jesus said that a tree which does not bear fruit will be cut down and cast into the fire. As the tree is much more than the fruit which it bears, so Christianity is more than Christian morals, but most of us are as ready as Jesus to curse a tree in leaf which bears no fruit; we expect Christianity to produce good conduct.

This was not always so. The high ethic of Judaism had entered into Christianity to be sure, but when the gospel ventured out into the Greek world it came into contact with cultic practices and religious doctrines of a very different order. In some of these, drunkenness and sexual promiscuity were used as a means of mystic union with the divine. This was true of Dionysian cult and at the temple to Aphrodite on Acro-Corinth. These cultic practices, together with a sophisticated theology known as Gnosticism, for a time invaded the church and threatened it from within. It was this threat from sophisticated immoralities in the name of Christianity which provoked our present book, The Letter of Jude. The letter itself does not give a name or a label to the heresy which it is attacking, but scholars in subsequent ages have called it Antinomianism. It is also known as Libertinism. As one studies this book of the New Testament, he begins to understand that the high Christian ethic which is now generally taken for granted as an integral part of the Christian religion was given its assured place in history only after a severe struggle. We, today, are the spiritual descendants of the Puritans and the inheritors of many ages of ethical Christianity. It is hard for us to realize that there was ever a possibility of Christianity's growing in another direction. The Letter of Jude shows us a small but determined party which would have taken Christianity into free thought and free love. That will be the subject of our study in this chapter.

I. WORKING YOUR WAY INTO THE BOOK

Libertines

It is clear from the beginning that The Letter of Jude is written against heretics.

Read Jude 3, 4.

The author, he tells his readers, had planned to write a treatise on salvation, but a virulent threat to the gospel had arisen which caused him to set aside this cherished project in favor of a trumpet call to defenders of the faith. "Ungodly persons who pervert the grace of God" were attacking the church from within. The danger constituted an emergency placing "the most holy faith" in deepest peril.

From the letter itself, it is difficult to get a definite picture of the threatening heresy, for nowhere does the author give it a name or set forth its doctrines in outline. Nowhere does he answer the heresy by argument. Instead, he uses invective, warning and exhortation. His letter is not a systematic theological treatise, but a battle cry.

We know enough about the threatening heresy, however, to understand Jude's allusions and to give it a name. It is Antinomianism or Libertinism. This was immorality with a sophisticated philosophical base. Antinomianism—a nihilistic rejection of moral law—took its departure from Paul's teaching, "But if you are led by the Spirit, you are not under the law" (Gal. 5:18). The Christian was free; the law had no power over him, for he had been saved by grace through faith. The reasoning of the Antinomians had been anticipated and spurned by Paul at the outset: "What shall we say then? Are we to continue in sin that grace may abound? By no means! How can we who died to sin still live in it?" (Rom. 6:1 and 2). Nevertheless, the heresy which Paul had anticipated and denounced in advance actually developed. These doctrinaire, moral anarchists had a motto: "All things are lawful for me."

Read 1 Corinthians 6:12; 10:23.

The mistake of the Antinomians consisted in oversimplifying the alternatives before a Christian. They thought of two—legalism or Libertinism, of which they chose the latter. Paul had showed that there were three—legalism, Libertinism and true liberty. True liberty was an inward faith or spirit which could not be measured by law or imposed by law, expressing itself in moral deeds, which were fruits of the spirit (Gal. 5:13, 16 and 17). This was Paul's definition of true liberty and it became normative for the later church.

Read Revelation 2:14-15.

Here, influenced by pagan religious practices, is the same moral license we have been talking about. In the Nicolaitans it was dignified into a philosophy. According to the church fathers, the Nicolaitans were the followers of Nicolaus of Antioch, one of the seven in Acts 6:1-6 who according to legend had become an ascetic and held that Christianity was not an ethic, but an ecstasy. The letter of Second Peter deals with the same heresy. These men boasted of freedom; and they were free from the Jewish law, but they had become slaves of something worse—now they were the slaves of their own passions. They had left a naïve and untaught immorality only to return to immorality upon sophisticated grounds. So doing they were doubly enslaved: by their passions and by their perverted reasoning. Second Peter uses violent language against these men; if they were going to be Christians on these terms, it had been better for them to remain in paganism. (See II Pet. 2:2, 13, 14, 18, 22.)

From the above it can be seen that the heresy of Libertinism or Antinomianism made itself felt in several New Testament writings— in First Corinthians, in Revelations, and in Second Peter as well as in our present epistle.

BELIEFS

From the New Testament itself we never do get a very clear idea about the systematic beliefs of these Antinomians. We are dependent upon the writing of the church father, Irenaeus, in his book, *Against Heretics*. He gives an account of the "Party of Simon Carpocrates," an Egyptian sect of Christianity whose teachings in the second century A.D. are strangely parallel to those indicated in Jude and the other New Testament allusions. They were gnostics of a sort. They taught that mankind is divided into three classes, the "spiritual" who were assured of salvation because they possessed "the Spirit," the "sensuous" who did not possess the spirit but possessed merely mind, *psyche*, and who in consequence might or might not be saved according as they used or misused their free will. The sensuous class of mankind therefore, was, under the law, whereas the spiritual class was above the law. The third part of mankind was the material or worldly class who were incapable of salvation on any grounds. Regarding the "Party of Simon Carpocrates," Irenaeus said, "They hold that good behavior is necessary for us members of the church (being merely sensuous), since otherwise we cannot be saved; they themselves will be saved, however they behave, because they are by nature spiritual."

The heretics taught that the world was created by an inferior god, the god of the Old Testament, together with his angels. The law was the code of this inferior creator god and its sway was canceled by the act of redemption in Christ. It was canceled, however, only for those who attained to a special knowledge or spirit. The members of the sect claimed this special status for themselves. Thus rejecting the creator and his angels as inferior; they also rejected the moral law which had sprung from them. They gained freedom to do as they pleased in morals. Faith came to mean a special kind of knowledge of an ecstatic sort. According to Irenaeus, they believed that Jesus was born of human parents. Other forms of gnosticism have taken an opposite view, that Christ only appeared to be a man but that he was really above the world and the flesh. Either doctrine amounts to a denial of the lordship of Christ.

With such a background in mind we are able to understand better a number of the allusions appearing in The Letter of Jude itself. Let us now look at some of these.

Read Jude 4.

We can see that the heretics are actually in the church, having insinuated themselves into it surreptitiously. We can see further that they are people who abuse the grace of God as an opportunity for immorality and that in one way or another they deny the lordship of Christ.

Read Jude 7.

The immoralities of the Antinomians are now likened to those of Sodom and Gomorrah. This means sodomy, sexual immorality and perversion.

Read Jude 8.

The heretics were visionaries who appear to have made some pretension to mystical dreams. They also rejected church authority, and mocked the angels. It is supposed that the reference, "reviled the glorious one," signifies the angels of creation. This fits what we know about the Carpocratians just mentioned.

Read Jude 10.

A life of sexual indulgence is here indicated. The heretics displayed animal instinct for self-gratification. But they were arrogant about it. They reviled and mocked any other interpretation.

Read Jude 11.

The heretics are here identified with three Old Testament villains. They are like Cain who by Jewish tradition became the type of self-seeking skeptics who do not believe in moral retribution or an after life. They are like Balaam, a pseudo-religionist, who cashed in on visionary errors and who prophesied for gain. They were also like the sons of Korah who rebelled against divine authority.

Read Jude 12.

The perfect commentary upon this abuse of the fellowship supper in the early church is to be found in 1 Corinthians 11: 17-22. The church suppers had become pagan banquets for these heretics.

Read Jude 16.

This catalog of vices labels the heretics as a very unlovely people.

Read Jude 19.

It is not surprising that such people caused church divisions. Jude turned back some of their language upon them, accusing them of being worldly people devoid of the spirit in spite of their claims to possess the spirit.

Literary Sources

We are beginning to see that The Letter of Jude, although it is exceedingly small, is filled with quite a number of allusions requiring a rather extensive knowledge for interpretation. In addition to the above allusions to the heresy of Antinomianism, there are others which we ought to notice before completing our study of the letter. The allusion in Jude 5 is to the Korah's rebellion in Numbers 16. The legend of the angels referred to in Jude 6 is from the Old Testament apochryphal book of Enoch, chapters 5-16, 21, 54, 64, 67. This can be read in *The Apocrypha: An American Translation* by Edgar J. Goodspeed. As we shall see, the Letter of Jude makes other uses of the book of Enoch. Jude 7 refers to Genesis 19:24.

The legend of the archangel Michael referred to in verse 9 is to be found in the pseudepigraphic Old Testament book, The Assumption of Moses. In verses 14 and 15 Jude quotes directly from the apocryphal book of Enoch, 1:9 and 27:2. Jude 16 is a quotation from the pseudepigraphic Assumption of Moses 5:5 and 7:7 and 9. The quotation from the apostles found in Jude 18 does not appear anywhere else in the New Testament. Yes, The Letter of Jude is an exceedingly small book, but it is very rich in allusions and quotations.

The identity of the churches addressed by The Letter of Jude is completely uncertain. From the fact that the "Party of Carpocrates" was located in North Africa and that other gnostic tendencies of the same kind were found there, it has been reasoned by some scholars that the churches addressed were located in that region. It sounds like a logical deduction, but there is no other historical evidence in support of it.

AUTHOR

The author of the letter calls himself Jude, the brother of James, but this does not help us to identify him. Jude or Judas was a common name among Hebrew Christians. There was a Jude in the reign of the Roman emperor, Hadrian, who was bishop of the Jerusalem church. The New Testament tells us about a number of other Christians of the same name. There was a Jude among the brothers of Jesus. (See Matthew 13:55 and Mark 6:3.) This particular Jude who was the brother of Jesus was, of course, also the brother of James; but one would expect him to claim kinship to Jesus rather than to James, although James had been a very noted leader of the Jerusalem church. One of the disciples was a Judas, who was the son of James. (See Luke 6:16 and Acts 1:13.) Saul lodged with a Judas in Damascus (Acts 9:11). Thus we are able to see that the name was a very common one and that we have no clear guide as to whether the author of our letter was any one of these or still another Christian who may have had rather great authority and prestige in the church toward the end of the first century. It is now generally supposed that the letter was written somewhere around the year A.D. 90. The letter was not accepted as canonical for some time. Jerome, toward the end of the fourth century, says, "Because Judas draws a testimony from the aprocryphal book of Enoch, his epistle is rejected by very many." It was one of the last books to get into the New Testament.

The Letter of Jude is short, simple and unified. It is written to certain unidentified Christian churches to guard them against people that we may call Christian subversives who were undermining the high moral character of the Christian community. The author reminds his readers that divine judgment upon erring children of God is certain. He then goes on to give a characterization of the subversives, and ends by calling Christians to be loyal to the authority of the apostles and to continue in the main tradition of the new religion. He ends with a doxology.

Outline of the Letter

Introduction: Salutation, 1-2
    I. Reasons for writing, 3, 4
        A. To exhort Christians to uphold the faith
        B. To warn against Christians perverting grace of God as excuse for immoralities (Antinomians)
    II. Condemnation of Antinomians, 5-16

    A. Examples of God's past punishment of such backsliders, 5-7

    B. The Antinomians denounced, 8-16

  III. The duty of Christians, 17-23

    A. Remember apostles' warnings, 17-19

    B. Build their lives on faith, prayer and love of God, 20-21

    C. Try to save the heretics, 22-23

Conclusion: Doxology, 24-25

KEY PASSAGES

Brief as the letter is, it hardly seems necessary to summarize it in a few verses chosen from the whole. Nevertheless, when verses 3, 4, 20 and 23 are taken together, they do supply rather satisfactory summation of the complete letter. Read them in that light.

II. PREPARING YOUR BOOK SERMON

CARDINAL IDEA

We must be on guard against any interpretation of the gospel which tends to relax the high moral code of Christianity. To be genuine, Christianity must express itself in the Christian ethic.

SHAPING YOUR PREACHING OUTLINE

It may seem to the modern reader that the book of Jude is nothing but ancient history. To be sure, now and then we find a small group of misguided Christians appearing here or there in Christian history who advocate something of the kind, but they never have a far-reaching influence. In the seventeenth century, for example, there was the sect of Ranters in England who are reported to us by John Bunyan who said of them, "These would condemn me as legal and dark, pretending that they only had attained perfection that could do what they would, and not sin." He goes on further to report that one of them "gave himself up to all manner of filthiness, especially uncleanness . . . and would laugh at all exhortations to sobriety. When I labored to rebuke his wickedness, he would laugh the more." There is perhaps no such sect anywhere in contemporary Christendom. The main tradition of Christianity—that of a high ethical religion—has won out. Such immorality as there may be among Christians is a lapse from their faith rather than an expression of it. We may continue to have our Elmer Gantry's, but it is doubtful if we will ever get a sophisticated advocacy of free love and moral anarchy as a proper expression of the Christian spirit.

What then is the message of the book of Jude to the twentieth century? It may seem that what we have said excludes the letter from the pulpit as a message to present-day Christians. One value, of course, is the insistence of the book upon Christian ethics as an integral part of the Christian religion. There may not any longer be a pretension to Christian faith which does not demonstrate itself in a Christian way of life. The other value lies in a warning against the tendency which may exist even within Christianity to place undue emphasis upon some doctrinal or institutional aspect of our religion at the expense of ethical sensitivity. It may be said that there are five strains in religion: mystical evperience, doctrine or belief, ritual, ecclesiastical organization and ethics. A lopsided emphasis upon doctrine or belief may result in very unbrotherly behavior as in the case of the Council of Nicaea, where one of the Christian bishops slapped the aged Arius in the face because of his heretical doctrines. We have seen all kinds of breaches of Christian brotherhood in the name of orthodox belief. This is one way by which Christianity leads into certain kinds of behavior contrary to the Christian ethic. Similarly, an undue emphasis upon the ecclesiastical institution may result in a Sunday religion which is identified with going to church and the proper observance of one day out of seven rather than everyday application of certain principles and attitudes to common behavior.

Sacramentalism and liturgy may sometimes lead to a dulling of the ethical sense. During the spring of 1954, the writer, while living in Manila, Philippines, witnessed example of this emphasis. The Black Madonna of Quiapo, a very ancient and venerated statue of the virgin, was taken on its annual airing in the streets at fiesta time. Thousands gathered for the procession, trampling one another in their efforts to touch the statue for the supposed blessing deriving therefrom. Not a few of the devotees brought their sweepstake tickets to rub upon the Madonna to make them magically effective in the coming races. Here we have an example of the Christian religion used for unethical ends. From the above it would seem that the danger to Christianity in our time is not that of a doctrinaire Antinomianism, but that of misplaced emphasis leading to a weakened ethical sensitivity. This is the point of relevance at which a book sermon on the Letter of Jude may begin.

There is still another way in which Christianity may lose its moral fervor. This happens when talking about Christianity becomes a substitute for being Christian. This can happen to preachers. The figure for it in The Letter of Jude is "fruitless trees in late autumn, twice dead, uprooted." When Christianity becomes nothing but talk or high-flown philosophy, it is both without root and without fruit. This may be another point of modern relevance from which the sermon on The Letter of Jude may begin.

One approach to the outline of this sermon may be taken through a topical treatment of the three main movements within the letter itself. These are: the error, the task of guarding the faith from error, the winning back of the errorists. The error has already been set forth, both in its ancient and modern forms. It is the danger of reducing the moral demands of Christianity or of abrogating them in the interest of some other demand. The defender of the faith is one who watches his own faith seeing that it is kept strictly in line with the main Christian tradition of high ethical monotheism. This defender of the faith is to love the errorists while hating their error and to exert every influence to win them back to true Christianity.

Another approach to the sermon may be made through the outline of the letter itself. There are five main steps in such an outline: (1) guarding the gospel once for all delivered so that it does not become foreign to itself; (2) the judgment of God upon backsliders; (3) the heresy of Antinomianism and its manifestations; (4) the positive duties of Christians; (5) the doxology. Since the letter is so very short, it should be possible for a preacher to present the whole letter in total, interlining it throughout with relevant modern illustrations.

A third outline largely from a topical point of view, but echoing the phrases of the letter itself, will call for a three-point sermon. (1) Know the danger, (2) Look after your own faith. (3) Save whom you can.

Modern Title

It is difficult to find any one topic which seems satisfactory for this particular book. At the head of the chapter we have called it "Christianity and Moral Riot." Another possible topic is "Religious Immoralities." "Religion *versus* Morality" may also be suggestive.

28

FIRE ON THE EARTH
The Revelation of John

THE COLLAPSE of an empire is an awe-inspiring spectacle. It is as
though a "mighty angel took up a stone like a great millstone
and threw it into the sea" (Rev. 18:21).

The merchants . . . who gained wealth from her, will stand far off,
in fear of her torment, weeping and mourning aloud,
  "Alas, alas, for the great city
  that was clothed in fine linen, in purple and scarlet,
  bedecked with gold, with jewels, and with pearls!
  In one hour all this wealth has been laid waste."
And all shipmasters and seafaring men, sailors and all whose trade is on
    the sea, stood far off and cried out
  "What city was like the great city?"
And they threw dust on their heads, as they wept and mourned, crying
    out,
  "Alas, alas, for the great city. . . ."

[Rev. 18:15-19]

Of explanations of the decay and fall of empires there is no end,
but one that deserves more than passing thought is the religious one,
such as the verdict that Victor Hugo pronounced upon Napoleon,
"God grew tired of him!" This is the view of the book of Revelation:

We give thanks to thee, Lord God
　　almighty, who art and who wast,
That thou hast taken thy great power and
　　begun to reign.
The nations raged, but thy wrath came . . .
for rewarding thy servants, the prophets and
　　saints, and those who fear thy name,
　　both small and great,
and for destroying the destroyers of the earth.
　　　　　　　　　　　　　　　[Rev. 11:17, 18]

I. WORKING YOUR WAY INTO THE BOOK

A rapid "first" reading of the book of Revelation is apt to be a
pulse-quickening, spine-tingling experience. One is caught up into a
tense drama enacted on a cosmic stage; he is dazzled by brilliant,
kaleidoscopic imagery, and inspired by sublime poetry. To read this
book is to be captured by the rhythm and the exultation of Handel's
Hallelujah Chorus: "The kingdom of the world has become the
kingdom of our Lord and of his Christ, and he shall reign for ever
and ever" (Rev. 11:15). It is not hard to understand why this highly
charged emotional writing has aroused the imagination of readers
down the centuries. It has the sweep and power, the mystery and
grandeur, and the triumphant hope which we want our religion to
give us. Readers instinctively feel that it is a writing for them, not
alone for Christians in the first century, and that its relevance to
questions of human destiny is present, real and urgent.

But the very factors that have made Revelation so inspiring have
also made it the happy hunting ground for cranks, visionaries and
misguided prophets. It would take a very long sheet of paper, for
example, to list the identifications of the beast of the thirteenth
chapter. In various interpretations down the centuries he has been
successively Mohammedanism, the Papacy, Napoleon, Kaiser Wil-
helm II, Hitler, and even Herbert Hoover. And how many times
have arithmetic and calendar been applied to the book to set a date

for the end of the world? Disagreements among these prophets and the failure of their prophecies never seem to discourage them.

We will be delivered from these and kindred difficulties only as we are able to answer a few questions: Who were the original readers of this book? What was their situation? Why was the book composed? What kind of literature is this? Let us take the last question first.

TYPE OF LITERATURE

The type of literature is *apocalyptic*, a kind of writing which flourished in late Palestinian and early Christian times. Two biblical books belong *in toto* to this peculiar kind of writing; these are Daniel and Revelation. But there were apocalyptic elements in the Prophets, such as Isaiah 6:1-6; Ezekiel 1:1-3:27; Joel 2:28-3:17. It is in The Pseudepigrapha of the Old Testament, however, that we find most of the Jewish apocalyptic writings, such as The Book of Enoch, The Assumption of Moses, The Secrets of Enoch, The Apocalypse of Baruch, IV Ezra, and the Sibylline Oracles.[1] As a preparation for the book of Revelation, a reading of The Book of Enoch is especially rewarding; it pictures the Messianic woes, the victorious Messiah descending to earth, the new Jerusalem, the resurrection of the dead and other elements so important to the framework of the Christian writing. Still belonging to this same type of literature are three additional Christian apocalypses: Mark 13, The Apocalypse of Peter and The Shepherd of Hermas. To these may be added three relatively modern books: Dante's *Divine Comedy*, Milton's *Paradise Lost* and Bunyan's *Pilgrim's Progress*.

When these writings are taken together and read as a group, they will be seen to shed light upon one another. All are characterized by ecstatic feeling, by allegory of an extremely bizarre variety, so

---

[1] R. H. Charles, *The Apocrypha and Pseudepigrapha of the Old Testament in English* (Oxford University Press, 1913).

extreme in many instances as to lead into an obscurity which serves to heighten the sense of mystery. There is also a peculiar fondness for numbers. All the writings deal with a cosmic drama showing two worlds in conflict; they abound in prayers and hymns; they are visions; and they are tracts for time of crisis. They have a pastoral aim, to encourage the faithful in a period of persecution and danger. Much of the imagery of these books is standard; for example, beasts quite generally represent nations or empires.

ORIGINAL READERS

Who were the original readers of this book? We are not left in doubt:

Read Revelation 1:4, 11.

They are members of seven churches of the Roman province of Asia, who are in the midst of, or are about to enter, a general persecution:

Read Revelation 2:10 13; 3:10, 12, 21; 6:9-11; 13:10; 14:12; 17:6.

Only one martyr is mentioned by name; he is Antipas of Smyrna. But others are anticipated. The author himself is on Patmos, which is a tiny island at the entrance of the Aegean Sea; it is the seat of a penal colony:

Read Revelation 1:9, 10.

His book is an account of a vision he had on a Lord's Day while in prison for his faith. He writes in ecstasy under great stress about things that "must soon take place" (1:1). His central message to his hard-pressed readers is, "Be faithful unto death, and I will give you the crown of life" (2:10).

PERSECUTIONS

But what is this persecution which Christians are called to endure? It is persecution by the Roman state. The immediate occasion seems to be the refusal of Christians to worship the Emperor:

Read Revelation 13.

There are two beasts in this chapter, one emerging from the sea, 3:1-10, the other from the earth, 3:11-18. The first is clearly the Roman Empire with its seven emperors and its ten tributary kings. (See also 17:9-12.) This was Rome who ruled the world (13:7b, 8) and made war upon the church (13:7a). The second beast was the cult of emperor worship, which "makes the earth and its inhabitants worship the first beast." There is a boycott against those who refuse to worship the emperor: Those who do not possess the official mark or certificate will be refused at the markets (13:16, 17). Thus everyone in a region would soon be driven by economic necessity to get a certificate proving that he had worshiped the emperor. Those who refused were killed (13:15).

It is practically certain that the mystical number of the beast in 13:18 means "Nero," but this does not date the persecution in Nero's reign. There are two reasons: (1) There was no general persecution of Christians under Nero, only a local purge relating to the burning of Rome. (2) This emperor is represented by the thirteenth chapter as wounded and healed (13:3). As amplified in 17:9-11, this verse is a clear reference to the Roman superstition that Nero, who had died by suicide under mysterious circumstances, was really in hiding and would return again to take up his diabolical rule. A like rumor about Adolph Hitler grew up and circulated for a time after World War II. We can easily understand the Nero legend in the light of this modern example.

The first persecution of Christians by the Roman state for refusal to worship the emperor took place in the last four years of the reign of Domitian, that is, between A.D. 92 to 96. Even in Rome Domitian required his subjects to call him "Our Lord and God." In consequence, the book of Revelation is most frequently dated in this period.

With this background we have the fundamental key for grasping the meaning of Revelation. Church and State are in conflict, with the church resisting idolatrous secular power with marytrdom; faith pitted against force, losing the battles but winning the war. This conflict is lifted by the book into cosmic significance; it is fought not only on earth but also in heaven, where the celestial victory is the forerunner and guarantee of earthly triumph.

WRITER'S ASSUMPTIONS

Other keys are needed. These consist of the fundamental assumptions of the writer and the meaning of some of his images. Consider the assumptions: God rules in history, but he does not move by smooth transitions in a gradual progress; he moves by judgment, destruction and renewal, cataclysmically. God will bring his kingdom on earth. The breakup of "the kingdom of his world," however, will be a fearful tumult attended by messianic woes both in human society and in the realm of nature. As a part of the turbulence, just before the Kingdom appears, evil will reach its height incarnate as a man, a messiah of Satan, Antichrist. (In the book this Antichrist is Nero revived.) God will achieve his victory by the power of the true Messiah, the Christ, but he will win it through the holy community, the church.

The images of the book are partially explained by the book itself: *Read Revelation 1:20; 4:5; 5:6; 7:13; 12:17; 13:18; 17:7; 19:8.*

We can also be assured that the Lamb is Christ, that the two witnesses of chapter 11 are Moses and Elijah, that the woman of chapter 12 is the church, that the dragon in the same chapter is Satan, of whom the Roman beast in chapter 13 is an agent. Babylon in chapters 17 and 18 is Rome. The seals, the trumpets and the bowls are various messianic woes. These must not be separated too meticulously, for there are numerous repetitions whose main effect is to show the long duration and the mounting horror of the judgment falling upon the perishing earthly kingdom. When we are tempted to press for an exact meaning of every symbol in the book, we must remember the deliberate multiplication of images to increase the sense of mystery which characterizes this type of literature. For example, the seven thunders of 10:4 are surely introduced in this way. Thus, it is not necessary to understand Revelation minutely in order to read the book meaningfully.

OUTLINE OF THE BOOK

Introduction: How the vision came and for whom it is intended, 1:1-20
    I. Letters to the seven churches, chapters 2 and 3
       (Christ can only help the church in its coming crisis if it is faithful)
    II. Prologue in heaven, chapters 4 and 5
       (God entrusts judgment to Christ)
    III. The seals: judgment pictured, chapter 6
First interlude: the church's safety assured, chapter 7
    IV. The trumpets: judgment proclaimed, chapters 8, 9
Second interlude: the church's safety, 10:1-11:14
       (Judaism to perish; the church to conquer but through marytr- dom.)
Third interlude: the church and her enemies, chapters 12 and 14
       (The church wins the war in heaven against Satan, but cast to earth the war continues. Satan is now operating through the Roman Empire and emperor worship, which are the second and third beasts. The church is assured of victory in this conflict)
    V. The bowls: judgment poured out, chapters 15 and 16
    VI. The fall of Rome, chapters 17-19
    VII. The millennium, 20:1-10
    VIII. The end of the world and the Judgment, 20:11-15
    IX. The New Jerusalem, 21:1-25
Conclusion: Authentication and warning against revision, 22:6-21

At this point we would suggest a rapid reading of the entire book of Revelation.

KEY PASSAGES

"Be faithful unto death, and I will give you the crown of life" (2:10). To this central passage others may be joined, for example, 3:19-21; 11:15.

II. PREPARING YOUR BOOK SERMON

CARDINAL IDEA

When the church stands under the condemnation of secular society and even suffers an exterminating persecution its seeming weakness is lifted into conquering power by its God and Christ who will have the last word in history, if the church can keep the faith.

SHAPING A PREACHING OUTLINE

One sermon may be based upon the material in the preceding section on "Working Your Way into the Book." There is a need for a correction of false views of this writing which are widespread in our own apocalyptic twentieth century. To show what is relevant and what is not may be a worthy aim of a single sermon, whose main units might deal with: wrong interpretations that plague and confuse us, the original circumstances of writing, the meaning of the central images, the structure of the book, its central message for us.

Henry Sloan Coffin in *Communion through Preaching* undertakes a four-point summary of the message of Revelation, as follows:

1. The certain downfall of the dominant secular culture. Rome, the all powerful, is viewed by this prisoner in one of her concentration camps as doomed. "She glorified herself"—the fatal self-sufficiency of all secularism. "Strong is the Lord God which judged her."

2. The continuing instability to be expected when a great culture breaks up. [Dr. Coffin refers to the messianic woes in chapters 6-16, then goes on to say,] Here is a profound insight into history. When a civilization collapses—like the Roman Empire or the industrial world of nineteenth- and early twentieth-century Europe and America—tranquillity is not soon regained. Earth reels under blow on blow. This is not good news to our generation, but it is God's truth and must be faced. Christians must prepare themselves to take it and take it and take it again.

3. The Church, through which God carries out His main purpose in history, is represented in chapters two and three by seven flickering lamps shining against the black darkness of a doomed world. [This

Church, weak and faltering as it may be, can be strengthened for the conflict by its faith.]

4. The climax of history is the arrival of the city of God. . . . That is our hope—not of a commonwealth marred by human ignorance and sin, but of a society whose architect and builder is God. . . . And if one asks what is this heavenly society like, the answer is subsumed briefly: "The throne of God and the Lamb shall be in it." Life is completely harmonious with the will of God manifest in Jesus of Calvary. And what of its citizens? Three things are plainly said: They are useful— "His servants shall serve Him"; they are companiable, companiable with God and therefore with one another—"they shall see His face": their characters reflect clearly the Divine—"His name shall be in their fore- heads." This society is the end product of human history, the fulfillment of the purpose of the incoming and always active God.[2]

A third way of outlining the sermon is to base it upon the drama of the book itself following the main features of the action. Whether this is done in the words of the book itself or not, modern relevance must not be sacrificed along the way. Such a treatment might well group the messianic woes and treat them much more briefly than in the original.

Much may be said for a plan which ends with the messages to the churches. In the light of the church's place in God's design for history, what kind of church do we have? How does it need to be strengthened? Which of the weaknesses of the seven are we in- volved in? The sermon will then close with that magnificent scene of Christ standing at the door and knocking (Rev. 3:12-22).

Finally, a sermon can be built upon the songs and prayers of the book, which are its sublimest passages. A slight regrouping of these sections seems necessary, thus:

The sovereignty of God, 4:8; 7:12; 15:3-4; 4:11
The messiahship of Christ, 5:9, 10
The cry of the martyrs for vindication, 6:9, 10
The assurance of salvation, 7:10

---

[2] Coffin, *Communion through Preaching*, pp. 106-9. Copyright, 1952, by Charles Scribner's Sons; used by permission of the publisher.

The great tribulation, 7:14-17
  The cry of the wicked, 6:16
Power over the nations, 11:17-18
  The seeming might of the state, 13:4
  Judgment upon empires, 13:10
  The conquest of Satan, 12:10-12
  The fall of Babylon, 18:2-3
Come out of her my people, 18:4-8
Lament for Babylon, 18:10
  Her vanished splendor, 18:14, 16-20
  The seal of her doom, 18:21-24
The heavenly song of triumph, 19:1-3, 5, 6-8

Modern Title

"The Church against the World" and "Fire on the Earth" suggest themselves almost automatically. The clue in Alpha and Omega may lead us to "The First and Last Word about Human History." The imagery of the book itself will suggest many other titles.

29

A BOOK SERMON ON EPHESIANS
An Example

Note: *The following sermon is appended in an effort to provide an example of the preaching that this book advocates. Based upon the principles laid down in Chapters 1 and 2, it expands one of the outlines suggested in the chapter on Ephesians beginning on page 110. Therefore, the sermon will be read most meaningfully as a sequel to Chapters 1, 2, and 13.*

THE GOAL OF HISTORY

"The mystery of the ages" is this: What is history all about? A cynic has said, "All that we learn from history is that no one learns anything from history." From Spengler to Toynbee our age is busy in the making of philosophies of history. Some of them are hopeful; others are pessimistic, echoing the mood of the grief-stricken Macbeth after the death of his queen:

> Tomorrow, and tomorrow, and tomorrow
> Creeps in this petty pace from day to day
> To the last syllable of recorded time;
> And all our yesterdays have lighted fools
> The way to dusty death. Out, out, brief candle!
> Life's but a walking shadow, a poor player,
> That struts and frets his hour upon the stage
> And then is heard no more. It is a tale
> Told by an idiot, full of sound and fury,
> Signifying nothing.[1]

[1] Act V, sc. 5.

Not so for Paul. The goal of history had been obscured in darkness through long ages, he said, but at last its meaning had been unveiled. He wrote wonderingly of this revelation: "To me, though I am the least of all the saints, this grace was given, to preach to the Gentiles the unsearchable riches of Christ, and to make all men see what is the plan of the mystery hidden for ages in God who created all things . . ." (3:8, 9). Again, "When you read this you can perceive my insight into the mystery of Christ, which was not made known to the sons of men in other generations as it has now been revealed to his holy apostles and prophets by the Spirit . . ." (3:4, 5).

Since the design of history has at last come to light, what does Paul say it is? Hear it in his own words: ". . . that is, how the Gentiles are fellow heirs, members of the same body, and partakers of the promise in Christ Jesus through the gospel" (3:6). "For he has made known to us in all wisdom and insight the mystery of his will, according to his purpose which he set forth in Christ as a plan for the fullness of time, to unite all things in him, things in heaven and things on earth" (1:9, 10). We might say it in our own words somewhat differently: "Christ is the focal point of the universe, of all history, and of all being; all things, as they are brought into their true relation to him, are also brought into their true relation to one another and so into an all-embracing harmony." Or, to put it as briefly as possibly: "The goal of history is one world in Christ through the Church Universal."

John Oxenham once called the cross of Christ "God's signpost." It points the way that God wants us to go. During World War II a serviceman from my church wrote me somewhere in England, "I should like to tell you where I am, and I suppose I could plead military secrecy as an excuse for not telling you, but the truth is, the signposts are down and I don't know where I am." Precisely; when the signposts are down we are lost in history. But since Golgotha God's signpost has been pointing the way. There is no need to be lost.

Paul's Letter to the Ephesians falls naturally into two parts, chapters 1 through 3, which are doctrinal; and chapters 4 through 6 which are ethical. Let us summarize these first three chapters quickly: "The plan of God for humanity was a mystery hidden for ages until it burst upon the world in Christ and his church. Now the plan is revealed, and it is this: the hostile sections of humanity can be reconciled and the world can become one world through the church. Has not the church already proven that it can overcome the most violent hostility in the Roman world—that of Jew and Gentile? It will be equal to other hostilities in time to come, and so long as its life is hid with Christ in God, it will lead the way for all the word from ethical darkness to light and from strife to peace." History a tale told an idiot? Far from it. It is God's drama, and we have an important role to play in it.

There is a single phrase which is repeated in Ephesians no less than thirty times; it is "in Christ." Taking it as a key, we shall gather the message of the letter into three topics: Out of Christ; in Christ; life in Christ.

1. *Out of Christ.*

The best we can achieve out of Christ is a kind of selfish competitiveness, a condition in which we are "strangers to the covenants of promise, having no hope and without God in the world" (2:12). In Romans and Galatians Paul had said that men in such a case are enslaved to their unregenerate selves, slaves of sin and death. Here he uses another figure. He says that we are strangers and aliens to one another, to God, and even to ourselves.

"Strangers to ourselves?" you ask. "How can that be?" It happens every day. Several years ago as I was counseling a young man who felt himself threatened by his brother's success, he came to me burning in envy and jealousy. I taunted him, "So you love yourself so much?"

"Love myself?" he flared back at me; "I don't love myself. I hate myself." He buried himself under a mountain of invectives.

After a time I broke in to say, "You are not as bad as all that. You ought to get to know John Brown [his own name]."

"But I don't know him," he almost shouted. "Who is he? I've never met him. He's a stranger."

In our selfish competitiveness we stand over against one another, over against ourselves, as strangers. But it is the best we can achieve out of Christ, for it is the natural order of life without the touch of God. Our selfishness is more than natural; it is stubborn.

> The Lord said, "Say we";
> But I shook my head,
> Hid my hands tight behind my back, and said,
> Stubbornly,
> "I"

> The Lord said, "Say we";
> But I looked upon them grimy and all awry—
> Myself in all those twisted shapes? Ah, no!
> Distastefully I turned my head away,
> Persisting,
> "They."[2]

The word *we* is not in the vocabulary of natural man. In such a state men do not stand together; they stand against each other with barriers between them. Paul called this division the wall, "the middle wall of partition." We use another word now—curtain, the iron curtain, the bamboo curtain. In Paul's day the curtain was lowered between Jews and Gentiles. In ours there are other curtains.

During the Korean War while I was aboard ship in Kobe, I was introduced to a cultured Japanese gentleman, an antique dealer. We fell to discussing the war. "It's all a waste, a big mistake," he said. "The Koreans are not worth fighting for. Koreans are not human beings." A week earlier I had learned from missionaries in Tokyo that Korean residents in Japan were greatly discriminated against

[2] "Pronouns" by Karle Wilson Baker, in *Burning Bush*. Copyright, 1922, by Yale Press, and used by permission of the publisher.

and that many of them were depressed into the criminal class. For that Japanese gentleman the curtain of prejudice shut Koreans out of the human race. What an irony, I reflected. Only a few short years ago when America was at war with Japan I remembered over-hearing Americans say more than once, "You know, I don't think the Japs are quite human, do you?"

All of us seem to have our scapegoats, our people "on the other side of the tracks," outside the pale. With the Filipino it is the Chinese. In Jordan it is the Jew. In Israel it is the Arab. It used to be the Samaritan, the Moabite and the Edomite. In southwestern America it is the Mexican; on the West Coast, the Japanese; in the northeast, it is the Jew; and throughout much of the land it is the Negro. Yes, we have reason to know about walls and curtains. Stuart Chase in *Roads to Agreement* has recently sketched a "Sky-scraper of Conflict" with personal quarrels in the basement and the cold war in the upper stories. In this same book he reports a study which "indicates that 80 per cent of all adult Americans have marked prejudice against various groups of their fellow citizens." Yes, Paul, we know about barriers and human strife. How well we know!

Out of Christ our lives are accurately described by Thomas Hobbes as "the war of each against all" and as "nasty, brutish and short." Out of Christ, we are strangers, even enemies.

2. *In Christ.*

In Christ these enmities are reconciled. Let Paul tell it:

For he is our peace, who has made us both one, and has broken down the dividing wall of hostility . . . that he might create in himself one new man in place of the two, so making peace, and might reconcile us both to God in one body through the cross, thereby bringing the hostility to an end. And he came and preached peace to you who were far off and peace to those who were near; for through him we both have access in one Spirit to the Father. So then you are no longer strangers and sojourners, but you are fellow citizens with the saints and members of the household of God, built upon the foundation of the apostles and prophets, Christ Jesus himself being the chief cornerstone, in whom the whole structure is joined together and grows into a holy temple in the Lord; in whom you also are built into it for a dwelling place of God in the Spirit. [2:14-22]

The reconciliation which is achieved begins with persons, and not with those who are on the other side of the world merely. Reflecting upon the 900,000 Russians, 2,000,000 Jews, 700,000 Negroes, 400,000 Poles, 230,000 Puerto Ricans, 500,000 Irish and 500,000 Germans living in New York City, Stuart Chase sees this largest of our American cities as "a permanent exhibit of the phenomenon of One World. . . . The city has to be tolerant, otherwise it would explode in a radio-active cloud of hate and rancor and bigotry."[3] To a lesser extent, the same may be said of nearly every community in our land. We are a melting pot of world peoples; the stranger is not in faraway places; he is in our midst.

But what we do with him here will also affect our world brotherhood abroad. It happened that I was in Manila, Philippines, when Vice President and Mrs. Nixon came on their tour of good will to Southeast Asia. One evening the Vice President addressed five hundred Americans in the Manila Polo Club. He told them that Americans abroad, whatever their official status, were ambassadors of good will or of ill will for their country and that they should conduct themselves accordingly. The same issue of the *Manila Bulletin* that reported Nixon's speech carried an Associated Press dispatch from Louisville, Kentucky, telling of a petition to exclude a Filipino mother and her children from their own newly purchased home in Louisville, an alderman taking the initiative. This incident completed Nixon's speech. It showed that Americans at home are also ambassadors. A world press and world radio spotlight our actions for every people on this globe these days. What a person

[3] Stuart Chase, *Roads to Agreement* (Harper, 1951), p. 212.

does about his neighbors can aggravate or alleviate the cold war itself, for in this matter of brotherhood we are all ambassadors of good will or of ill will.

Christian reconciliation is aimed at the sore spots. It is meant to work where the strife is the most severe. There are those who say, "Christianity is a beautiful religion and if ever the world gets to rights perhaps we can follow it, but not while there is so much hatred and strife." They miss the whole point. Christianity came to destroy hostility and to bring peace.

One memorable day in the Christmas season of 1953 I stood in the office of Bishop Leonard Dia, General Secretary of the United Church of Christ in the Philippines, as he told of his own home missionary penetration into a wild mountain region in the province of Cotabato, on the southern island of Mindanao. The natives there carry spears and continue their age-old tribal warfare. They live in isolation even from one another; a tribe consists of those forest huts within the sound of the chieftain's bell. These animistic peoples proved to be a ripe harvest field for Bishop Dia and his companions, and in a short time there were four hundred converts, including five enemy chieftains. One day the bishop got all these chieftains together. They stood stiffly in a circle, eyeing one another suspiciously. Finally one spoke up, pointing at the man to his right,

"Is he a Christian?"

"Yes," the bishop answered.

"But he is my enemy. He tried to kill me," he said, indicating a scar on his left arm not far from his heart.

"It's true that he was your enemy," the bishop answered, "but not any more. Now he is your brother."

The chieftain looked at his old enemy again; his face lit up in understanding. That night the second chieftain slept in the hut of the first. "It is not good for you to sleep out in the woods without a shelter or a blanket. Come to my hut; take my blanket." Christ "is our peace, who has made us both one, and has broken down the dividing wall of hostility . . ."

To be reconciled means a new relationship, and the new relationship creates new man. It also brings peace—not armistice, but peace. Our modern world is a world of armistice lines, the boundaries where fighting reached a stalemate or where exhaustion overtook the foes. In Korea, Indochina, Germany, around Berlin there are armistice lines. Right down the middle of the Holy Land there is an armistice line. Visiting Jerusalem recently I was awakened in the dead of night by the sound of firecrackers, only they were not firecrackers. We had seen the armed patrols on both sides, and the barbed wire; we had walked through the bombed-out, shell-shattered buildings in Jerusalem's no-man's-land. Armistice, but not peace. Peace is a positive thing. It comes from reconciliation. It comes from something better than mutual exhaustion and from something better than the victory of either side. It is a third alternative. "For he is our peace . . . that he might create in himself one new man in place of the two, so making peace, and might reconcile us both to God in one body through the cross, thereby bringing the hostility to an end" (2:14-16).

3. *Life in Christ.*

We turn now to the second division of the letter, the ethical portion in the last three chapters. Our heading is "Life in Christ." When men are reconciled to one another and are drawn together as new persons, their life in Christ will express itself in at least four ways:

First, they belong to a new spiritual community, the church. The church is the completely candid, undefensive meeting of two persons in the presence of Another. "Where two or three are gathered together in my name, there am I in the midst of them" (Matt. 18:20). It is within such a context that the former individualist learns to say "we."

The Lord said, "Say we";
And I,
At last,
Richer by a hoard
Of years and years,
Looked in their eyes and found the heavy word
That bent my neck and bowed my head,
Like a shamed schoolboy then I mumbled low.
"We," Lord.[4]

How shall we improve upon the language of Ephesians itself?

I therefore, a prisoner for the Lord, beg you to lead a life worthy of the calling to which you have been called, with all lowliness and meekness, with patience, for bearing one another in love, eager to maintain the unity of the Spirit in the bond of peace. There is one body and one Spirit, just as you were called to the one hope that belongs to your call, one Lord, one faith, one baptism, one God and Father of us all, who is above all and through all and in all. [4:1-6].

[We come together and we stay together] until we all attain to the unity of the faith and of the knowledge of the Son of God, to mature manhood, to the measure of the stature of the fullness of Christ. . . . speaking the truth in love, we are to grow up in every way into him who is the head, into Christ, from whom the whole body, joined and knit together by every joint with which it is supplied, when each part is working properly, makes bodily growth and upbuilds itself in love. [2:13, 15-16]

Yes, life in Christ means belonging to a new spiritual community, the church.

It also means living by the code of Christ. Christianity expresses itself in a distinctive morality. Have you supposed that American ethical standards just happened, that they are a part of the topography? Go abroad and wander through the world, particularly through the Far East. You will come back saying, "Thank God for our Puritan forefathers." You will then begin to see how dependent we are upon the ethical heritage of the Judeo-Christian religions. Anyone who reads his New Testament carefully will see that the

---

[4] Karle Wilson Baker, *op. cit.*

battle with paganism was not easily won within the church. In the Roman world religion did not necessarily mean high ethics; rather, it meant ecstasy and ritual. But the Christian religion does mean a high ethic; life in Christ involves living by the code of Christ:

> Therefore, putting away falsehood, let every one speak the truth with his neighbor, for we are members one of another. Be angry but do not sin; do not let the sun go down on your anger, and give no opportunity to the devil. Let the thief no longer steal, but rather let him labor, doing honest work with his hands, so that he may be able to give to those in need. Let no evil talk come out of your mouths, but only such as is good for edifying, as fits the occasion, that it may impart grace to those who hear. And do not grieve the Holy Spirit of God, in whom you were sealed for the day of redemption. Let all bitterness and wrath and anger and clamor and slander be put away from you, with all malice, and be kind to one another, tenderhearted, forgiving one another, as God in Christ forgave you. [4:25-32]

Life in Christ is a high ethical adventure.

Moreover, it means the building of Christian homes. We do not follow the details of the Ephesian picture too willingly, for what we see there is a patriachal family and a household with slaves. But we can follow the principle disclosed, which is mutual love. "Be subject to one another out of reverence for Christ" (5:21). "Let each one of you love his wife as himself, and let the wife see that she respects her husband" (5:32). "Children obey your parents in the Lord. . . . Fathers do not provoke your children to anger" (6:1, 4). Life in Christ means building homes in which we are "subject to one another out of reverence for Christ."

Finally, life in Christ means a church militant and missionary. The Christian soldier in the last chapter of the letter is not an individual Christian; he is the whole church mobilized as God's army. The war he wages is not defensive. Instead he fights to conquer the earth for Christ.

> Finally, be strong in the Lord and in the strength of his might. Put on the whole armor of God, that you may be able to stand against the

wiles of the devil. For we are not contending against flesh and blood, but against the principalities, against the powers, against the world rulers of this present darkness, against the spiritual hosts of wickedness in the heavenly places. Therefore take the whole armor of God. . . ." [6:10-13]

The church is mission; its aim is world conquest.

Thus endeth the reading of the Ephesian letter. "And this is the stuff of destiny?" you ask. To see the church in its true light, to belong to it because one has been drawn to Christ and into his new life, is to see God's design unfolding.

For he is our peace, who has . . . broken down the dividing wall of hostility . . . that he might create in himself one new man in place of the two, so making peace, and might reconcile us both to God in one body through the cross, thereby bringing the hostility to an end. [2:14-17]

An Indian churchman, after a recent visit to America, published a book in which he holds up a mirror to church life in the United States.

There is in America great loyalty to churches, i.e., to the local churches and perhaps to the denominational organizations; but church consciousness is not strong. By church-consciousness is here meant a consciousness of belonging to a great ongoing historic reality that proceeds on its path of witness while kingdoms rise and fall and philosophies pass away like a breath of wind.[5]

To read Ephesians aright is to see the church like an army with banners spread out on the battlefield of the universe. It is to see the church living and conquering "while kingdoms rise and fall and philosophies pass away." It is to catch the exultation of Handel's Messiah as a huge choir and orchestra lift our hearts to the inspiration of the Revelation hymn: "The kingdom of this world is become the kingdom of our Lord and of his Christ and he shall reign forever and ever."

[5] Sabapathy Kulandran, *The Message and the Silence of the American Pulpit* (Pilgrim Press, 1949), p. 46.

INDEX

Acts of the Apostles: author, 61; cardinal idea, 65–66; episodic nature, 61–62; cf. Gospel of Luke, 60, 63; Holy Spirit, 63; key verses, 64; names for, 67; outline, 62–63; sermons on, 66–67; speeches, 64; spirit of, 59; universalism, 65
Address to Diognetus, 142–43
Angels, worship of, 129, 132
Anti-Marcionite Prologues to the Gospels, 36
Antichrist, 145–46, 247
Antinomians; *see* Libertines
Anton, Paul, of Halle, 151
Apocalyptic, 146, 244–45
Archippus, 127
Aristotle, 79
Arius, 239
Armistice lines, 259
Ascension, 44–45
Asceticism, 128
Augustine, 8, 55
Authority, apostolic, 202–3, 223

Backsliding, 171, 175
Bacon, Benjamin, 23
Baker, Karle Wilson, 255, 259
Beloved disciple, 50
Benevolence, 184
Bibliolatry, 5
Bicknell, E. J., 146–47, 149
Blackwood, A. W., 15
Blood, 76
Bunyan, John; *see* Ranters

Buttrick, George Arthur, 15

Campbell, Alexander, 185
Cerinthus, 215, 216
Change and permanence, 170–78
Charles, R. H., 183–84
Chase, Stuart, 256, 257
Church, 26; administration, 224; attendance, 171, 177; as community, 65, 134–41, 195, 210, 218–19, 226, 259–60; expansion of, 64, 66; philosophy of, 113; strife, 88; universal, 110–18, 225, 253
Christian liberty; *see* Freedom
Clement (of Rome), 205
Coffin, Henry Sloan, 249–50
Colossae, 126–27
Colossians, Letter to: author, 128; bearers, 127; cardinal idea, 131; key verses, 129, 130; purpose, 128; sermons on, 131–33
Conscience, freedom of, 88
Consistency, Christian, 180–89
Corinth, 81–83
Corinthians, First: cardinal idea, 87; date, 82; key verses, 86; names, 90; occasion, 83–85; outline, 86; previous letter, 83; sermons on, 87–90
Corinthians, Second: cardinal idea, 97–98; occasion, 91–92, 93; names for, 99; Joyful letter: key verses, 96; occasion, 95; outline, 95; purpose, 95–96; Severe letter: key verse, 94; outline, 92

Set in Linotype Janson
Format by Marguerite Swanton
Manufactured by The Haddon Craftsmen, Inc.
Published by HARPER & BROTHERS, *New York*